D0909213

Buying antiques in Europe

What to buy and where

Buying antiques in Europe

What to buy and where

Carol Kennedy

BOWKER
London and New York

First published 1976 in Great Britain by Bowker Publishing
Company Limited, Epping, Essex and in the United States of
America by R. R. Bowker Co., 1180 Avenue of the Americas, New
York, NY 10036

ISBN 0 85935 018 5

Library of Congress catalog card number 76-49706

The author and publishers have used their best efforts in
collecting and preparing information for inclusion in *Buying
Antiques in Europe*. They do not assume, and hereby disclaim, any
liability to any party for any loss or damage caused by errors or
omissions in the publication, whether such errors or omissions
result from negligence, accident or any other cause.

Printed and bound in Great Britain by
REDWOOD BURN LIMITED
Trowbridge & Esher

Contents

*To my mother, Grace Kennedy, for
her unfailing encouragement and
enthusiasm*

Introduction

The collecting urge crosses all international frontiers, and it has never been more widespread than today. There is a desire everywhere to connect with the past, to put roots down from the rootless present, even if the connecting link is only an old flatiron from London's Portobello Road market or a watercolour of Brighton Chain Pier in the 1860s. Throughout the cities of Northern Europe it is noticeable how people have taken to collecting old agricultural and domestic implements; in many cases the reason is to decorate the country cottages that come with affluence, but it nevertheless expresses a yearning for a more settled and rustic way of life.

Other motives have contributed to the growth in collecting, chiefly worldwide inflation which in the last few years has bred a powerful desire to put money into things that will at least have a chance of retaining, if not increasing, their value while currencies fluctuate and fade. The prime attribute of a work of art is its uniqueness, which cannot ultimately be affected by a fall in the dollar or the price of gold. As Lord Eccles, a former Minister for the Arts in Britain, wrote in his delightful little book *On Collecting*, governments can go on printing banknotes and bonds but they cannot increase the supply of Botticellis.

The principle behind this has led to a great boom in investment collecting, a postwar phenomenon which first became apparent in the 1950s and really took off in Britain in the late 1960s. Antique-dealing became a 'trendy' occupation; a whole new profession of art-investment consultancy and broking was born; companies began to put surplus funds into fine art; and television cameras moved into the big London salerooms to record historic bids like the £2.3 million paid for a Velasquez by Norton Simon of California. World records, it seemed, were being broken almost daily. Some sections of the art market, notably impressionists and early Chinese porcelain, inevitably became overheated and some rash investors burned their fingers, but the result of the shakeout was a healthier and steadier trade.

As the purchasing power of money continues to depreciate, however, there remains a strong attraction for many people in what is known around the salerooms as the 'small, portable investment'—small objects of high value and international convertibility which can be carried conveniently in a pocket and 'cashed' anywhere in the Western world where currencies are still strong. Rare stamps, coins and precious stones obviously fall into this category, along with certain small art objects such as fine antique watches, jewellery and snuffboxes. All these areas have shown amazing growth in the last few years.

But this is not collecting for its own sake. Although it is a natural human wish to see one's own judgement vindicated in hard cash—a personal fancy backed, as it were, by the experts—the soundest principle is still to buy only what one likes. After all, even a Ming vase pays no dividends except pleasure; if at the end it also realizes a profit, that is pure bonus to the years of enjoyment in its possession.

It does make sense of course, unless one is very wealthy, to look for an unfashionable area to start in and then to specialize—always remembering the important thing is to buy quality. For those who travel a lot in Europe it's worth following political trends with an eye to the market; coin collectors, for instance could have picked up Portuguese 18th-century gold issues in 1975 for 60 per cent less than they commanded before the left-wing coup.

The enormous spread of collecting, operating on the relentless law of supply and demand, has brought many things within the definition 'antique' which would have been scorned as junk not so long ago. The 'frontier' for an antique used to be 1830, but when the US Customs revised its definition to include objects made 100 or more years ago it gave a tremendous boost to the values of everything produced in Victoria's reign. Another milestone came with the opening in 1971 of Sotheby's Belgravia branch in London, dealing in objects from 1830 to 1930, and four years later the strictly regulated Grosvenor House Antiques Fair in London finally abandoned its rigid 1830 requirement by opening a special section for art nouveau and art deco. Subsequently the other great

London saleroom, Christie's, opened a branch in South Kensington to handle such formerly unthinkable 'antiques' as old gramophone records, postcards, railwayana and car mascots.

Almost anything is collectable nowadays, which means that almost anyone has the means to be a collector. No longer is collecting an elite matter of a young lord on the Grand Tour picking up a couple of Raphaels in Rome or Gibbon's library in Lausanne, or of a landed gentleman hanging Stubbs horse paintings in his stately home and filling cabinets with Chinese porcelain acquired on a voyage to the East. Today, as a stroll through any European city's flea market will show, people collect buttons, old bottles, early photographs, matchboxes, First World War tobacco tins, brass weights, posters, sewing machines and all kinds of ephemera which generations consigned to the dustbin. Even commercial packaging has been accorded the status of a special exhibition at London's Victoria and Albert Museum—and the man behind it is still collecting examples of present day cereal and soup packets. Sometimes it seems as if we will end up being afraid to throw anything away.

This book, however, concentrates on the traditional areas of collecting, specifically on a dozen principal fields: silver, ceramics, paintings, prints and maps, glass, clocks and watches, jewellery, coins and medals, bronze, pewter, firearms and books. Furniture has been deliberately left out, important though this is to the antique tradition of England and many other countries, because this book is designed for travellers and packing a Queen Anne commode in a suitcase is clearly not a practical idea.

This book is not for specialists nor for dealers who will already know their field and where the sources are. It has been written primarily with the travelling businessman or woman in mind—the person on a busy schedule but with a taste for browsing in antique shops and markets who may, on a hurried trip to Barcelona or Budapest, find an hour or so to see what that city has to offer and what the best things are to buy.

Each major country in Europe therefore has a general introduction outlining some of its contribution to art history and the traditions of European craftsmanship, with indications of what visitors can expect to find in its antique shops and galleries.

For each country also, under 'Specialities', are listed particular national contributions to the main categories of art object (e.g.

Introduction

Gallé glass in France, Berlin and Vienna porcelain, Dutch maps, Irish silver) as well as specialities of minority interest with a strong national aspect (e.g. lace in Belgium, 19th-century dolls in France).

The cities and towns for which dealers, markets, fairs and auctions are then listed are mainly those which business travellers would be most likely to visit; not included are holiday resorts as such, which would be unlikely in any case to yield the best bargains. The choice of dealers inevitably has had to be selective and somewhat arbitrary as listing all the thousands of dealers in all the major cities of Europe would have been physically impractical. The choice of names was governed initially by those appearing in the standard directories of international antique dealers such as the French *Guide Emer,* British *International Antiques Year Book* and West German *International Directory of Art.* These were further weeded down to make a representative sampling and to avoid duplication—too many silver dealers, say, or too many picture galleries. By virtue of their inclusion in these annual directories the listed dealers are established names—often being members of the appropriate national association of antique dealers, which carries a stamp of respectability and experience. But it should be stressed that in general they are not personal recommendations.

Following national specialities and dealers are also listed some lesser-known museums of special 'collector' interest—containing, for instance, a fine collection of portrait miniatures, 18th-century coins, musical instruments, Meissen porcelain, Italian silver or French snuffboxes. In general, these do not include the world-famous institutions such as the Prado in Madrid or the Louvre in Paris, which will already be well known to any visitor with an interest in the arts. Occasionally, however, attention is drawn to specialist sections in such a museum—London's Victoria and Albert Museum for instance, is a mine of valuable information for collectors in many different fields.

Finally for each country there is a reading list of useful books dealing with the art and antiques of various countries. For practical purposes these lists are restricted to books published mainly in the last 20 years, earlier ones usually being out of print or obtainable only at specialist libraries.

The 'General reading' list which follows this introduction includes useful books dealing with the art and antiques of Europe

x

generally. As far as travel guides are concerned, the Fodor series generally contains extremely useful advice on shopping for antiques as well as for other items, and the books are regularly and efficiently updated. Nagel guides are strong on art historical background, especially in Eastern Europe, in which the Fodor guides cover only Yugoslavia, Czechoslovakia and Hungary.

No collector can now expect to find a secret corner of Europe where antiques come at pre-Second World War prices. The international growth of interest in antiques—even the Soviets have become avid collectors—has resulted in a shrewd sense of what the market will bear, even in state-controlled Eastern European shops. Where antique dealers haven't penetrated, tourists probably have, and one would be lucky nowadays to find the remotest Transylvanian village without a clue as to the value of its early farm implements or primitive pottery. Nevertheless it is always possible to make a find—which is the essential lure of the chase for collectors—so happy hunting!

Acknowledgements

Many people and organizations have helped in compiling the information for this book. They include saleroom staff, dealers and associations of dealers in several countries, collectors, journalists and various experts all over Europe. In alphabetical order, particular thanks are due to: the Austrian Institute, London; Richard Barber; Signor Giuseppe Bellini, Florence; Douglas Bennett, Dublin; John Calabrini; Christie's staff, especially Susan Rose of the press office; Marietta Coleridge; David Coombs; Robert Deardorff, Rome; Dr Ingrid Detter-Delupis; Virginia Devine, *Washington Post* correspondent, Vienna; William Dillon, Dublin; Judy Emrich; C. J. Fox; Jack Franses; Eleanor German, Brussels; J. A. Maxtone Graham; Marissa Harris; Carole Hazlewood, Brussels; Audrey Hobson; Henry Kahn, Paris; Matti Kohva, Helsinki; Peter Krause, West Berlin and Frankfurt; Kultura (Hungarian Trading Co.), London; Herbert Lass, Vienna; Beata Levy, Paris; Phillips and Co.; the Polish Embassy, London; the Polish Institute, London; Michael Simmons; Sotheby's staff, particularly Rosamund Hinds-Howell of the press office; Richard Stone; and John Veatch, West Berlin. Grateful acknowledgement is made to the following for permission to use photographs: Douglas Bennett Valuations (p.199), Central Office of Photography, Sofia, and Bulgarian Embassy, London (p. 335), Christie's and A. C. Cooper Ltd (pp. 111, 192, 299 and 369), Foto R. Nohr, Munich (p.2), Galerije Primitive, Zagreb (p.383), Sotheby Parke Bernet & Co. (pp. 2, 44, 78, 216, 254, 266, 318, 341, 348, 360 and 372), Victoria and Albert Museum, London (pp. 18, 234 and 284).

General reading

Bacci, Mina, *European Porcelain* (London: Hamlyn, 1969)
Baynton-Williams, Roger, *Investing in Maps* (London: Barrie & Jenkins, 1969)
Charleston, R. J. (ed.), *World Ceramics* (London: Hamlyn, 1968)
Collector's Encyclopaedia (London: Collins, 1974)
Encyclopaedia of Antiques (London: Collins, 1973)
Gros-Galliner, Gabrielle, *Glass: A Guide for Collectors* (London: Muller, 1970)
Hughes, Graham, *Modern Jewellery 1890–1967* (London: Studio Vista, 1968)
Middlemas, Keith, *Continental Coloured Glass* (London: Barrie & Jenkins, 1971)
Radford, P. J., *Antique Maps* (London: Garnstone Press, 1971)
Snowman, A. K., *18th-Century Gold Boxes of Europe* (London: Faber & Faber, 1966)
Taylor, Gerald, *Continental Gold and Silver* (London, 1967)
Tooley, R. V., *Maps and Mapmakers*, 4th edition (London: Batsford, 1970)
Tyler, E. J., *European Clocks* (London: Ward Lock, 1968)

Part One
Western Europe

Attributed to Christian Greiner, this carved figure of St Valentine, with an epileptic at his feet, was recently sold at Sotheby's for £5000

1
Austria

Introduction

It is only a little over 50 years since Vienna was the capital of an empire stretching from eastern Poland to the Adriatic, and this rich mix of cultures makes Austria today a uniquely attractive country for the collector – apart from anything else it is a great entrepot for the now largely forbidden treasures of Eastern Europe. In the antique shops of Vienna's inner city can be found Polish coins, coloured Bohemian glass, Silesian porcelain, German jewellery, carved wooden statues in ebullient Austrian baroque, Biedermeier furniture and knick-knacks, Italian ma jolica and antique maps of Vienna showing the city under siege by the Turks.

The selling-up of the Austrian past was first brought about by the poverty of the nation after the Second World War. Nowadays Austrians enjoy a high standard of living and fewer national treasures from ruined castles and manor houses are leaving the country. Prices are certainly not cheap for foreign collectors, though lower than in France or the Federal Republic of Germany. Bargaining is always advisable, and it pays to be accompanied by an Austrian friend as this may save as much as 20–30 per cent. But the range of goods is unsurpassed in Europe, and both Vienna and regional centres like Graz and Linz offer plenty of good things.

Austria's decisive victory over the Turks in 1683 set the Habsburg stamp upon the country's artistic development for centuries to come. The great baroque architectural works that flowered in the subsequent economic boom placed Austria in the front rank of European art, and the baroque and rococo styles went on to dominate everything in Austrian creativity, from silver to furniture to clocks to guns to bookbindings. They are the very spirit of Vienna and at most Vienna antique shops can be found expressed in bronze, silver, paint or wood (but buyers should beware the many fake baroque carvings on offer).

Biedermeier (from *der biedere Meier,* the bourgeois of comfortable means) was the style which came in around 1820 in reaction against baroque and rococo. At first it was simple and classic; later it developed neo-gothic characteristics. In furniture, early Biedermeier is much sought after with its fine veneer, especially in cherrywood. The Biedermeier period naturally affected painting as well.

Austrian collectors today display curiously contradictory desires: on the one hand they go for inlaid baroque furniture, Austrian marquetry and classic Biedermeier styles, and on the other for folk art and rustic painted furniture. Impromptu farmyard displays of painted country furniture can often be found by the road in the Austrian countryside.

The most important movement in Austrian art was the Vienna Sezession of 1897 – a Morris-like association of architects, artists and designers who quit the Viennese Society of Visual Artists in disillusionment with its conservatism. Their work was strongly influenced by the art nouveau manner and the movement subsequently produced the Wiener Werkstätte and Wiener Keramik. The Sezessionists, led by Gustav Klimt, came in the end to influence every kind of design from tea services to jewellery.

Austria has a strong tradition of fine craftsmanship in firearms, porcelain, enamel work, petit-point embroidery, clocks, carved wooden statues, silver, glass and all manner of objects in Jugendstil (the German term for art nouveau). The Wiener Werkstätte (Vienna Workshop), an offshoot of the Sezessionists, was an association of artists–craftsmen modelled on C. R. Ashbee's Guild of Handicraft in England. Established in 1903, but closed in 1932, its aim was to apply artistic design to the widest range of articles. Its products included textiles, furniture, metalwork, architecture and jewellery.

Collectors with only a few hours in Vienna should visit the Dorotheum, the state-run auction house founded by Emperor Josef I 250 years ago which draws its stock from pawnbrokers' unredeemed pledges. It is not as good as it used to be, say the Viennese – prices are up and there is less on offer – but the four-storey baroque building with its rooms crammed full of late-Biedermeier furniture, horse brasses, copper pans, clocks, phonographs, musical instruments, rugs and jewellery should not be missed. Under the graceful stone staircase may be found art deco chairs, marble-topped washstands and other unconsidered trifles of interwar Vienna going begging for a handful of schillings.

Vienna's flea market in Am Hof Square is also worth a visit, as genuine bargains can be had here among the makeshift stalls where penurious students sell off family treasures. Brass beds, antique wooden wine presses, old carpenter's tools and much of even less commercial value may conceal a fine Meissen dish or rare piece of Austro-Hungarian silver, dark and oxidized with age. The atmosphere is jolly and *gemütlich*.

Vienna is probably one of the most richly museum-endowed cities in Europe. It even has one devoted to the history of the Vienna horsecab trade. Among them, of special interest to weapons collectors is the finest municipal collection of firearms and armour anywhere in the world with the oldest horse armour and oldest German armour (all in mint condition). There is.the incomparable Albertina with its Dürer drawings and a state collection of furniture, as well as a clock museum and several museums devoted to the lives of composers.

Specialities

Art Nouveau (Jugendstil)

See 'Introduction' for notes on the Wiener Werkstätte and its influence. Jugendstil is today highly fashionable and expensive, but nice pieces can occasionally be picked up at a reasonable cost in Vienna in the Dorotheum and Alt-Wien Kunst auction rooms or at the Am Hof market.

Carvings

In many Viennese antique shops can be found carved wooden baroque statues of saints and cherubs – expensive but very characteristic of the country. St Florian, the saint who protects against fire and is always represented with a burning house, is a · perennial subject. But buyers should be on their guard against fakes as this is a favourite field for the unscrupulous.

Clocks

English influence predominated from 1680 to 1780, and bracket clocks in the English manner were decorated with typically Austrian baroque. French influence took over in the 19th century, and exquisite ormolu work can be found in late examples. Apart from carriage and long-case clocks, the characteristic Austrian design for mantel clocks was *Stockuhr*, introduced in the mid 18th century. It had supporting columns and often a mirror behind. Dolphins and the imperial eagle were featured as decorative motifs in the years 1815–30. From around 1780 a type of wall clock called the 'Vienna regulator' was popular, with a long pendulum, glass-fronted door and often an enamel dial. (Andreas Huber was a leading maker.) The *Zappler*, a miniature clock about 6.4 cm (2½ in) high, was made after 1800 in many shapes in embossed brass, mother of pearl and other materials. It was noted for its rapid pendulum movements.

Coins

Vienna is an excellent centre for Eastern European coins, especially Polish, which are now difficult if not impossible to take out of Poland itself.

Embroidery

Petit point is a distinctive Viennese tradition which originated when ladies of the manor were left behind by knights going to the Crusades. It had a maximum of 36 points per square centimetre (232 per square inch) compared with 16 (103) for gros point, seen on tapestries. Embroidered evening bags of the Biedermeier period, often sewn with pearls, make an interesting and unusual buy.

Enamel Work

Enamel work is still being made to Biedermeier patterns as

demitasse services, jewellery, etc. The old jewellery, ornamented with diamonds and semiprecious stones such as garnets, is well worth hunting for.

Firearms

Firearms are still a leading craft industry in Austria. The village of Ferlach in southern Carinthia has since 1558 been entirely given over to the making of guns – almost every house is a workshop. At the time of the Turkish wars it was the principal gun-making centre in the West; during 1800–15 it produced 300 000 guns to defeat Napoleon. Now it makes mostly sporting pieces. The distinguishing marks of a Ferlach gun are its carving, engraving and inlaid ivory work on the stock, often featuring mythological scenes. Vienna has the world's finest dynastic collection of firearms, formed by the Habsburgs, almost every piece of which can be traced back to its original owner. But the market for antique guns has been contracting over the past 15 years and prices are now very high.

Glass

Vienna was famous for its enamelled glass, makers of which included Gottlob Samuel Mohn (1789–1825), Hoffmeister and Anton Kothgasser. Earlier there was the Bohemian *Zwischengold* decoration: gold foil enclosed between the double walls of a faceted beaker, engraved and sometimes highlighted with coloured lacquer. Joseph Mildner of Gutenbrunn refined the technique by inserting miniature portrait panels and medallions in the hollow glass walls and sometimes enclosed parchment miniatures a speciality of his. The typically blue Biedermeier glass is popular with Viennese bargain hunters, but the Jugendstil era produced some truly outstanding glass artists, with the advantage that the maker and sometimes the artist usually signed or had his name marked on the piece. Louis Lobmeyr of Vienna hired the finest Austrian and Czech glass designers to work for him, and the firm still makes some of the best glass in the world. The accent with Austrian Jugendstil was on colour and iridescence.

Jewellery

Apart from the enamel jewellery already mentioned, gold jewellery fashioned from antique ducats – coins made of 986 parts of pure gold – is worth searching for. Hoffmann, a maker who belonged to the Wiener Werkstätte, made jewellery set with unusual semiprecious stones such as malachite and coral. Collectors should especially look for his work in geometric style – the mark was WW, usually with the designer's monogram.

Paintings

The great baroque and Biedermeier periods naturally affected painting. Famous Austrian baroque painters included Johann Michael Rottmayr, Franz Anton Maulpertsch, Martin Johann Schmidt (Kremser Schmidt), Paul Troger and Daniel Gran. In the Biedermeier period (early stage 1820–50, less-expensive later stage 1850–80) they included the outstanding but strictly representational landscape painter George Ferdinand Waldmuller (1793–1865), Thomas Ender (1793–1875) and Rudolf von Alt (1812–1905), a watercolour artist who became president of the Vienna Sezession movement and painted attractive popular views of Vienna. Both Ender and von Alt worked with an exact minute attention to detail.

Regarded as exceptional among 19th-century artists but relatively little known was the painter-writer Adalbert Stifter (1805–68), while early 19th-century romantics included Ferdinand von Olivier (1785–1841), who painted sensitive Alpine landscapes, and Moritz von Schwind, responsible for the loggia of the Vienna Opera House.

Genre painting, a long-established tradition in Austria, was notable for the work of Peter Fendi (1796–1842), who made lyrical studies of young girls and bourgeois families; Carl Schindler (1821–42), who painted mainly soldiers and peasants, and Josef Dauhauser (1805–45).

The second half of the 19th century saw the rise of the wealthy middle classes who bought Franz Defregger's Tyrolean scenes and Hans Makart's sensual paintings in the manner of Rubens and Delacroix (his canvases and frescoes can be seen in the foyer of the Kunsthistorisches Museum in Vienna). These became lumped together patronizingly under the label of the 'Ringstrasse manner'.

Modern painting, a crucial part of Vienna's cultural life, began with the Sezessionists, who broke away from established conventions in 1898 under the leadership of Gustav Klimt. Egon Schiele and Oskar Kokoschka were distinguished successors, as was Richard Gerstl, who lived only from 1883 to 1908. The expressionists who followed included Anton Faistauer, Max Oppenheimer (known as Mopp), Anton Kolig and Albin Egger-Lienz, a Tyrolean painter of the First World War. The inter war period produced an interesting group of painters called the *Neue Sachlichkeit,* among whom were Rudolf Wacker and Wilhelm Thony.

Porcelain and Pottery

Austria's porcelain manufactory, the second oldest in existence, lured away the foreman from Meissen and a Meissen influence is undeniable. The Vienna hard-paste factory, founded in 1719 and closed in 1764, produced exceptionally thin and translucent porcelain with a greenish tinge. Its mark was often shaped like a beehive. After the Austrian state took it over in 1744 it made figures including dwarfs in the Meissen manner and *Commedia dell'Arte* characters. Its best-known modeller was Johann Josef Miedermayer. Bednarczyk has the best selection of Vienna porcelain in Vienna.

It is also worth looking around for the black-and-white majolica, decorated with cubist motifs, made by the Wiener Keramik workshops, an offshoot of the Sezession movement or 'sacred spring' of the early years of this century.

Silver

Vienna silver prior to 1815–20 is extremely rare because most gold and silver objects were melted down for patriotic reasons during the Napoleonic wars. Even church vessels with very few exceptions met this fate. Immediately after the Congress of Vienna silversmiths were allowed to produce silver again, and the mid 19th century was a great collector's period when Vienna was one of the richest financial centres in the world. Silver in the 19th century was first classic then baroque in style. The dark unpolished relics of Austria-Hungary's upper-class families, from teaspoons to coffee pots, can be found in Vienna antique shops, but Innsbruck is reputed to be the best centre for buying silver.

Snuff Boxes

Based on French models, there were gold boxes – very few of them marked – and some porcelain boxes were made by the Vienna porcelain factory between 1725 and 1735 in a variety of fantastic shapes; they were often painted with gaming motifs.

The trade

Graz

Dealers

Franz GRABNER, Mariahilferstr 7 (86579).
Clocks. Open 0800–1230, 1420–1800.

Ernest KINDLER, Hofgasse 8 (72454, 33451).
General antiques. Open 0930–1230, 1500–1800; appointment advisable.

Franz KRITZINGER, Mandellstr 3.
Works of art.

Ulrich MOSER, Hans-Sachs-Gasse 14 (87220).
Antiques, works of art.

Lanz MUNZHANDLUNG, Hauptpl 14/1 (86852).
Coins, specializing in medieval coins of Austria and the Holy Roman Empire; medals, decorations, numismatic books. Open Mon.–Fri. 0900–1230, 1500–1800; Sat. 1000–1200; appointment advisable.

Georg SCHMEE, Grillparzerstr 7 (33416).
Works of art.

Walter SIMENTSCHITSCH, Sachstr 34.
General antiques.

Wolfgang STEEB, Leonhardstr 3 (339412).

Innsbruck

Dealers

Kurt BRUNHUMER, Schubertstr 6.
Coins.

R. GREUSSING, Neurathgasse 5 (225565).

Ivana KATHREIN, Lieherstr 3 (22335).
General antiques.

Hans KONZERT, Erlestr 15 (24324).
Antiques.

Walter PRAUSE, Sparkasse Passage 2 (28410).
17th-century Dutch masters and antiques.

Georg TRAUTNER, Pfarrgasse 4–6 (21323).
Pictures.

WAGNER'SCHE Universitäts-Buchhandlung Museumstr 4 (05222, 22316).
Antiquarian books, especially of Tyrolean interest; decorative prints.

Linz

Dealers
Horst BEGSTEISER, Marienstr 5 (255057).
General antiques.

Otto BUCHINGER (Johann Karl Pohlmann & Co.), Bethlehemstr 5 (20278).
Antiques, works of art.

EIGL KURT, Dametzstr 25 (70270).
19th/20th-century oil-paintings and drawings of upper Austria, costumes, flowers. Open Mon.-Fri. 0800–1800; Sat. 0800–1200.

Engelbert & Pauline *JAHN*, Altstadt 2–17 (269287).
General antiques.

Karl *PFATSCHBACHER*, Leopold-Hasner-Str 30 (56065).

Salzburg

Dealers
Friederike *BRENNER*, Sigmundspl 3 (85195).
Oriental and Persian carpets.

Max *GROTJAN*, Goldgasse 13 (83301).
General antiques, works of art.

Georg *HASLAUER*, Getreidegasse 34 (84823).
Pictures, arms, furniture.

Dr Fritz *HOFNER*, Mozartpl 6.
Old masters.

R. L. *SCHUBERT*, Burgerspitalgasse 2 (43160).
Furniture, rugs, silver, jewellery, porcelain, paintings, mirrors.

Johann *STOLLNBERGER*, Goldgasse 5 (85496).
Rustic furniture, wrought iron. Open 1000–1200, 1500–1800;
appointment advisable.

Norbert *TROETSCHER*, Exnerstr 9 (34397).
General antiques.

Galerie *WELZ SALZBURG*, Sigmund Haffnergasse 16 (87031).
Old pictures, modern drawings.

Vienna (Wien)

Dealers
Herbert *ASENBAUM* (Zum Antiquar), Karntnerstr 28 (522847).
Paintings, sculpture, jewllery.

Inge ASENBAUM, Hafengasse 1a (737113).
Jugendstil.

Czeslaw BEDNARCZYK, Dorotheergasse 12 (524445).
General antiques, silver, porcelain, glass, icons, paintings; Vienna porcelain specialist.

Friedrich DEUTSCH, Dorotheergasse 13 (522371).
General antiques, militaria, French furniture. Auctions.

Ernst DITTMAR, Herrengasse 6 (636268).
18th/19th-century paintings

Johann EDELBOCK, Resselgasse 4 (572130).
General stock, furniture, porcelain, glass, sculpture.

Inga FUCHS, Stallburggasse 2 (5240262).
Jugendstil glass.

HACH-SAZENHOFEN (J. Sazenhofen), Dorotheergasse 12 (525953; private 6320853).
General stock, rustic furniture, folklore antiques, weapons.

Ernst HAMMER, Spiegelgasse 23 (5220232).
Furniture, paintings, glass, silver, porcelain.

Reinhold HOFSTATTER, Dorotheergasse 15 (528984) and Braunerstr 12.
Specialist in baroque furniture, wood-carvings and sculpture. Open 0900–1800; appointment advisable.

B. HORN, Habsburgergasse 14 (525339).
Porcelain, general antiques.

HOROWICZ & Co., Sonnenfelsgasse 7.
Coins, medals.

Franz HRUSCHKA, Gluckgasse 2 (521705).
18th/19th-century paintings, furniture, porcelain, silver.

Helmut KLEWAN, Dorotheergasse 14 (522898).
17th/18th-century paintings.

Kunstgalerie Dr Tomasz METLEWICZ, Seilergasse 14 (522746).
Specialist in 17th-century Dutch paintings; other 17th/
18th-century paintings, silver, French furniture, glass. Open
Mon.-Fri. 1000–1300, 1500–1800; Sat. 1000–1300; also by appointment.

E. M. MAUTNER, Herrengasse 2 (631224).
Specialist in Russian icons.

NAGEL, Messepl Kiosk (933140).
Arms, militaria.

Ingo NEBEHAY, Annagasse 18 (521801).
Books, autographs, engravings.

Rudolf OTTO KG, Lainzerstr 53 (821515).
Specialist in 19th-century paintings; contemporary artists.

Galerie Friederike PALLAMAR, Dorotheergasse 7 (525228).
Important stock of 17th-century Dutch and Flemish masters.
Exhibitions yearly in Nov. Auctions.

Walter PODWINETZ & Co., Halbgasse 18 (934161).
Oils, watercolours.

Leopoldine PRINZ, Dorotheergasse 8 (524719).
Wood carvings, pottery, small antiques.

Erika REITZNER, Braunerstr 11 (529143).
Old Vienna art. Auctions.

Galerie SANCT LUCAS (Dr Robert Herzig), Josefspl 5 (528237).
Old masters. Open Mon.–Fri. 1000–1300, 1500–1800; Sat.
1000–1300; also by appointment (always advisable). Auctions.

Galerie SCHEBESTA, Plankengasse 7/1 (525818).
19th/20th-century paintings.

August SIEDLER, Kohlmarkt 3 (521741).
General antiques, paintings, sculpture.

Wilhelm SMOLKA, Spiegelgasse 25 (5230773).
Paintings, baroque furniture, sculpture. Restorations.

Johann STOHR, Volkerpl 14 (2437335).
Specialist in clocks.

Agob J. TARJAN, Karntnerstr 30 (528710).
Persian and Oriental rugs and carpets.

*WIENER KUNSTSALON (Wolfgang Siedler), Spiegelgasse 3
(523805)*
14th- and 18th-century sculpture, furniture, tapestries, paintings.

Josef ZAHN & Co., Salesianergasse 9 (732126).
Old metal and crystal chandeliers.

Markets
Flea market (FLOHMARKT), Am Hof Sq.

Auctions
ALT-WIEN KUNST, Braunerstr 11 (529143).

Friedrich DEUTSCH, Dorotheergasse 13 (522371).
See 'Dealers'. Sales periodically.

DOROTHEUM, Dorotheergasse 11 (523129).
Vienna's famous state-run auction house, where about a third of
the goods are pawnbrokers' unredeemed pledges. The profits go
to charity. Sellers are charged 12% commission and buyers 20%.
Catalogue lots are marked with the price at which the auctioneer
will start accepting bids. Viewing Mon.–Fri. 1000–1800; Sat.
1000–1200. Sales Mon.–Fri., 1400.

Galerie Friederike PALLAMAR, Dorotheergasse 7 (525228).
See 'Dealers'. Sales periodically.

Galerie SANCT LUCAS (Dr Robert Herzig), Josefspl 5 (528237).

See 'Dealers'. Sales periodically.

Museums

Graz

LANDESZEUGHAUS am Landesmuseum Joanneum, Herrengasse 16.
An exceptional collection of arms and armour. Built in 1642 as the Styrian Armoury it possesses 27 000 pieces of armour and weaponry (Styria was famous for its wrought iron) and could fully equip 3000 men.

Vienna

ALBERTINA, Augustinerstr 1.
The world's largest collection of drawings, engravings and prints from the Middle Ages onwards – particularly strong on Dürer but also on Raphael, Michelangelo, Rubens, Rembrandt and da Vinci.

BEETHOVEN-ERINERRUNGSRAUME, Mölkerbastei 8.

BUNDESSAMMLUNG ALTER STILMOBEL, Mariahilferstr 88.
Magnificent collection of antique furniture, baroque to Biedermeier, formerly in the possession of the imperial Habsburgs.

FIAKERMUSEUM
History of the Vienna horsecab trade.

GEYMULLERSCHLOSSL, Potzleinsdorferstr 102.
Empire and Biedermeier furniture, old Vienna clocks.

HAYDN-MUSEUM, Haydngasse 19.

KUNSTHISTORISCHES MUSEUM, Heldenpl.
Fine arts, including paintings and frescoes by Hans Makart.

MOZART-ERINERRUNGSRAUME, Domgasse 5, Figarohaus.

MUSEUM FUR VOLKSKUNDE, Laudongasse 15–19.
Alpine folk art and country furniture.

NEUE HOFBURG, part of the Kunsthistorisches Museum, Heldenpl.
Probably the world's finest display of medieval arms and armour, including the oldest horse armour and oldest German armour, all in mint condition; superb collection of antique musical instruments.

SCHUBERT-MUSEUM, Nussdorfer Str 54.

UHRENMUSEUM DER STADT WIEN, Schulhof 2.
Watches and clocks from the earliest times to the present.

One of a pair of lappets in pillow-made lace, with an intricate pattern of leaves, blossoms and fruit. Brussels, 18th century

2
Belgium and Luxembourg

Introduction

Belgium is perhaps the richest and most complex source of antiques in Europe after Britain and is regularly combed by
dealers from other countries. Cross-fertilized by its two cultures,
French and Flemish, and historically at the crossroads of
north-west Europe, Belgium's hundreds of antique shops and
markets abound with treasures from France, Germany, the
Netherlands, Britain, the Far East and Africa.

In its own right, of course, Belgium has a rich heritage of
Flemish paintings – names like Hans Memling, Jan van Eyck,
Pieter Brueghel, Jacob Jordaens and Sir Anthony van Dyck.
Belgian artists pioneered art nouveau in 1884 (indeed the
Belgian magazine *L'Art Moderne* coined the phrase) and were in
the forefront of this century's surrealist movement with the work
of Delvaux and Magritte. Collectors around the world also look
to Belgium for antique lace and tapestries, firearms, antiquarian
books and Tournai porcelain.

Comparatively young as an independent nation, Belgium
before 1830 was ruled by Spain, Austria, France and the
Netherlands, and the country's legacy of antiques reflects all
these influences. In this century, there have been the short but
traumatic German occupations of the two world wars. Despite
this scarred history, however, Belgium remains an exceedingly
prosperous country with a great number of wealthy art collectors
who have managed to retain their treasures. There are far more
things in private possession than ever come on the market and

family chateaux often hide many treasures such as Aubusson carpets in almost mint condition.

Visiting collectors therefore have stiff competition at the top end of the scale, but on a more modest level may have good hunting despite the rising cost of antiques which Belgium shares with most of Western Europe.

Jacques Haumont, managing director of the Antiques Center market in Brussels and compiler of a handy guide to the country's antique and bric-à-brac dealers (the latter known as *brocanteurs*), has claimed that antiques are cheaper in Belgium than in any other EEC country except Britain: 'certainly they are cheaper than any other western country on the Continent aside from Spain. Buying in Belgium is simply a matter of good business.' However, when sterling is low against European currencies it is probably true, as Sotheby's representative in the Netherlands has suggested, that a British collector can usually buy 'at the same or lower price at his local antique shop'. This should not deter collectors, however, from looking out for things that may not easily be found at home.

The main antique centres of Belgium are in Brussels, which has about 1000 dealers and at least 285 listed shops, and the predominantly Dutch-speaking cities of Antwerp, Bruges and Ghent. English is however, widely understood and spoken in Belgian shops. Liège, a French-speaking city, is a 'must' for firearms enthusiasts, having been a renowned centre of the gun trade for centuries. Also, during the summer, when all fashionable Belgium moves to the coast, dealers appear in resorts such as Knokke and Ostend.

In Brussels the main area for antiques is around the place du Grand Sablon, which has a colourful weekend open-air market and scores of antique shops in neighbouring streets. High-class dealers are found on avenue Louise, chaussée d'Ixelles and chaussée de Charleroi, among other thoroughfares. One confusing thing about the Brussels antique trade – which is notoriously volatile with businesses opening and closing within days – is that some of the best antique shops do not even have a name or sign up to attract attention. Collectors with minimal time to spare had best go to one of the covered markets, where a number of dealers under one roof cater for a wide range of interests and price tags. There are comparatively few specialists among Belgian dealers; silver, for instance, is found mixed up with a variety of other stock. Covered markets started in Brussels in 1968 and at least five are now in business there. The regular *galeries* or shopping arcades, a feature of Brussels, also sell antiques among much else. Most visitors seek out the traditional open-air markets: the *marché aux puces* (flea market) in the place du Jeu-de-Balle and rue Radis, and the Sablon market which is particularly good for book hunters.

Winter is traditionally the season for foreign dealers to scour Belgium for antiques and bric-à-brac. They come especially from the Netherlands and Federal Republic of Germany, though the Japanese have recently arrived in force also, often paying higher prices than US buyers. The Dutch buy up all kinds of goods, especially copper, pewter, heavy Flemish furniture, cast iron and old handmade farm implements. They also look for bowl and pitcher sets in good condition and at the top end of the market go for fine 17th- and 18th-century Oriental porcelain and 18th-century Dutch marquetry with its intricate inlaid designs – this was nearly all exported at the time of manufacture. Belgium's own speciality in furniture is the elaborately-carved Liège furniture (*meubles liègeois*), often large and bulky and featuring glass panes decorated with delicate traceries of wood. Highly popular locally, it commands big prices; for example, a tall 18th-century desk with glass doors enclosing a library top would cost at least 150 000 francs. The Salon des Antiquaires in Liège is a good place for furniture enthusiasts to become acquainted with the style.

Auction catalogues often refer to *haute époque,* which was the 16th-century period just prior to Louis XIII. The term mainly describes tapestries and furniture, both very expensive. Antwerp and Brussels are the main centres.

When Belgian dealers want to replenish their own stock they often go to the Ardennes area, so for foreign visitors a trip to this picturesque wooded countryside may prove profitable as well as pleasurable. In a radius of 30–50 km (19–31 miles) around the resort of Spa, small dealers can be found every few kilometres selling mainly 18th- and 19th-century rustic antiques and modern ironwork.

Antique collectors should also certainly try to attend one of the many auction sales held in the major centres, particularly the mixed-goods sales where unexpected bargains can often be picked up. At these sales pieces which arouse no response at their opening bids are sometimes offered at a descending rate by the auctioneer, until an item which started at, say, 3000 francs may be literally given away at 1 franc. These are known as 'lost sales' but are often bulky items of little interest to foreign visitors, such as a tattered set of Flemish dining chairs or a three-piece suite. The monthly mixed-goods sales held at the Galerie Moderne in Brussels are attended almost exclusively by flea market dealers, who often sell items to each other after having a mixed lot knocked down to them. Mixed-goods sales are held regularly at several Brussels salerooms. Anyone who does not trust his French or Dutch enough to join in the bidding can give an order to an attendant to bid on his behalf. It should be noted that saleroom prices in Antwerp and Ghent are often higher than those in the capital. It is advisable to check sale days and auction times on the spot, a useful guide being the English-language weekly *Brussels Times,* whose saleroom feature 'Going, Going, Gone' covers big out-of-town sales as well as those in the capital.

Belgian collectors themselves have recently been going heavily for so-called 'new antiques', particularly art deco of the interwar years. Brussels was the cradle of art nouveau and still has plenty for sale, as well as an art nouveau museum. The Belgian architect Victor Horta designed the revolutionary art nouveau Tassee house in Brussels, while the famous artist and teacher Henri van de Velde also turned his hand to the design of art nouveau furniture.

Although unlikely to be a target for the visiting collector, English furniture sells briskly to Belgians and can be found in various centres at dealers with distinctively English names, such as Hampshire House Antiques in Keerlergen, 28km from Brussels, Windsor House Antiques in Antwerp, Cornish in Brussels and Jacobean Antiques in Knokke. The British embassy often directs inquirers to Neuver Antiques and Decoration in Brussels which generally has a good supply of English desks, chests and silver. A thriving trade in English imports is also carried on by Brussels dealer Steppe, who has also recently been specializing in Buddhas and other Oriental temple ornaments.

To sum up: Belgium is a fruitful and varied source of antiques, though prices are considerably higher than a few years ago. The Belgians are accustomed to bargaining so it is worth following their example and trying to get the best possible price.

Specialities

Art Nouveau

Brussels was the seedbed of art nouveau and three of its original fruits – houses designed by the pioneering architect and furniture designer Victor Horta – can still be seen at 224 avenue Louise, 6 rue Paul-Emile-Janson and 25 rue Americaine (the latter being Horta's own house, now the Musée Horta). Perhaps nowhere else in Europe is the organic quality of art nouveau so brilliantly apparent, with architectural and decorative features growing out of one another. Among other innovations, Horta pioneered the concept of open-plan living.

Art nouveau objects are heavily collected in Belgium and prices are consequently high, though still cheaper than elsewhere. The dealer L'Ecuyer in Brussels is the leading specialist and there is another specialist in the Antiques Center market, also in Brussels. One less expensive and very characteristic field is Belgian art nouveau posters, foremost artists in which were Privat-Livemont, Rops, Rassenfosse, Victor Mignot and Fernand Toussaint. The Stedelijk Museum in Amsterdam has a representative collection of both Belgian and Dutch art nouveau posters.

Books

Belgium is a noted centre of the antiquarian book trade and carries on a sizeable export trade in rare books, mostly on scientific subjects. Topography, folklore and local history also have a strong interest for Belgian buyers. There are about 40 firms of book dealers, mostly located in Brussels and Liège. Book auctions are held at Galerie Falmagne in Brussels.

Bottles

Like Britons, Belgian collectors have recently realized the attractions of old glass bottles, especially the soda-pop type with glass-marble stoppers which sell at up to 300 francs. Markets are the place to look.

Bronze

Art nouveau is again the dominant style and L'Ecuyer in Brussels usually has a good stock.

Clocks

Mainly ornate French and Dutch mantel clocks are to be found. Dealers to try are: Galerie Roosens and Baptiste (Brussels). Antica and de Mot (Antwerp) and L'Etoile d'Or (Namur).

Firearms

Liège is a world-renowned centre for firearms and edged weapons. The Musée d'Armes there has more than 8000 examples showing the gunsmith's technique over the centuries. The leading Liège dealer is La Rapière, which also restores weapons.

Glass

Pâte de verre and art nouveau glass generally are very popular and L'Ecuyer in Brussels is the place to go – expensive but worth it. The Argus stand in Les Vieux Sablons market (also in Brussels) has a good selection as well.

Jewellery

Art Nouveau was a strong influence on jewellery in Belgium, its most distinguished exponent being Philippe Wolfers whose family firm, Wolfers Frères, were crown jewellers to the Belgian kings. Philippe made no pieces after 1908 and his work has always been keenly collected. Henri van de Velde was another leading art nouveau jeweller, who worked in an abstract style as opposed to the naturalistic forms of Lalique in France. Leading Belgian dealers include: Delplace and van der Leenen (Brussels) and Hansenne, Huysmans and Smeets (Antwerp). Antwerp is of course a world diamond centre.

Lace

Lace is probably the first thing one associates with Brussels or

Bruges, but there is not much genuine old lace to be found today outside museums. One recommended dealer is de Valkeneer in Brussels.

Oriental Art

Oriental art is well represented in Belgian antique shops. There is a large amount of Dutch East India Company porcelain, as in all the Low Countries, and many temple ornaments such as Buddhas. It is said that many of the Buddhas have been stolen and that the supply may not last.

Paintings

Landscapes, portraits and genre scenes of the Flemish school are obvious choices. Top galleries include those of Finck and Willems (Brussels) and van Herck (Antwerp).

Pewter

Pewter is very much a Belgian speciality, as in all the Low Countries. It is known in Dutch as *tin*. The town of Huy is famous for its modern and reproduction pewter. Antique pieces are expensive but Antwerp is a good place to find it, dealers there including Michiels, who also does restoration, Beullens, Mullendorf, Avonds and Zeberg. (Note: many Antwerp pewter dealers speak only French or Dutch.)

Porcelain and Pottery

Soft-paste creamy-white Tournai porcelain is the national speciality, made in Tournai from 1751; some porcelain was also made in Brussels. A number of Tournai styles were copied from Sèvres and Meissen ware and there are figure groups resembling Chelsea work. A fine underglaze blue was typical of the tableware, now much sought after by Belgian collectors. Marks included a roughly-drawn tower or a version of Dresden's crossed swords with crosses in each opening.

A group of late 19th-century Belgian artists known as *Les Vingt* (The Twenty) produced some excellent pottery, one of their members, A. W. Finch, making rough but attractive plates in red, green and brown. Another potter, Isidore de Rudder, modelled masks of theatrical or folklore characters in porcelain or stoneware, some in editions of up to 50. He also made portrait panels of women subjects in art nouveau style in blue, pink and white. Many leading Belgian artists also worked for the German company Villeroy und Boch, which had one of its three factories in Luxembourg and produced earthenware and stoneware, especially mugs for export to the USA during 1860–1900. The firm was noted for its *Mettlach* ware – art pottery, mainly beer steins, decorated with inlaid clays in contrasting colours. Villeroy und Boch are still in production in Luxembourg.

Delft ware is also widely available in Belgium's Dutch-speaking cities, specialists including: Golbert and Smeets (Antwerp); de Vooght and Michot (Bruges); Bruggeman-Deruyter (Kortrijk); Old Flemish Art (Ghent); and Finkielstejn (Liège). A leading porcelain dealer in Brussels is van Hove.

Prints and Maps

Prints and maps are another Low Countries speciality. Galerie Alex Finck and Willems in Brussels have a wide selection. Old prints of Ostend can be found at Galeyn in Ostend. Other good sources include Broes and Duprez in Bruges, and antique maps can be found at van der Weghe in Brussels.

Silver

Silver is an excellent thing to buy in Belgium – Belgians buy it by weight and often ignore a good piece of plate. Collectors should look out especially for Victorian silver, known in Belgium as 'Louis Philippe' or 'Napoleon III'. Leading dealers include van Hove in Brussels and Cappriccio dell'Arte in Antwerp, but the covered markets are as good a source as any.

Tapestries

Tapestries have been a speciality of Flemish weavers since 1500. Oudenaarde tapestries, characterized by the absence of red tones, can be found at the major antique fairs and in the area around the Sablon market in Brussels. Some lovely examples from the 17th and 18th centuries can still be found – expensive, but cheaper than outside Belgium. Dealers to try include Le Brun and two of the van Hove shops in Brussels. Brussels became Europe's main tapestry centre under the Habsburgs and the major designer was Jan van Roome. Early patterns (from the 15th century) included religious and chivalric subjects; later came decorative gothic-style compositions, hunting scenes and allegorical subjects.

Wood Carvings

Wood carvings are typical of the Flemish heritage and mainly of religious subjects.

Wrought Ironwork

Wrought ironwork is a typical craft of Belgium and (especially) Luxembourg, along with other forms of metal-working. Dinant has long been a famous centre for beaten and engraved copper, and brass is also extremely popular, particularly the Flemish-style chandeliers which are eagerly snapped up at auctions. Ermans in Brussels specializes in both wrought and cast iron. Belgian collectors are very interested in old farm implements – part of the craze for the rustic past very noticeable in Northern Europe. In some cases these have been converted into modern decorative objects.

The trade

A useful book is that compiled by dealer Jacques Haumont, *Guide des antiquaires et brocanteurs de Belgique*. It lists chiefly those firms registered for value added tax (though there are many smaller unlisted ones), indicates which languages are spoken at the dealers, and gives business hours and telephone numbers. It covers the whole country, even the smallest towns.

Antwerp

Dealers

ANTICA, Conscienceplein 16 (321822).
Clocks.

AVONDS, Mechelsesteenweg 78 (385186).
Flemish oak furniture, Delft, pewter. Restorations.

Michel BASCOURT, Mechelsesteenweg 17 (337120).
Paintings, furniture, porcelain, faience, 16th/19th-century objets
d'art. Open Mon.–Sat. 1000–1230, 1430–1830; also by appointment.

BEULLENS, Vleminckveld 48–50 (330187).
Pewter.

Galerie CAMPO, Meir 47–55 (321225)
19th-century romantic and modern paintings.
Open 1000–1230, 1400–1800. Auctions.

CAPPRICCIO DELL'ARTE, Groendalstr 20 (339007).
Silver.

GOLBERT, Arenbergstr 16 (320567).
Delft.

HANSENNE, Breughelstr 12 (392505).
Jewellery.

Jan van HERCK, Leopoldstr 20 (333185) and 57 (333275).
Antique furniture, Delft ware, Chinese porcelain, sculpture,
Dutch paintings, tapestries. Restorations of furniture and paintings. Auctions.

HUYSMANS (Le Petit Grenier), Leopoldstr 17 (333188).
China, Delft, old jewellery, furniture. Open 0900–1800; closed
Sun.

*LIBRAIRIE DES ARTS ET GALERIE, Nouvelle Galerie de la rue
des Tanneurs 61–2 (322450).*

Fine antiquarian and modern illustrated books, 1st editions, fine bindings, drawings, paintings, engravings. Auctions.

LUNA Antica, Maanstr 33 (390452).
Specialist in Delft and icons. Closed Sun. Also in Brussels.

MICHIELS, Mechelsesteenweg 76 (378794).
Pewter, copper, Delft, French provincial furniture. Restoration of pewter and furniture.

de MOT, Isabellalei 29(302672).
Clocks.

MULLENDORF, Oude Kerkstr 28 (375381).
Pewter.

SEGERS, Hopland 7–9 (330609).
Antique weapons, Oriental porcelain, 17th/18th-century French and Dutch furniture. Open Mon.–Fri. 0900–1900; Sat. 0900–1300; also by appointment.

SEYMUS, Justitiestr 12 (385766).
Clocks. Restorations.

SMEETS, Maalderijstr 1 (338464).
Pewter, pottery, brass, jewellery, furniture. Open 0900–1830; closed Sun.

STANDAARD Boekhandel, Huidevetterstr 57.
Antiquarian department specializing in history, philosophy, folklore and early Belgian books.

Axel VERVOORDT, Vlaaikensgang, Oude Kornmarkt 16(336780/90).
Silver, furniture, objets d'art. Open 0900–1900; closed Sun.

WINDSOR HOUSE Antiques, 35 St Jorispoort (312074).
English furniture.

ZEBERG, Melkmarkt 37–9 (338230).
Pewter.

Markets
Antique market, Hendrik Conscienceplein.
Open Sat., Easter-Sept.

Auctions
Galerie CAMPO, Meir 47–55 (321225).
See 'Dealers'.

Jan van HERCK, Leopoldstr 20 (33185) and 57 (333275).
See 'Dealers'.

LIBRAIRIE DES ARTS ET GALERIE, Nouvelle Galerie de la rue des Tanneurs 61–2 (322450).
See 'Dealers'.

Bruges

Dealers
BROES, Stevinpl 12 (333774).
Old prints. Open 0900–1200, 1430–1830; closed Sun.

DEPREZ, Kraanpl 4 (330882).
Prints.

Galerie GARNIER, Korte Zilverstr 8 (330196).
Furniture, pictures, antiques. Open 0900–1200, 1400–1900; closed Sun. and 15 July to 15 Aug. Auctions.

Marc MICHOT, Groenelei 3 (339720).
17th/18th-century Delft ware, Chinese porcelain, 12th/19th-century art objects, 17th/18th-century pewter.

VLAEMINCK, Genthof 25 (335262).
Pewter. Open 0900–1200, 1330–2000; closed Wed.

de VOOGHT, Katelijnestr 47 (331079).

Fairs
Antique fair, Boudwinjnpark.
Yearly in 1st fortnight in Aug.

Auctions
Galerie GARNIER, Korte Zilverstr 8 (330196).
See 'Dealers'.

Brussels

Dealers
ARGUS, 244 chaussée d'Ixelles (483634).
Antique and secondhand glass. Restorations.

L'ARMORIAL, 16 pl du Grand-Sablon (5133724).
Tournai and Chinese porcelain, furniture, wood-carvings,
faience, pictures. Open 1000–1230, 1400–1830.

ASIE-AFRIQUE, 42 rue de la Régence (5124607).
Sculpture from India, Nepal, Cambodia, China and Japan;
Tibetan bronzes, primitive art. Open Mon.–Sat. 1400–1830; also
by appointment.

Georges BAPTISTE, 11 rue St-Jean (5127174).
Specialist in English antiques, especially clocks, watches, pistols,
sundials, furniture. Appointment always necessary.

A. BELLEY, 1 rue Van Moer (5124706).
18th-century ceramics, especially Tournai, porcelain, clocks,
mirrors, silver, tapestries, furniture.

BERRY, 24 rue Ernest-Allard (5124903).
Faience, Continental and Chinese porcelain, 18th/19th-century
furniture.

BOSKOVITCH, 13–15 rue Ravenstein (5380975) and 5 ave Louise.
Ceramics, jewellery, glass, tapestries, furniture, Flemish
paintings, 12th/18th-century sculpture.

Le BRUN, 26 blvd de Waterloo (5124704, 5113017).
Fine 18th-century furniture and porcelain, tapestries, wood-
carvings, bronze, objets d'art, engravings. Open 0900–1230,
1400–1830.

CALOU, 30 Galerie Louise (5115766).
Oriental carpets, 17th/18th-century Chinese porcelain, French 18th-century furniture. Open 1000–1900; closed Sun., also Mon. in Aug.

CLIQUET, 27 rue du Pépin (5122295).
Chinese and Japanese lacquer furniture, 18th/19th-century Chinese and Japanese bronzes, weapons, cloisonné, ivories, hardstones, 18th-century Dutch marquetry.

J. CORNISH, 14 rue de Joncker (377937).
English furniture.

Robert COURTOY, 19 rue des Minimes (5132115).
Tapestries, early furniture. Open 1100–1230, 1500–1900; closed Sun.

DECOSTER, 102 rue Royale (5172637).
Jewellery, silver. Restorations.

Georges DEDONCKER, 43 rue du Lombard (5128061).
Arms, militaria, Congolese works of art. Open 1000–1200, 1400–1700; closed Sun.

Mme Lucien DELPLACE, 4 rue de la Longue-Haie (5111392).
Prints, drawings, watercolours. Open 1000–1200, 1400–1800; closed Mon., also Sat. in summer and 1st fortnight in Aug.

Paul DELPLACE, 30 rue de Namur (5122070).
Antique jewellery, Oriental works of art. Open 1000–1230, 1400–1830.

Francis DEVAUX, 4 rue de Naples (5122253).
Old and modern paintings. Closed July. Restorations.

L'ECUYER, 107 and 187 ave Louise (5375063, 6480684).
19th-century decorative items, art nouveau and art deco posters.

ERMANS & Fils, 71 rue Hôtel-des-Monnaies.
Specialist in wrought and cast iron.

Galerie Alex FINCK, 28 ave Louise (5124276).
Flemish paintings, 15th/20th-century. Chinese porcelain. Open 1000–1200, 1430–1830; closed Aug. Restorations.

FRANCESCHI & Fils, 10 rue de la Croix-der-Fer (2179395).
Numismatic specialist. Closed Aug.

HARPER'S Bizarre, 4 rue des Chevaliers (5124068).
Watches, scientific instruments, music boxes, unusual collector's items.

de HEUVEL, 2 rue de la Longue-Haie (5111727).
Leading specialist in old masters. Open 0700–1200, 1400–1700; closed Sun.

van der HEYDEN, 1 rue Ernest-Allard (5120294).
Clocks, watches. Restorations.

Henri van HOVE, 6 rue du Pépin (5120602) and rue Cap. Crespel.
Silver, furniture, porcelain, tapestries, works of art.

de JONCKHEERE-ANDRIES, 10 pl du Samedi (2180802).
Flemish and French old masters, especially 16th/17th-century. Flemish works. Open 1030–1200, 1400–1800; closed July.

LALOUX-DESSIN, 115 ave Louise (5379944).
Bronze, ivory, silver. Closed 15 July to end Aug.

van der LEENEN, 19 rue de Joncker (5381728).
Bibelots, glass, primitive art. Closed Sun., and Mon. mornings.

A. van LOOCK, 51 rue St-Jean (5127465).
Old and rare books, engravings, maps, drawings, views, decorative prints. Closed Sun.

LUNA Antica, 11 rue Lebeau (5132649).
Specialist in faience and icons. Closed Aug. Also in Antwerp.

MARKET 223, 223 ave Louise (497435).
Open 1000–1900; closed Sun. and 15–31 Aug.

J.-P. MEULEMEESTER, 50–2 rue de Rollebeek (5124801).
Paintings and drawings. 11th/19th-century.

Louis MOORTHAMERS, 124 rue Lesbroussart (6478548).
Drawings, engravings, maps, atlases, books. Closed weekends.

NACKERS Market, 28 chaussée de Wavre (5127280/9688).
Open 1000–1900.

NEUVER Antiques and Decoration, 114 blvd Général Jacques.
English furniture and silver.

PAULUS, 11 rue Ropsy-Chaudron (5214612).
Coins, medallions. Closed weekends and 15 July to 15 Aug.

P. van der PERRE, 21 rue de la Régence (5118245).
Books, autographs, engravings, 19th-century pictures. Auctions.

Galerie ROOSENS, 167 chaussée de Charleroi (537862).
Clocks.

Maison SAHAKIAN, 30 rue de l'Ecuyer (5172780).
Antique carpets, especially Caucasian. Open Tue.–Fri.; closed 1
July to 20 Aug.

STEFANOVICH, 38–9 Galerie Louise (5129429).
Fine porcelain, paintings, 18th-century furniture.

Karl STEPPE, 1302 chaussée de Waterloo.
English items; specialist in Buddhas and other Oriental temple
ornaments.

THYRION, 42 rue de Trèves (5113767).
Antique weapons.

TULKENS, 21 rue du Chêne (5130525).
Antiquarian books and manuscripts of 15th–20th centuries, fine
modern illustrated editions. Closed Sat.

VALENCAY, 4 pl du Grand-Sablon (5135154).
Bronze, silver, furniture, curiosities. Open daily.

de VALKENEER, 82 rue du Tabellion.
Old lace.

Pierre VANDERBORGHT, 9 rue Ravenstein (5124860).
Old jewellery, prints, bibelots, old and new books. Closed Sun., and Mon. April–Sept.

Au VIEUX SOUBISE, 202 ave Brugmann (3449302).
Earthenware, pewter, bronze, collectors' items. Closed Mon. mornings

J. van der WEGHE, 9 rue des Sablons (5119046),
Maps, views, 17th/18th-century prints, 16th/17th century atlases. Closed 1–21 Aug.

Jean WILLEMS, 47 rue des Petits-Carmes (5120353).
Old masters, 19th-century paintings. Open Tue.–Sat.

Markets and fairs
Antique market, pl du Grand-Sablon.
Open Sat. 0900–1900; Sun. 0900–1300.

Flea market, pl du Jeu-de-Balle.
Open daily 0800–1300.

Flea market, rue Radis.
Open Sun. morning.

ANTIQUARIUS, 6 pl de la Chapelle (5127161).
Permanent antique and bric-à-brac market with 50 stalls. Open Sat.-Thur. 1000–1830; Fri. 1000–2200.

ANTIQUES CENTER (Salons Stephanie), 79–81 ave Louise (5377320).
Permanent antique market with 40 stalls. Open 1100–1900; closed Mon. and public hols. Yearly fair in Oct.

Au ROUET, 22 rue Bodenbroek (5118915).
Covered antique market with 20 dealers. Closed Mon.

Galerie du SABLON, 35 pl du Grand-Sablon.
Market with 15 stalls. Open daily; closed early Sun.

Les VIEUX SABLONS, pl du Grand-Sablon.
Permanent antique market with 13 dealers. Crystal, antique silver, weapons, art nouveau, art deco, Chinese porcelain, jewellery, etc.

Auctions

Salle de Vente de BEGUINAGE, 10 rue du Rouleau (2181742).
Mixed goods. Sales Wed.

Galerie FALMAGNE.
Books.

Galerie FERBACH, 215 chaussée d'Ixelles (6477683).

Galerie MODERNE, 41 rue des Petits-Carmes, 3–7 rue du Parnasse and 6 rue du Grand-Cerf (5139010).

P. van der PERRE, 21 rue de la Régence (5118245).
See 'Dealers'.

Salle de Vente PORTE D'ANVERS, 24 chaussée d'Anvers (2170756).
Sales Mon. and Thur.

Ghent

Dealers

H. E. van HOECKE, Onderbergen 6 (233305).
17th/18th-century porcelain, faience. Closed 15 July to 1 Sept.

G. MORANT, Kortrijksepoorstr 25 (255597).
Antique Chinese art — porcelain, jade, bronze. Closed July.

OLD FLEMISH ART, Limburgstr 10 (250176).
Antique weapons, porcelain, copper, brass, pewter, silver. Open 1000–1200, 1400–1830.

Galerie ST BAVON, St Baafspl 12 (250176).
Porcelain, pewter, icons, old furniture.

Markets and fairs
Flea market, pl du Marché.
Open Fri.–Sat.

Antique fair, St Pietersabdij.
Yearly in March-April.

Antique fair, Koornleigund.
Yearly on 3rd weekend in Sept.

Auctions
Galerie STAMPAERT, Vliegtuiglaan 5 (512561).

de VOS, Ziniastr 37 (264581).

Keerbergen

Dealers
HAMPSHIRE HOUSE Antiques. 62 Tremelobaan (52646).
English furniture. Closed Thurs.

Knokke

Dealers
JACOBEAN Antiques.
English furniture.

Kortrijk

Dealers
BRUGGEMAN-DERUYTER, Kapitelstr 1 (221359).
Delft-ware specialist.

Liège

Dealers

CHAMBORD, *14b rue St-Remy (523597)*.
Delft, paintings, engravings, silver boxes.

DEMOULINS, *12 rue de la Casquette (236987)*.
Engravings, antique jewellery, Liègeois furniture, Oriental and Delft porcelain, 17th/19th-century paintings. Restorations.

FINKIELSTEJN, *27 rue de la Casquette (236987)*.
Specialist in Delft.

Guy GENARD, *12 rue des Clarisses (322674)*.
Coins, faience, porcelain. Open 0900–1900; closed Sun.

Librairie HALBART, *11 rue des Carmes (235428)*.
History, art, maps, engravings. Open 0900–1830; closed Sun.

L. V. PLANCHAR, *16 rue St-Remy (236722)*.
Liègeois furniture, German faience, silver. Restorations.

La RAPIERE, *26 rue St-Thomas (321127)*.
Fine antique weapons. Open afternoons and Sun. mornings; also by appointment (always advisable). Restorations.

RICHTERICH, *28 rue des Dominicains (234124)*.
Jewellery, curios.

SALON DES ANTIQUAIRES.
Liègeois furniture.

WALTHERY, *30 rue Darchis (234949)*.
Delft, 18th-century Liègeois furniture. Open 1400–2000.

Markets
Market, quais de la Bulle.
Open Sun. 0700–1900.

Auctions

Maison ISTA – MARECHAL, 49 rue des Champs (431765).

WIERTZ, 35 rue aux Chevaux (270382).

Luxembourg City

Dealers

ART CHINOIS, 18 rue du Marché-aux-Herbes.

Jen BADU, 1b rue Beaumont (27036).

MICOLAY-MOOTZ, 4 rue Wiltheim (22478).

NUMIA, 12 rue Duchschen (481765).
Coins.

Nicola ROMANO, 1 rue de la Loge (40910).

Namur

Dealers

A L'ETOILE D'OR, 400 chaussée de Dinant (74319).
Clocks.

Ostend

Dealers

GALEYN.
Prints, including old prints of Ostend.

Museums

Apart from its big famous collections, Belgium offers a variety of smaller museums of particular interest to collectors of, say, old maps, Delft ware or firearms.

Antwerp

ROYAL MUSEUM OF FINE ARTS, pl Leopold de Wael.
A formidable collection of Dutch and Flemish masters plus the best of contemporary Belgian work – offers the world's finest opportunity to study the work of Peter Paul Rubens in its historical perspective.

RUBENS HOUSE, Rubensstr 9 (off the Meir).
Paintings by Rubens and his pupils contained in a house designed by the master.

SMIDT VAN GELDER HOUSE, Belgielei 91.
This 18th-century house, bequeathed in 1949 to the city with all its contents, offers the rare opportunity to see the home of a collector of superb taste, with its fine antiques – furniture, china, paintings – untouched in their original setting. Open on odd-numbered days of the month.

Bruges

BRANGWYN MUSEUM, Dyver Canal.
An unexpected 20th-century English touch amid a rich harvest of Flemish paintings and the purest medieval setting in Northern Europe. Sir Frank Brangwyn, who worked there, left many of his paintings and drawings to the city.

Brussels

ARMY MUSEUM, parc du Cinquantenaire.
Militaria and arms collection, mainly from the First World War.

BODART OPTICAL MUSEUM, 33 rue Royale.
This optical firm's museum contains exhibits ranging from early

spectacles made of rock crystal to a marvellous collection of jewelled, inlaid and miniature opera glasses.

INSTITUT ROYAL DU PATRIMONIE ARTISTIQUE, 1 parc du Cinquantenaire.
The first body in the world to study the scientific preservation and restoration of works of art; the venture is sponsored by UNESCO.

MUSEES ROYAUX D'ART ET D'HISTOIRE, ave des Nerviens.
Notable among other things for one of the finest collections of Delft ware in the world, also the rare Arnhem pottery, Tournai porcelain, Brussels and German wares, and an outstanding collection of lace, embroideries and textiles.

MUSEE HORTA, 25 rue Américaine.
Lived in and designed by Victor Horta, pioneering architect and furniture designer; now a museum of art nouveau.

ROYAL CONSERVATORY OF MUSIC, 17 pl du Petit-Sablon.
Over 4000 musical instruments, both European and Oriental. Free 'period' concert on Wed. night.

Dinant

ADOLPHE SAX HOUSE.
Adolphe Sax, inventor of the saxophone, was born in 1814 in this town, famous for its metalwork, especially beaten and engraved copper; his home is now a small museum of interest to collectors of musical instruments.

Liège

MUSEE D'ARMES, 8 quai de Maestricht.
The most complete collection of small arms in Europe, with over 8000 examples showing the development of the gunsmith's art over the centuries. Closed Tues.

Mons

MUSEE DU CHANOINE PUISSANT, rue Notre-Dame – Debonnaire.
Unique collection of old lace.

Namur

MUSEUM OF ARTS AND CRAFTS, rue de Fer.
Arts and crafts of the middle ages and the renaissance. Meuse region gold plate, wooden statues, liturgical ornaments, copper ware. Includes works by the Belgian painter Felicien Rops.

MUSEE COMMUNAL D'HISTOIRE MILITAIRE DU COMTE DE NAMUR, route Merveilleuse de la Citadelle.
6000 antique weapons.

MUSEE DE CROIX, rue Joseph Saintraint.
18th- and 19th-century local crafts.

MUSEE DIOCESAIN ET TRESOR DE LA CATHEDRALE, 1 pl de la Cathédrale.
The work of Mosan silversmiths (who lived along the river Meuse) – famous for their craftsmanship – and some outstanding Dinant copperware.

Sint-Niklaas

CITY MUSEUM.
Map collectors will be interested in the two rooms devoted to Mercator, the geographer who was born in nearby Rupelmonde in 1512 – includes his famed navigational planisphere, along with some rare maps.

Tournai

MUSEE DES BEAUX ARTS, 18 Enclos St-Martin.
The best in Tournai arts, including the famous porcelain, tapestries, brass, copper and ironwork.

Further reading

Baar, A., *Rétrospective de la verrerie artistique belge* (Liège, 1930) – for glass collectors.

Beurdeley, M., *Porcelain of the East India Companies* (London, 1962).

Honey, W. B., *European Ceramic Art* (London: Faber & Faber, 1952).

Hulst, Roger d', *Flemish Tapestries* (Cambridge, 1967).

Imber, D., *Collecting Delft* (London: Arco and New York: Praeger, 1968)

Jonge, C. H. de, *Delft Ceramics* (London: Pall Mall Press, 1970).

Klamkin, Marion, *The Collector's Book of Art Nouveau* (Newton Abbot: David & Charles, 1971) – a good introduction to art nouveau.

Soil de Moriame, E. J. and Desplace de Formanoir, L., *Les Porcelaines de Tournay* (Tournai, 1937)

Tavernor-Parry, S., *Dinanderie* (London, 1910) – still the definitive book on Dinant metal-working.

Thomson, W. G., *A History of Tapestry* (London, 1930 and New York, 1931).

Now worth several hundred pounds, art deco posters like this one of Maurice Chevalier published in 1937 are eagerly sought by collectors.

3
France

Introduction

Few parts of Europe are as exciting for collectors as France where, as befits the country which invented the flea market, every sizeable town has its *marché aux puces* and every region its own tradition of antiques. In the world of the *haut antiquaire* France offers a great heritage in furniture-making, clocks, jewellery design, tapestries and objets d'art such as the magnificent 18th-century snuff box. In this century, art nouveau and art deco are both predominantly associated with France – even today in Paris the sinuous wrought-iron entrances to many metro stations remain monuments to art nouveau, and artefacts from the 1900s to the 1930s are avidly collected. While Louis XVI furniture and clocks, impressionist paintings and Cartier jewellery of the 1920s will be beyond the resources of most visitors, much pleasure is to be had from browsing round the markets and, in Paris, through the narrow streets of book and print dealers on the Left Bank of the Seine.

The sprawling complex of five markets at St Ouen on the outskirts of Paris, at the end of the metro line running to porte Clignancourt, is well worth a day of anyone's time and Paris dealers themselves comb it regularly, though to the uninitiated many of the stalls may appear to be littered with reproduction ormolu and expensive fake antique weapons. To save time and energy it is important to sort out the different markets and select a target. The Marché Biron, good for firearms and armour, is the most sophisticated of the five, with carefully-selected and presented merchandise priced at a level similar to that in the antique shops in central Paris. Collectors are more likely to find bargains in the Marché Paul-Bert and Marché Vernaison, which are messy and dirty but frequented by dealers and where the knowledgeable can often make a marvellous find. The Vernaison is oldest of the five markets. Dealers incidentally tend to visit the flea markets on Saturdays, when the serious trading takes place; Sunday is for sightseers and Monday – so it's said – for bargains when dealers are packing up after the bulk of the weekend's business is done.

A Paris trade dealer who sells to the public at flea market prices is Liss. Bargaining is accepted by all French antique dealers, not only at the flea markets but also in the grandest shops with the biggest price tickets.

As well as the famous flea market at St Ouen, there are open-air markets outside Paris – the annual Foire à la Feraille and Foire du Jambon, which take place in the early spring in Pantin, and the Foire des Brocanteurs (secondhand dealers) at Chaton are worth visiting. There is a lot of junk here certainly, but the professionals go through them carefully and there are lots of foreign buyers. Nothing new is allowed to be sold; lots of Napoleon III furniture and 1900 paste jewellery is found.

In France, the sign *occasion* outside an antique dealer's can mean both 'bargain' and 'used'; *rossignol* (literally, nightingale) means in dealer's slang something left over from the best stock, i.e. those period pieces that are not quite antiques.

In Paris, antique markets on the London pattern have sprung up, with prices usually on the high side. The Faubourg St-Honoré market (Cour aux Antiquaires) – not to be confused with the exclusive shops in the same street – has stalls run by well-to-do middle-aged ladies and is a pleasant place to drop into after the expensive shops. The Porte Maillot market attracts tourist trade from two big new hotels nearby and is also patronized by residents of the western suburbs – definitely not cheap, but worth looking at. An old-established feature of Paris life is the Village Suisse market, which is very accessible and much more elegant and expensive than it used to be, with lots of plants and fountains. It is certainly less exhausting than the flea markets, but buyers should beware of reproductions, especially in furniture.

All around the former site of Les Halles, the famous old vegetable market, there are lots of secondhand shops in the rue St-Denis and the 'passage' at rue St-Honoré. They contain a varied choice, from sheer junk to excellent 18th-century stuff, but are definitely worth a couple of hours. There are also a number of antique shops in the new Porte Maillot shopping centre, the Palais des Congrès, dealing with furniture, glass and porcelain. Antique shops in central Paris are concentrated in three main areas: the 6th and 7th arrondissements on the Left Bank of the Seine, a wonderful hunting ground for collectors of rare books, prints, posters, scientific instruments, maps and manuscripts; the fashionable 8th arrondissement, especially boulevard Haussmann; and the 9th arrondissement, where there is a cluster of small but interesting shops around the St Georges metro station.

The sales at Hôtel Drouot, France's premier auction centre, were a Paris institution for 123 years, but for some time the 70 or so auctioneers who used the premises had found themselves bursting at the seams, and prestige sales were held at the Georges V Hotel and the Palais Galliéra. The auction house had now moved completely to the old Gare d'Orsay building and is known as Drouot Rive Gauche, whose smartly decorated new salerooms offer a variety of auxiliary services. At the Drouot, those auctions *without* a catalogue tend to be the ones where bargains are found.

There are also two auctions held at Versailles at weekends, an increasingly popular excursion for Parisians. Maître Bache specializes in pictures; the other auctioneers go in for everything. Announcements of Paris sales can be found in the national press and *Gazette de l'Hôtel Drouot*, published three times weekly. French auctions are organized very strictly, with the official auctioneers fulfilling the role of civil servants. All auctions have to be held under auctioneers' own names rather than a company name such as Sotheby's or Christie's. Buyers pay a tax of 16 per cent on amounts up to 6000 francs. 11.5 per cent on amounts between 6001 and 20 000 francs, and 10 per cent on amounts above that.

Outside Paris, excellent antique fairs are held in Lyon, Marseille and Toulouse. The latter is particularly good for 18th-century furniture and other treasures from the big houses in the hinterland where upper- and middle-class families are now feeling the economic pinch. Tours is another very good provincial centre, especially for 18th-century Provençal furniture and ceramics, and tapestries of excellent quality. Aix-en-Provence is a first-rate antique centre, but prices are likely to be high as this attractive town is full of affluent commuters with offices in Marseille. The regions of France each have their particular interest for collectors.

Here are some of the regional specialities, listed with the cities given in 'The trade'.

Bouches-du-Rhône (Aix-en-Provence, Marseille)

Far Eastern objects (much in demand by French collectors); rustic Provençal furniture in carved walnut; porcelain and fine glass of the 18th century; Provençal oil lamps in glass, earthenware and Marseille ceramics; painted draught screens; Roman and Greek coins; finds from excavations.

Gironde (Bordeaux)

Bordeaux faience (18th-century) products, including pharmaceutical and domestic implements; a local hard-paste porcelain (late 18th-century) and cream earthenware (1834–45), mainly transfer-printed; mahogany furniture of the 18th century and Restoration periods; Bordelaises commodes in mahogany of the Louis XV period; knick-knacks of the romantic period; old plate signed '*Vieillard*'.

Nord (Lille)

Ceramics, especially earthenware, from Lille, St Omer, Tournai, Valenciennes and Delft; Flemish and Dutch paintings; Flemish furniture; weapons (in Lille).

Rhône (Lyon)

15th/16th-century fine furniture; Lyonnais wardrobes; 17th/18th-century panelling; old faience from Bresse, Roanne, Meillonnes, Charolles, Lyon; tapestries; engravings; paintings of the Lyon school.

Alpes-Maritimes (Nice)

Provençal furniture; Biot jars; Provençal glassware; faience from

Moustiers, Marseille, Avignon; modern paintings (especially in Nice). The area between Nice and Monaco has been enriched for more than a century with art objects from many parts of the world; Beaulieu has developed into a particularly good centre for buying and selling.

Ille-et-Vilaine (Rennes)

A region rich in cupboards, tables and cabinets in a local style which recalls Louis XV, mostly carved and some signed and dated; empire and restoration furniture; East India Co. porcelain, brought back to the area by sailors in the 18th and 19th centuries; rare antique faience from Rennes and Quimper.

Seine-Maritime (Rouen)

Norman furniture; cabinets, chests, chairs and other items of Empire and Louis-Philippe periods; ceramics from Rouen, Strasbourg, Lunéville; iron firedogs; copperware; country clocks; statues and pictures of the *haute-époque* (renaissance) era; antique dolls of the region; terracotta from Grailloc.

Bas-Rhin (Strasbourg)

Faience; lead soldiers; pottery and stoneware implements of the wine grower's trade; glass from Vallerysthal; 18th-century locks; pewter; *pâte de verre*.

Specialities

Art Deco

This style originated in Paris, at the Exhibition des Arts Decoratifs of 1925, and took off as a collecting field with an anniversary exhibition in 1966 which coined the term 'art deco'. Prices are now very high and quality perhaps not what it was. Gallé and Daum glass and Majorelle furniture are especially popular. A leading Paris dealer is Levy.

Autographs and Manuscripts

Autographs and manuscripts are a strong Paris speciality, to be found among the rare book dealers in the rue Bonaparte and rue de Seine area.

Books

In Paris, the area around rue Bonaparte is full of dealers in rare books. The twice-yearly Bordeaux book fair should not be forgotten.

Bronze

The French speciality here is the 19th-century school known as Les Animaliers sculptors who produced fine, lifelike animal figures. Leading artists were Antoine-Louis Barye, P. J. Mêne, Christophe Fratin, Emmanuel Fremiet, and Rosa and Isidore Bonheur. Some of the highest prices are paid for the rare impressionist-style bronzes of Rembrandt Bugatti, brother of Ettore who founded the car firm. Deschamps in Paris is a leading dealer in animalier bronzes.

Clocks and Watches

French clocks are prized for their ornamental qualities, particularly those of the prolific Louis XV and XVI periods. Typical of the first era was the bronze rococo clock with abstract decorations of flowers or shells. Top Louis XV makers include Baillon and Leroy, those of the succeeding reign Janvier and Caron. The French made the finest watches in Europe from the 16th century until 1675, when the main centre shifted to London. Bréguet was the outstanding name. The French also made the finest small clocks at an early stage, and the French carriage clock is famous.

Coins and Medals

There is tremendous French interest in this field. The Paris dealers can mostly be found clustered, appropriately enough, round the Bourse. The coinage of Louis XIII was particularly beautiful, and the Louis XIV period medals resemble Roman coins in the quality of their portraiture. Jean Varin was the outstanding medallist of the time.

Dolls

The antique-doll market is almost entirely French, the 19th-century maker Jumeau being the top name. Dumas is a leading specialist dealer in Paris.

Firearms

By the end of the 17th century French gun-makers had the reputation of being the best in the world. Among stylistic and technical innovators were Bertrand Piranbe and Isaac de Chaumette. Mouton of Nancy made all-metal pistols. Leading 19th-century makers were le Page and Nicolas-Noel Boutet, gun maker to Napoleon and the finest decorative gun-maker in Europe, whose work has never been surpassed. Lille is a good centre for antique weapons, also the markets of Paris.

Glass

France was comparatively late into the field of fine table glass, Baccarat in 1765 being the first to produce it. French glass really came into its own in the late 19th century with *pâte de verre* and opaline ware, and later with art nouveau and art deco glass by Gallé, Daum and Lalique – the latter still produced, but less interesting to collectors since the death of René Lalique in 1945.

French glass paperweights are notable and costly collectors' items. Baccarat, St Louis and Clichy being the three main factories. The earliest weights are attributed to St Louis (1845–49), the most prized variety being those in overlay glass, cut through as in cameo glass. All factories produced the popular millefiori type, with bunches of multicoloured glass canes cut to resemble posies of flowers; Baccarat millefiori weights date from 1846 (1849 being the rarest year). Clichy's swirl pattern is instantly recognizable and the Clichy flower sprays are rare and expensive. Weights are priced according to the rarity of their colour and design; the market has fluctuated considerably in the last ten years.

Plate glass was a French invention in 1688, and consequently early French mirrors were the best in the world. Another glass speciality of the 17th century was *verre filé de Nevers* – figurines and toys made of glass threads at Nevers – which continued to be produced for at least three centuries.

Pewter

Pewter is less important than in Britain, Low Countries and Federal Republic of Germany. The best pewter dealer in Paris is Boucaud.

Porcelain and Pottery

The French are great collectors of their native ceramics: pottery from Nevers, Rouen, Lyon, Marseille, Moustiers, Niderviller and Lunéville; porcelain from the Paris factories, Sèvres and Limoges. Many wealthy French families have splendid inherited collections.

The earliest centre for soft-paste porcelain was Rouen in 1673, but in the 18th century factories sprang up at St Cloud, Chantilly and Mennecy, all in or near Paris. Mennecy paste was of a lovely deep ivory and the glaze had a brilliant wet look. Some of Europe's finest rococo figures were made here. The earliest patterns were lacy arabesques in underglaze blue, developing at St Cloud into raised gold decoration with coloured enamel, a style copied at Meissen. Oriental themes followed; plum blossom in white relief or, at Chantilly, a simple form of Japanese decoration, very clear and bright. The unique quality of Chantilly lay in its opaque milky glaze, a marvellous background for painted decoration but not suitable for underglaze work. Few figures were produced at these factories on account of the difficulty of working the soft paste in the round.

Vincennes, whose white biscuit ware had a texture like marble, transferred to Sèvres in 1756 where it still flourishes. The royal cipher of two crossed L's was introduced in 1753, six years before Louis XV bought the Sèvres factory. The world's greatest collection of Sèvres is owned by the Queen. Characteristic of this factory were paintings enclosed in panels on coloured grounds of exceptional richness and depth. The first 14 years of the factory are considered to be the finest. Each year had its own colour:

turquoise was introduced in 1752, jonquil yellow in 1753, pea green in 1756, 'Pompadour rose' pink in 1757, and the magnificent royal blue in 1758, so brilliant that its effect was sometimes deliberately softened by an all-over pheasant's eye pattern.

The first French hard-paste porcelain was made at Limoges, where the right kind of clay was found. It was predominantly creamy with a flower-sprig type of decoration. Limoges had earlier been the centre of European enamel production during the 12th–14th centuries and 16th–17th centuries. Reproductions were made in Paris of Limoges enamels in the 19th century.

Tin-glazed earthenware (i.e. faience) was first developed at Rouen in imitation of Chinese porcelain. *Faience blanches* (i.e. everyday ware decorated with simple paintings or coats of arms) was introduced to France from Italy (from Faenza, hence the name) and made in Lyon and Nevers. A white or cream-coloured, lead-glazed earthenware of English type was made at Chantilly and Lunéville.

Collectors of East India Co. porcelain, ordered in quantity by the French nobility during the reign of Louis XV, can usually find good but pricy examples along the quai Voltaire and rue St-Honoré in Paris.

Posters

The French were undisputed masters of the art nouveau and art deco poster, from the works of Alphonse Mucha and Toulouse-Lautrec to those of A. M. Cassandre, who designed for the Compagnie Générale Transatlantique and French Railways. The latter are particularly prized by collectors now; some in London have fetched around £500. Around the rue de Seine and surrounding streets in Paris, good examples can often be picked up more cheaply than in London, despite competition from US dealers. Other top poster designers of the interwar years included Charles Kiffer and Caddy.

Silver

Very little early silver survives, as it was mostly melted down to pay for various wars. The 18th-century silver was nearly all lost in the Revolution, so most of what can be found is 19th-century. Collectors should look out for coffee and chocolate jugs (*chocolatières*), the latter with a little hole in the lid for a wooden spoon to stir the thick hot chocolate. One of the greatest names in French 18th-century silver was Robert-Joseph Auguste. Juste-Aurèle Meissonier was the supreme silversmith of the rococo period.

Snuff Boxes

Snuff boxes were very much a French speciality, especially those made in gold in the 18th century, often with relief work in four-colour gold, by makers such as Ducrollay, George and Drais. After 1750 the shapes were predominantly oblong, circular and oval, sometimes with inset miniature paintings or enamelled. Enamel work in blue or purple shades denoted the 1780s, after which the Revolution put a stop to such frivolities. Gold boxes were also engine-turned, usually with horizontal lines.

Porcelain boxes were made at St Cloud (1723–50), Chantilly, Sèvres and Mennecy. Lacquered 'Vernis Martin' boxes were popular from 1744 to 1764; they had gold mounts and crimson or dark-green backgrounds painted with pastoral or genre scenes.

Tapestries

France was the first country in Europe to develop high-warp loom tapestry. By the mid 18th century the main centres were Paris, Tours and Rouen, but Paris was always the leader; the Gobelins buildings in the Faubourg St-Marcel continued production into the 20th century. Until the Revolution, Beauvais supplied the nobility and court officials of France, while Aubusson catered for the wealthy middle classes. Beauvais was nationalized in the third year of the Republic.

The trade

Aix-en-Provence

Dealers
Serge BADY, 13 rue Mignet.
Antiques, coins.

Philippe BESANCON, 19 rue Cardinale (262983).
General antiques.

Lucien BLANC, 44 cours Mirabeau (260053; private 401199).
Old masters, modern paintings, fine antique furniture, objets
d'art. Open Tues.–Sat. 0900–1200, 1400–1900; also by appointment (always advisable).

J.–L. BOUZON, 2 rue Joubert (261869).
Important stock of Midi faience ware, other objects of quality.
Trade terms.

Marcel COLAS, passage Agard (260398).
Old books, coins.

LEREST & MATHIEU, 54 cours Mirabeau (261672).
18th-century French furniture, paperweights, etc.

LORENZACCIO, 19 cours Mirabeau (274531).
Fine 17th/19th-century furniture, antiques, paintings. Open
0900–1200, 1500–1900; appointment always advisable.

Les PARIS d'HELENE, 4 rue Joubert (261269).
Silver, jewellery, antiques.

J.–L. REYNAUD, 3 rue Matheron.
Clocks, antiques.

Armand VALON, route nationale 7 (à Lignane) (246185).
18th/19th-century English and French bronzes, books and antiques.

Markets
Flea market, pl du Palais and pl de Verdun.
Open Tues., Thur. and Sat. morning.

Bordeaux

Dealers
La Galerie d'ART, 39 rue Palais-Gallien (448152).
Paintings.

Galerie Noel BONNET, 29, 31 and 44 rue Bouffard (486182).
Paintings, 16th/19th-century engravings.

CAROL, 6 rue des Remparts (483480).
Coins, medals, stamps.

CHOTTARD, 74 rue Naujac (486256).
Books.

ELVE (Lucien Vigneau), 25 rue Bouffard (485808).
18th-century ceramics. (Vigneau also has shops in Paris and Nice)

Galerie du FLEUVE, 38 cours du Chapeau-Rouge (485010).
Prints, engravings.

Galerie IMBERTI, 47 rue Porte-Dijeaux (482781).
Prints, drawings, old masters, 19th-century paintings.

KERTIGHIAN, 36 rue Bouffard.
Coins, medals.

MARONNE, 37 rue Bouffard.
Books.

PASSICOUSSET, 35 rue Bouffard (483453).
Antiques, faience.

Paul ROUGIER, 61 rue des Renparts (520139).
Scientific instruments.

Markets and fairs
Bric-à-brac market, pl Meynard (nr church of St Michel).
Open Mon. and Wed.–Fri.

Antique fair.
80 exhibitors. Twice yearly in mid Feb. and Oct. (2nd-3rd Sun.).

Book fair, pl des Quinconces.
Twice yearly in March and Oct.

Auctions
Auction room, 16–20 rue Delurber (442146, 480410).
Sales Tues., Wed. and Fri., 1400.

Lille

Dealers
ASMODEE, 29 rue Royale.
Specialist in the period 1900–30, jewellery of all periods.

Philippe BOUHIN, 23 rue de Paris (552737).
Antique weapons.

DESPLATS, 4 rue Basse (553415).
Ceramics.

DUPONT, 141 blvd de la Liberté (548560).
Books.

LACASSE, 5 rue Curé-St-Etienne (553585).
Antique pewter, copper and brass; coins, medals.

LAHOUSSE, 8 rue Basse (556351).
Coins, medals.

MISCHKIND, 7 rue Jean-sans-Peur (573049).
Paintings, lithographs, sculpture.

RAMART, 4 rue Sec-Arembault.
Drawings, engravings.

VANLERBERGUEL 35 rue J.-B.-de-la-Salle.
Clocks.

Pierre VASSE, 76 rue Esquermoise (551849).
Paintings, prints.

Markets
MARCHE DE LA TREILLE, 23–5 rue des Chats-Bossus.
Bric-à-brac market with over 20 stalls.

MARCHE DE WAZEMMES (flea market).
Open Sun. morning.

Auctions
Auction rooms, 2 rue Ste-Anne (552543).
Sales Mon. and Wed., 1400.

Lyon

Dealers
L'AIGLE D'OR (Gerard Romestant), 29 pl de Bellecour (372679).
Antique arms, Louis XIII and provincial furniture.

Galerie CARACALLA, 12 rue du Boeuf (370314).
Important stock of engravings from earliest examples to 19th century; drawings, watercolours. Open 1000–1200, 1400–1900.

CYVOT (La Sabretache), 260 rue Duguesclin (600759).
Antique weapons.

Roger GONNARD, 7 pl de Bellecour (378303).
Specializes in arms and militaria, scientific instruments. Appointment necessary.

C. A. GONNET, 44 rue Auguste-Comte (370203).
General antiques, especially ceramics.

Armand & Paul LARDENCHET, 10 rue Président-Carnot (374134).
Manuscripts, 1st editions, modern illustrations, fine bindings. Open Mon.–Sat. 0900–1900; appointment always advisable. Also in Paris.

MONTMORY, 11 rue Grenette (425900).
Antique jewellery, gold, silver.

Au ROUET D'OR (Mme Marthe Bernin), 12 rue Franklin (370384).
18th/19th-century faience and small items of furniture, 18th-century porcelain and bibelots. Open Oct.–May.

Galerie SAGITTAIRE (F. Lascoux), 23 rue Auguste-Comte(376268).*
Old paintings. Open 1000–1200, 1500–1900; closed Mon.

Galerie ST GEORGES, 22 rue St-Georges (377273; private 472027).
Paintings of old, modern and Lyon 19th-century schools. Closed Mon.

Paulette SECRETANT, 4 pl Sathonay (281322).
Antique weapons, military curios, orders, decorations and historical documents.

Galerie VERRIERE, 13 quai Romain-Rolland (374064).
Paintings, sculpture, tapestries. Open Mon.–Sat. 0900–1200, 1430–1930; appointment always advisable.

Markets and fairs
Flea market, 1 bis, rue Joseph-Merlin and Villerbanne, 115 blvd Stalingrad (527009).
Pictures, arms, faience, pewter, books, jewellery. Open Thur. and Sun. mornings; Sat. all day.

Antiques fair, Grand Palais.
Twice yearly in 2nd half of April and Oct.

Auctions
Auction rooms, 19 rue Confort and 6 rue de l'Hôpital (420134).
Sales daily, 1400 and 2000.

Marseille

Dealers
ALLEGRE, 45 rue de la Loge (597933).
Books.

CAPURRO, *47 rue St-Jacques (374652).*
Ceramics, weapons, pictures.

CHAIX-BRYAN, *23 rue Jean-Fiolle.(372609).*
Paintings.

GAILLETON, *43 rue Dragon (370883).*
Silver.

GONZALES, *3 rue Aldebert (535037).*
Arms.

GUILLON, *3 rue de Lodi (474106).*
Silver, clocks.

LAFFITTE, *156 La Canebière (596028).*
Books.

POLART, *4 rue Pommier (624949).*
Oriental antiques, tapestries, rugs.

PORCHER, *20 rue St-Saens (337794).*
Paintings.

REYNAUD, *37 rue du Dr-Escat (374380).*
Automata, old toys, music boxes, scientific instruments.

TEYSSIER, *370 ave du Prado (777609).*
Arms, ceramics, scientific instruments, marine antiques.

Markets and fairs
Flea market, Quartier St-Lazare, rue Peyssonnel, rue de Pontevée and rue Clary.
Open Sun. morning.

Antique fair.
Yearly in April.

Auctions
Auction rooms, 45 rue d'Aubagne (540945).
Sales Sun.–Fri., 0900 and 1430.

Auction rooms, 102 rue Cantini (776836).
Sales Wed. and Sat., 0900 and 1430.

Auction rooms, 19 rue Borde (772773).
Sales Wed., Fri. and Sat., 1430.

Auction rooms, 130 ave de Toulon (477532).
Sales Wed, and Sat., 1430.

Nice

Dealers
AUGIER, 10 ave de Verdun (877369).
Jewellery, silver.

AUSTERLITZ, 5 rue Dalpozzo.
Arms, orders, decorations.

BIANCARELLI, 26 rue Ségurane (855852).
Jewellery, silver.

DAMGAARD, 20 rue Catherine-Ségurane (809264).
Antique clocks, bric-à-brac.

Anne de FRANCONY, 16 blvd Victor-Hugo (887364).
19th-century and modern paintings and lithographs.

Jean HEKKING, 4 rue de Longchamp (878539).
Antique weapons.

HORNSTEIN (Aux Grands Siècles), 21 rue de France (886879).
Coins, medals, silver.

MATARASSO, 2 rue de Longchamp (877455).
Books, prints.

Au MIROIR DES SIECLES, 37 rue de la Buffa (884861).
Silver.

NIRY, 100 rue de France (870629).
Oriental works, tapestries.

PICHET D'ETAIN, 2a rue Antoine-Gautier, Village Ségurane (802014).
A leading French provincial dealer in pewter, copper and brass.

Galerie RECAMIER, 50 rue de France (881525; private 852717).
17th/19th-century paintings.

RENAULD, 60 bis, blvd Risso (809496).
Arms.

Lucien VIGNEAU, 11 ter, rue Maréchal-Joffre (878187).
Ceramics, Gallé glass, clocks. Also in Paris and Bordeaux.

Markets
Flea market, blvd Risso and quai du Paillon.
Open Mon.–Sat.

Paris

Dealers
Librairie de l'ABBAYE, 27 rue Bonaparte (0338999).
Antiquarian books and manuscripts of historical, literary and musical interest; specialist in autographs. Open Mon. 1400–1930; Tues.–Sat. 1000–1230, 1400–1930.

Mme ALTERO-VAILLANT, 21 quai Voltaire (5480271).
Specialist in glass; 18th-century furniture, objets d'art.

Aux ARMES DE FRANCE (Charles Marchal), 46 rue de Miromesnil (2657279) and Marché Biron (stand 20), St Ouen.
Antique weapons, orders, lead soldiers.

Galerie ARTEL, 25 rue Bonaparte (0339377).
Icons.

Huguette BERES, 25 quai Voltaire (5485632).

French 19th/20th-century paintings and drawings; Japanese prints a speciality. Open 1000–1300, 1400–1900; appointment always advisable.

BONNEFOY & Cie (Au Vieux Paris), 4 rue de la Paix (0731278).
Antique jewellery and silver.

Au BON VIEUX CHIC (René Johnson), 16 quai du Louvre (2365661).
Arms, military curios, decorations. Open 0900–1900; closed Mon.

Charles & Philippe BOUCAUD, 25 rue du Bac (5483539).
Pewter.

Emile BOURGEY, 7 rue Drouot (7708867).
Coins.

Alain BRIEUX, 48 rue Jacob (2602198).
Old scientific and medical books, scientific instruments, maritime antiques. Open daily 1000–1300, 1400–1900; appointment advisable.

Jean & Denise CAILLEUX, 136 faubourg St-Honoré (3592524).
Fine 18th-century paintings and drawings. Open daily 1000–1200, 1400–1800; also by appointment.

COULET & FAURE, 5 rue Drouot (7708487/638).
Antiquarian books and autographs. Open Mon.–Sat. Auctions.

Galerie DABER, 24 ave de Friedland (9242402).
19th-century French paintings. Open Mon.–Fri. 1000–1230, 1400–1830; Sat. 1000–1300; also by appointment.

Stéphane DESCHAMPS, 19 rue Guénégaud (6335800).
Art nouveau glass (Gallé, Daum, Mucha), 19th-century animalier bronzes.

Jean Baptiste DIETTE, 4 ave Matignon (3599890).
Antique clocks.

Philippe DUMAS, 26 rue Notre-Dame-des-Victoires (2360324).
19th-century dolls. Open 0900–1200.

ELEONORE, 18 rue de Miromesnil (2651781).
French and foreign silver and plate. Open 0930–2000.

Marc Sté GARLAND, 23 rue du Bac (2225057; private 2223821).
Antique jewellery. Open 1000–1900; also by appointment.

Galerie Joseph HAHN, 36 rue de Berri (3594534).
Old masters.

HALPHEN-MEYER, 241 rue St-Honoré (pl Vendôme) (2600938).
Antique jewellery, silver, gold boxes, miniatures. Open
0930–1900; appointment always advisable.

François HEIM SA, 15 ave Matignon (2252238, 3594926).
Old masters, sculpture. Also in London.

Georges HEIM-GAIRAC, 13 rue de Seine (3265750).
Old masters, Barbizon school, drawings, watercolours.

JADE Co. SA.
Chinese works of art, jade, hardstones, coral, turquoises, etc.
Also in Geneva and New York.

*Le KEPI ROUGE (Christian Blondieau), Village Suisse (stand 79),
rond-point de Lugano (15e) (5675983).*
Antique weapons, uniforms, military curios, prints, lead
soldiers.

*Armand & Paul LARDENCHET, 100 rue Faubourg-St-Honoré
(3591640)*
Manuscripts, first editions, modern illustrations, fine bindings.
Also in Lyon.

LEFEBVRE & Fils, 24 rue du Bac (2611840).
17th/18th-century porcelain and faience. Open daily 1000–1200,
1430–1900; appointment advisable.

Philippe LEROUX, 16 rue de Beaune (2220611, 2611824).
Glass.

Gérard LEVY, 17 rue de Beaune (2612655).
Art nouveau, art deco, Oriental works of art (chiefly paintings).

*LISS, 14 rue des Roulettes, Montreuil (nr metro Croix-de-Chavaux)
(2870595).*

G. LUBRANO & Fils, 5 rue des Lions (8874188).
Specialists in antique clocks. Restorations.

Galerie MARCUS, 20 rue Chauchat (7709123).
Large stock of old masters.

Alain MOATTI, 77 rue des Sts-Pères (2229104).
Medieval and renaissance works of art, bronze, scientific instruments, clocks.

NICOLIER, 7 quai Voltaire (2607863).
Large stock of 9th/19th-century faience and porcelain. Open
daily 1000–1200, 1430–1900; appointment advisable.

Librairie de NOBELE, 35 rue Bonaparte (3260862).
Antiquarian and modern books on the arts, collecting,
archaeology, Oriental culture and Egyptology. Open Mon.–Fri.
0900–1200, 1400–1900; appointment advisable.

Librairie PINAULT, 36 rue Bonaparte (6330424).
Literature, memoirs, cookery, maritime, illustrated books,
engravings, prints, Paris views. Auctions.

René PORTNOI, 240 faubourg St-Honoré (2271633).
Bronze, porcelain.

Paul PROUTE SA, 74 rue de Seine (3268980).
Specialist in original prints, etchings, engravings, lithographs
and drawings. Open Tues.–Sat. 0900–1200, 1400–1900.

Pierre de REGAINI, 6 rue de Beaune (5484267).

Porcelain, faience, 18th- and early 19th-century miniatures. Open 1000–1200, 1400–1900.

J. & A. SEMAIL, 10 rue du Cherche-Midi (5480382).
Watercolours, clocks.

SERPETTE, Marché Biron (stand 148, allée 2), St Ouen (6064969; weekday inquiries 2540655).
Ancient and modern arms. Open Sat.–Sun. 0930–1900; Mon. 0930–2200.

Jean-Pierre STELLA, Marché Vernaison (stand 122, allée 7), St Ouen (5484290) and 16 rue des Sts-Pères.
Arms, decorations, military documents, lead soldiers.

STUDIOS ATELIER, 2 rue de Lorraine (2054830/1).
Modern paintings. Open Mon.–Fri. all day; Sat. morning; appointment advisable.

TRESORS DU PASSE (Mme Polles), 3 rue des Saussaies (2654790).
18th-century ceramics, etchings, engravings. Open 0930–1900.

Pierre VANDERMEERSCH, 23 quai Voltaire (5482664, 2612310).
Antique porcelain, 16th/17th-century faience.

Librairie Jean VIARDOT, 13 rue de l'Echaude (6336007).
Old maps, views, atlases, prints, illustrated books. Open Mon.–Fri. 0900–1230, 1400–1830.

Au VIEUX CADRAN (R. Laforet), 59 ter, rue Bonaparte (3260107).
Antique jewellery, watches and clocks.

Lucien VIGNEAU, 2 rue des Sts-Pères (2607927).
Chinese porcelain, 18th-century French furniture, clocks, bronze. Closed Sun. Also in Nice and Bordeaux.

Jean VINCHON & Cie, 77 rue de Richelieu (7421611).
Important specialist in old and modern coins and medals. Open

Mon.–Fri. 0900–1200, 1400–1830; Sat. 0900–1200; appointment advisable.

Markets and fairs
Flea market, pl d'Aligre (12e).
Open daily to 1100.

Flea market, porte de Montreuil.
Open Sat.–Mon.

Flea market, porte Didot (14e).
Open Sat.–Sun.

Flea market, St Ouen.
Five markets, including Marché Biron, Marché Paul-Bert, Marché Vernaison. Open Sat.–Mon.

Antique market, porte Maillot.
30 stalls.

BICETRE, ave Paul-Vaillant-Couturier and ave Eugène-Thomas.
Market. Open Tues., Thur. and Sun.

COUR AUX ANTIQUAIRES, 54 faubourg St-Honoré.
Antique market. Open daily.

DES LILAS, ave des Bouleaux and ave de la Porte-des-Lilas (19e).
Market. Open Sun.

MARCHE BIRON, 18 ave Michelet and 85 rue des Rosiers, St Ouen.
Firearms, antiques. 200 dealers.

MARCHE PAUL-BERT, 18 rue Paul-Bert, St Ouen.
225 stands. Dealers' market open 0730–0800.

MARCHE VERNAISON, 136 ave Michelet and 99–101 rue des Rosiers, St Ouen.
300 dealers.

*VILLAGE SUISSE, 52 ave de la Motte-Picquet and 82 ave de Suffren
(15e).*
Market. Open Thur.–Mon.

Antique fair, Gare de la Bastille (inquiries to 15 rue de la Paix, 8e).
Yearly.

*BIENNALE DES ANTIQUAIRES, Grand Palais (inquiries to 11 rue
Jean-Mermoz, 8e).*
Yearly in Sept.–Oct.

FOIRE A LA FERAILLE, Pantin.
Yearly in early spring.

FOIRE DES BROCANTEURS, Chaton.

FOIRE DU JAMBON, Pantin.
Yearly in early spring.

FOIRE ST-LAURENT, near Gare de l'Est.
Yearly in June.

Auctions
COULET & FAURE, 5 rue Drouot (7708487/638).
See 'Dealers'.

DROUOT RIVE GAUCHE, 7 quai Anatole-France.
France's most important auction centre, comprising 20
salerooms and the services of banks, insurance offices and
valuers, and transport organizers. Sales daily, 1400 (25–30 sales
per season). More important sales on Mon., Wed. and Fri.
Viewing previous day. Three most important sales yearly in
March-April, May-June and Nov.–Dec.

*HOTEL DES CHEVAUX-LEGERS, Versailles (9505808, 9506982,
9503269, 9507504).*
Sales Wed. and Sun., 1400.

HOTEL RAMEAU, 5 rue Rameau, Versailles (9505506, 9507129)
Sales Tues. and Sun., 1400 in Winter; Tues. 1400 and Wed.
2100 in May and June.

Librairie PINAULT, 36 rue Bonaparte (6330424).
See 'Dealers'.

Rennes

Dealers
Jean BATTAIS, 11–12 pl du Palais (307522).
Pictures, jewellery, silver. Open Mon.–Sat. 0830–1200, 1400–1900; appointment always advisable.

BRUCHET-MERY, 56 rue d'Antrain (360372).
Antiques, curios.

CARADEC, 37 blvd Jean-Mermoz (509528).
Antiques, bric-à-brac.

DEVENYNS, 16 ave Janvier (303361).
Antique and modern weapons.

DURAND-NOEL, 17 quai Chateaubriand (303083).
Books.

GOURDEL, 5 rue Matte-Fablet (301497).
Jewellery.

PERROUAULT, 6 rue de la Monnaie (300007).

Au RELAIS DE LA BROCANTE (Mme Simon), 6 rue Thiers.
Furniture, knick-knacks.

Markets
Flea market, blvd de la Tour-d'Auvergne.
Open Fri.–Sat. and monthly public hols.

Auctions
Auction rooms, 5 pl du Champ-Jacquet and 32 pl des Lices (302221).
Sales Tues, and Thurs., 1400.

Rouen

Dealers
ANDRIEU, 9 rue Claude-Monet.
Prints, engravings.

Galerie CHAUVIDON, 11 rue Damiette (701020).
Six stalls of antiques, bric-à-brac, paintings.

HINARD-DARNAULT, 100 rue de la République (716790).
Antique clocks.

Irène HUISSE, 76 rue St–Romain (714426).
Old masters, drawings, watercolours, antiquities. Open
1000–2000; appointment always advisable.

Pierre METAIS, 2 pl Barthélémy (711148).
Faience of the Rouen area.

PERROT, 12 rue St–Romain (715795).
Ceramics.

PHALIPPOU-DELAPORTE, 11 pl de la Calende (717886).
Clocks.

RESSE, 11 rue Damiette (752322).
Ceramics.

WINTER, 7 pl Barthélémy (710337).
Scientific instruments, glass.

Markets
Flea market, pl St-Marc.
Open Sat.–Sun.

Auctions
Auction rooms, 20 rue Croix-de-Fer (715448, 703289).
Sales Tues., Fri. and Sat., 1400; occasionally Thur., 2100.

Strasbourg

Dealers

ANDRE, 1 rue Ste-Catherine (343703).
Books.

Galerie D'ARGENS, 15 rue du Bain-des-Plantes (326120).
Paintings.

ART ANCIEN, 7a rue des Frères.
Arms, coins, medals.

Antiquités CHENKIER, 10–11 rue des Dentelles (328276).
Arms, curiosities.

GANGLOFF, 20 pl de la Cathédrale (353957).
Prints, books.

Au LYS DE FRANCE (Jean Tindy), 4 rue des Dentelles (321067).
Paintings, earthenware, silver, antique jewellery. Open
1000–1200, 1500–1800; appointment always advisable.

PFIRSCH, 20 rue de la Nuée-Bleue (327273).
Ceramics, pewter, books, engravings.

RAUSCHER, 42 rue du 22-Novembre (322150).
Prints, engravings.

Markets
Flea market, pl du Vieil-Hôpital.
Open Sat.

Toulouse

Dealers
ANSAS DE PRADINES, 60 rue Pargaminières (217053).
Paintings (old masters and impressionists), silver, etc.

Jean BERTRAND, 25 rue du Rempart-Matabiau (222442).

BESAUCELE, 2 pl St-Scarbes (523487).
Chinese and Japanese porcelain, lacquer, netsuke.

Georges CEDOU, 39 rue de la Ste-Famille (478053).
Arms.

CHAPPE & Fils, 32 rue de la Pomme (226384).
Paintings.

Pierre FAURE, 5 rue Ninau (627645).
Silver.

FAUVEL, 10 rue Rempart-St-Etienne (226322).
Jewellery, silver.

FAVIER, 3 rue Baour-Lormiàn (428936).
Books.

FELIX, 26 rue Croix-Baragnon (520153).
Jewellery, silver.

Roger FOURNIALS, 31 rue Riquet (266382).
Coins, medals.

GRIMOUD, 10 pl St-Scarbes (221441).
Faience, prints.

Laurence LOCRE, 51 rue des Filatiers (526610).
Jewellery, paintings. Closed Sun.–Mon.

MONTAGUT, 5 pl Wilson (221040).
Arms, armour. Open Mon.–Sat. 0900–1200, 1400–1900; appointment always advisable.

THOUREL, 46 rue du Taur (220902).
Books, prints.

Mme VIGUERIE, 2 rue Philippe-Féral (524464).
Prints.

Markets and fairs
Flea market, pl St-Sernin (nr the Cathedral).
Open Sat.–Mon.

Antique market in Portet-sur-Garonne, 7 km (4½ miles) from Toulouse.

Antique fair (dates enquiries to 224025).
Held by Salon des Antiquaires for Languedoc-Midi-Pyrénées.
Yearly, usually in Nov.

Tours

Dealers
Edmond BACHELLIER, 70 rue de la Scellerie (051053).
Furniture and pictures. Closed Sun. 16th/19th-century.

BRILLET, 50 quai du Pont-Neuf (611049).

GRIZOLLE, 16 pl de la Résistance (056166).
Specialist in dolls.

KENT, 85 rue de la Scellerie (050330).

LEBODO, 31 rue de Bordeaux.
Prints, books.

QUANTIN, 27 rue Emile-Zola (057538; private 056177).
18th and early 19th-century furniture, barometers, mirrors,
knick-knacks. Open Mon. afternoon, Tues.–Sat. all day; appointment always advisable.

Markets and fairs
Bric-à-brac market, pl de la République.
Open Wed. and Sat.

FOIRE A LA BROCANTE.
Covered stalls on the Berry Canal hold items of value; others are
on open stands. Twice yearly in first half of May and first 3
weeks in Aug.

Auctions
Auction rooms, 20 rue Michel-Colombe (055059).
Sales Thur., 1400.

Museums

Aix-en-Provence

ATELIER CEZANNE, 9 ave Paul-Cézanne (262514).

Paris

ASSISTANCE PUBLIQUE, 47 quai de la Tournelle.
Historical documents, ancient medical and pharmaceutical instruments.

CERAMIQUES DE SEVRES, Pont-de-Sèvres.
Open 1000–1700; closed Tues.

JEU DE PAUME, Tuileries.
Not-to-be-missed collection of impressionists. Open 1000–1700.

MAISON DE BALZAC, 47 rue Raynouard, Passy (2245638).
Everything relating to the great 19th-century novelist. Open 1330–1800.

MUSEE DE L'ARMEE, Hôtel National des Invalides (7836070).

MUSEE D'ART MODERNE DE LA VILLE DE PARIS, ave du Président Wilson.
Adjoining museums contain modern French art, specializing in the Paris school.

MUSEE DES ARTS DECORATIFS, 107–9 rue de Rivoli (75001).
Silver, porcelain (especially Sèvres), art nouveau jewellery.

MUSEE CAMONDO, 63 rue de Monçeau.
Magnificent 18th-century furniture in the former home of a rich banker. Open Mon. and Wed.–Sat. 1400–1700; Sun. 1000–1200, 1400–1700.

MUSEE DU CINEMA, 82 rue de Courcelles, Passy.

MUSEE DU COSTUME, 11 ave du Président Wilson.
Costumes from 1700 to present. Open Mon.–Fri.

MUSEE DELACROIX, 6 rue Furstenberg.
The artist's studio preserved as he left it. Open 1000–1200, 1400–1800 (1 May to 1 Nov.).

MUSEE DES GOBELINS (7071002).
Open Wed.–Fri. 1400–1600. Visits to the workshops where the famous tapestries are made. Special exhibitions of tapestries are often held when the Gobelins Museum is open, 1000–1200, 1400–1700.

MUSEE INSTRUMENTAL DU CONSERVATOIRE NATIONAL DE MUSIQUE, 14 rue de Madrid (2921520).
Musical instruments. Open Thur. and Sat. 1400–1600; closed 14 July to 1 Oct.

MUSEE DE MARINE, Palais de Chaillot, pl du Trocadéro.
Ship models etc. Open 1000–1800.

MUSEE MARMOTTAN, 2 rue Louis-Boilly (2240702).
Magnificent collection of Monets. Open 1400–1700; closed Tues.

MUSEE DE LA MINERALOGIE, Paris Science Faculty (quai de Bercy), pl Jussieu.
One of the world's leading collections of minerals.

MUSEE MONETAIRE, Hôtel de la Monnaie, 11 quai de Conti (3265204).
Coins, medals. Open 1400–1700.

MUSEE POSTALE, 4 rue St-Romain.
Stamps. Open 1400–1800.

MUSEE RODIN, 77 rue de Varenne.
A charming old house in a garden, both filled with Rodin's sculpture. Open 1300–1700.

ORANGERIE, Tuileries.
Changing exhibitions, plus Monet's famous *Water Lilies*. Open 1000–1700.

PAVILLON DE MARSAN, Palais du Louvre (422284).
Silver, porcelain (especially Sèvres), art nouveau jewellery.

Rouen

MUSEE DES BEAUX ARTS ET DE LA CERAMIQUE, 26 bis, rue Thiers (712840).

PAVILLON ET MUSEE FLAUBERT, 18 rue Gustave-Flaubert.
Relics of the great novelist.

Toulouse

MUSEE PAUL DUPUY, 13 rue de la Pleau (216800).
Includes clocks, pharmaceutical implements, coins, engravings and drawings.

MUSEE DU VIEUX TOULOUSE, 7 rue du May (527580).
Ceramics of local workmanship.

Further reading

Cushion, J. P., *The Pocket Book of French and Italian Ceramic Marks* (London: Faber, 1965).

Dauterman, C. C., *Sèvres* (London: Studio Vista, 1970).

Davis, Frank, *French Silver 1450–1825* (London: Arthur Barker, 1970).

Edey, Winthrop, *French Clocks* (London: Studio Vista, 1967).

Landais, Hubert, *French Porcelain* (London: Weidenfeld, 1961).

Lane, Arthur, *French Faience* (London: Faber & Faber, 1970).

Lewis, M. D. S., *Antique Paste Jewellery* (London: Faber & Faber, 1970).

McCawley, Patricia, *Antique Glass Paperweights from France* (London: Spink & Son, 1968).

Mackay, James, *The Animaliers* (London: Ward Lock, 1973).

Reade, Brian, *Art Nouveau and Alphonse Mucha* (London: HMSO, 1967).

Weigert, R. A., *French Tapestry* (London: Faber & Faber, 1962).

Albrecht Dürer is one of the greatest names in German art, and his work is still accessible to collectors through the medium of the print. This engraving of Adam and Eve was sold at auction in 1973.

4

Germany, Federal Republic of

Introduction

The ravages of wars and inflation have turned German society upside down in the last 60 years, destroyed the old nobility, scattered their possessions and divided the old Germany physically into two countries. All this has caused considerable dispersal of the country's stock of antiques: the occupation troops of 1945 took a lot; Swedish dealers came into Berlin after the war and bought up much of the city's famous silver and almost all the good pewter at rock-bottom prices; much of the best china went to the USA; and a lot of faience went to France and Britain.

The general upheaval also instilled an earthy pragmatism in West German attitudes to buying antiques. 'A German will buy an antique chair as a farmer buys a cow – you know, slapping it on the rump to see how solid it is,' said one West Berlin antique dealer, only half-jokingly. 'A German will say, not how beautiful a piece is, but how useful.' On the other hand, West Germans do not buy antiques for investment nearly as much as the British do – perhaps because they have more confidence in the international soundness of their currency. When sterling started to fall on foreign markets, the flight from equities into internationally acceptable works of art and antiques became a marked phenomenon among British investors.

However, the West Germans are not unresponsive to the pull of the past. The nostalgia boom which has been gathering momentum for a few years has affected everything from reissues of Marlene Dietrich and Greta Keller records to trendy junk from the day before yesterday, such as old 78 dance records, photographs and interwar magazines. Bleibtreustrasse, a faded 1920-ish street off West Berlin's fashionable Kurfürstendamm, is full of shops selling this kind of thing. On a loftier plane, prices of up to 80 000 DM are paid for oil-paintings by the impressionist Lesser Ury (1861–1931) depicting the *jeunesse dorée* of pre-1914 Berlin strolling in the Tiergarten or Unter den Linden, while his earlier (some think finer) landscapes fetch only 10 000–20 000 DM.

A great surge of interest in antiques throughout West Germany generally has resulted in antique shops opening in almost every town and village – so much so that even British dealers are finding it profitable to open up in West Germany. Before the Second World War Berlin was a centre of art and antiques on a par with London, Paris and New York, but since the war and the partition of Germany, Munich has become the focus of the antique trade in the Federal Republic. Stuttgart, however, is *the* West German city for rare books.

West German taste varies enormously, according to the diverse pattern of the old independent states which only became forged into a German entity under Bismarck. South and west of the Main river, which forms something of a cultural frontier, the people are predominantly Roman Catholic, and the architecture in such cities as Munich, Würzburg, Freiburg and Cologne is rich in the gothic and baroque of the Holy Roman Empire. To the north a sterner simplicity of building is seen and taste tends towards the solid and classical.

West Berlin likes the classicist Biedermeier style of the first half of the 19th century (the word 'Biedermeier' itself reflecting middle-class prosperity: from *der biedere Meier,* the bourgeois of comfortable means). Hamburg, Frankfurt and Düsseldorf prefer English mahogany furniture, while Munich goes for oak and Bavarian baroque, the Rhineland for carved Liègeois pieces and Würzburg for decorated baroque. On the whole, West German collectors tend not to be so particular about the condition of pieces they buy as the British and – most of all – the Swiss.

German culture, so strong in music and literature, produced comparatively little in painting after its golden age in the 15th and 16th centuries (exemplified by the two Holbeins, Cranach, Dürer and Baldung), except for the remarkable Caspar David

Friedrich in the 19th century, some German impressionists and the later expressionist school.

European porcelain, on the other hand, was invented by Germans, Johann Friedrich Böttger being the first to produce a real porcelain of Chinese quality – at the Meissen factory he set up in Dresden in 1710. The five great names in German porcelain thereafter were the Meissen, Höchst, Frankenthal, Nymphenburg and Berlin factories. Inflation and the strong state of the deutschemark on the international exchanges mean that it may often be more advantageous to buy Meissen in the USA than in the Federal Republic – in fact, dealers have been bringing it from the USA to sell there. Also, some say that the best early Meissen is to be had in London, though the Federal Republic is still the place for good 19th-century Meissen and certainly for Berlin porcelain, in which there is strong local-collector interest (with prices to match).

Berlin used to be the great bargain centre for antiques. Before the Wall was built in 1961 refugees from the East used to stream in with their family treasures, and for years dealers used to flock there. There is still a trickle of things from the East, many of which come through diplomatic channels – small portable items like gold boxes, icons, small engravings and paintings – but East Berlin itself does not seem to hold much of interest to serious collectors. When in West Berlin, collectors should try to attend an auction at Leo Spik, one of the Continent's leading salerooms where amazing bargains can be found by the knowledgeable. Another auction house, Galerie Gerda Bassenge, is good for rare books, engravings and prints.

Most big German cities have a flea market or *Flohmarkt* (the largest being in Munich which also boasts the oldest auction house), but the West Berlin flea market is particularly colourful, situated in three or four original S-bahn carriages on a disused stretch of line above the underground station in Nöllendorfplatz. Prices are not necessarily cheap – indeed, 5000 DM have been known to change hands for a piece of Meissen – but Berliners love to go *trödeln* (i.e. bargain-hunting among the bric-à-brac) and around 11 a.m. on a Sunday 'all Berlin' can be found rummaging among the junk in the old cream-and-gilt railway cars.

What do West Germans themselves collect? Well, Jugendstil (the German word for art nouveau) is extremely popular – and expensive. Wood-carvings, an ancient German art, are always popular, especially carved Madonnas in Düsseldorf. There is also great interest in Berlin iron jewellery though very little is left now in West Berlin – Munich is the place to find good examples. West Berliners collect *Berlinois*–i.e. ephemera such as theatre programmes and other mementoes of *Alt Berlin* of the good old days. Collectors of children's toys are well catered for in the Federal Republic; the famous Marklin and Fleischmann model railways and clockwork playthings now fetch large sums in London salerooms. In addition, memorabilia of the Third Reich and Second World War are now becoming collected quite widely in the Federal Republic, including Nazi uniforms, badges and medals; these can be seen, along with militaria of the Kaiser Wilhelm era, at the West Berlin flea market.

Specialities

Books

Stuttgart, one of the oldest publishing centres in West Germany, is a good place to find rare books; dealers include Stuttgarter Antiquariat (incunabula, 16th-century books on humanism, illustrated books and German first editions), Neidhardt, Koehler & Volckmar, Felger, Muller & Graff and Plessing. In West Berlin, the leading specialist is Rittershofer and the auction house Galerie Gerda Bassenge is also a good source. Frankfurt and Munich are also good centres for bibliophiles.

Coins and Medals

Stuttgart and Frankfurt rank among the foremost European centres for coin collectors. Dealers include Kricheldorf in Stuttgart, Frankfurter Münzhandlung in Frankfurt and Kimpel in Düsseldorf. A coin fair is held every year in West Berlin.

Firearms and Antique Weapons

Germany has always been of the first importance in weaponry –

Saxon rapiers were famous and have been widely faked and the wheel-lock system of firearm ignition is thought to have been invented in Nuremberg. Good centres and dealers include: West Berlin (Flaschaar, Menz, Schliephake & Volker), Munich (Waffen Bavaria), Frankfurt (Christof, Stör, Numberger), Hamburg (Blass, Jagielski), Cologne (Rust) and Stuttgart (Nagel).

Glass

Germany was early famous for its green *Waldglas,* produced in the forest areas from Roman times on. Later, German glass became prized for its engraving and enamelling; a famous school of engraving was founded in Nuremberg by the Schwanhardt family in the 17th century, characterized by its delicate landscapes. Later the industry became concentrated in Silesia and Bohemia and the best factories were in what are now the German Democratic Republic and Czechoslovakia – notably at Potsdam, whose massive pieces were engraved for the court at Berlin. Potsdam's glass factory director Johann Kunckel developed an exotic gold-ruby process in 1680, in which gold ducats were originally melted down to give the red colour added richness. Bohemian *Zwischengold* glass of the 18th century sandwiched engraved gold leaf between two coloured layers. Later, the Biedermeier glass of the early 19th century was intricately cut and engraved on a coloured body, sometimes overlaid with enamelled panels.

Examples of Potsdam glass can still be found at the state-run Staatlicher Kunst in East Berlin, as well as at Western dealers. Henrich in Frankfurt is a leading glass specialist, and in Munich there are Oesterle, Pachtner and Rose among others.

Jewellery

Berlin iron jewellery, which became fashionable during the 1813–15 Franco-Prussian war when society women were asked to sacrifice their gold and jewels for the war effort, is keenly collected in the Federal Republic, but there is very little to be found in West Berlin itself. Some good pieces can usually be found in Munich.

Porcelain and Pottery

Johann Friedrich Böttger was the first European to produce a real porcelain of Chinese quality – at the Meissen factory he set up in Dresden in 1710. J. J. Kändler was appointed chief modeller at the factory in 1731, and so began the great period of Meissen figures and groups. Meissen ware, incidentally, is often called by the generic term Dresden in Britain and in France is known as Saxe porcelain. Meissen was the first factory consistently to mark its ware. Pieces stamped AR (for Augustus Rex of Saxony) are early and rare (1710–25), the usual mark being the blue crossed swords in the glaze. Motifs included the onion design (1740), vine leaf (1817) and red dragon. The factory, now in the German Democratic Republic, is still in production, though the ceramic tiles facing some of the monotonous office and apartment blocks in East Berlin cannot be numbered among its proudest modern achievements.

Höchst's best period was 1750–75 and its marks were various versions of a six-spoked wheel. The factory restarted production in 1965.

The Frankenthal factory, no longer in existence, produced figures distinguished by their subtle enamelling which included ballet and hunting subjects. Tableware was typically decorated with trellis, striped and chintz-type patterns, with a lot of crimson and green. Marks included PH and PHF impressed, a Palatine lion rampant and monograms J–AH, CT and VR.

The Nymphenburg factory is still in production in a baroque schloss near Munich. It was famous for its almost flawless and exceptionally white paste and went in for figure groups and moulded articles such as snuff boxes, mirror frames and candlesticks. Its early tableware was highly decorative in rococo style. Marks included variations of a shield impressed, a hexagram mark and a six-pointed star in underglaze blue.

The Berlin factory, founded by W. K. Wegely and Johann Benckgraff in 1752 and continued as the Berlin Porcelain Factory after 1761, produced strongly-coloured tableware and vases, mainly decorated with fruit, flowers and landscapes. It had as its marks (all in underglaze blue) a G (1761–63), sceptres (1763–1810) and KPM (Royal Porcelain Manufacture) under a red orb (1832 onwards).

Meissen ware is definitely worth buying, though it is expensive in the Federal Republic; Yokohama in West Berlin is a shop entirely given over to Meissen ware, and Pescoller-Kunstring in Munich also has a large stock. In West Berlin, Weick, probably the oldest dealer in the city, loves Berlin porcelain and always has some in stock; Dürlich has Berlin figures; and Krause usually has some good porcelain of various factories. Other leading porcelain specialists include Galerie Almas in Munich, Michel in Cologne and Meyer in Hamburg.

Porcelain collectors should visit the Porcelain Museum in Darmstadt and the Schloss Charlottenburg in West Berlin, where there is a spectacular collection of Berlin porcelain.

Faience production flourished in Berlin in the 17th and 18th centuries – developed, as in Brunswick, Frankfurt and Hanau, to compete with the fashionable blue-and-white ware from China.

In pottery, stoneware was established in the Rhineland by the late Middle Ages, reaching its peak of production in the 15th and 16th centuries. Cologne was an important centre with three stoneware potteries. 'Bellarmines', fat jugs with a bearded face at the neck, so called because of their supposed likeness to Cardinal Roberto Bellarmino, were made at Cologne and Raeren and there was a thriving export trade in them. English copies were made after the 17th century and German copies in the 19th century. Jugs which have a patch suggesting the removal of initials (HS for Hubert Schiffer, a 19th-century potter making Bellarmine copies) are masquerading as the earlier article.

Posters

Germany was a leader in poster design before the First World War, and posters are an integral part of the collecting trend for Third Reich memorabilia. There is a Poster Museum in Essen.

Prints and Engravings

Few countries have a richer history of print-making than Germany. Its woodcuts dominated the earliest days of the art, and the 15th century was a magnificent era of German engraving with a number of anonymous *Meisters* who signed with their initials, such as 'ES'. Martin Schongauer ushered in the golden age of the 16th century when Dürer towered above all Europe.

Some sources are: West Berlin – Galerie Gerda Bassenge

(auctions); Cologne – Kutsch, Leisten, Galerie Theo Hill; Düsseldorf – Lincke; Frankfurt – Fach, Trésor de Livres, Frankfurter Buchstube (maps); Hamburg – Das Bücherkabinett (maps), Hauswedell (auctions); Hanover – Galerie Christoph Kuhl (maps); Munich – Beisler, Hauser, Hugendubel, Muller (all maps); Stuttgart – Neidhardt.

Silver

Berlin was once famous for its silver but much disappeared in the aftermath of the Second World War. What survives tends to be heavy Victoriana. Augsburg was also a leading centre. German silver was largely of the 800 standard as opposed to the 925 of sterling, and has little interest for foreign collectors except for large serving pieces.

Watches and Clocks

Peter Henlein of Nuremberg (1479–1542) is credited with being the first maker of pocket watches, the earliest being spherical in shape with movements made of iron. Philipp Han (1730–90) was a noted 18th-century maker who incorporated repeating and calendar mechanisms. Black Forest clocks made of wood date from 1642 onwards and were mass produced from the mid 19th century. Junghans of Schramberg (still in existence) was one notable maker.

Munich is the best centre for dealers (Kastner, Jagemann, Schaller). Vogel in Düsseldorf should also be tried. There is a Clock Museum worth visiting in Wuppertal.

The trade

Bad Godesberg

Dealers
Irmgard & Wolfgang BARTEL, Moltkepl 4 (55827).
Oriental carpets, German furniture, glass, silver, porcelain. Also in West Berlin.

Bonn

Dealers
ALEFELD, Bonngasse 14 (55114).
Greek and Russian icons, antique jewellery, pictures, furniture, sculpture.

August BOEDIGER, Maargasse 4 (36940).
General stock, including Oriental. Open 0900–1230, 1430–1830.

H. G. KLEIN, Meckenheimer Str 24 (651550).
Good stock of high-quality 19th century silver, pictures, faience, glass, prints, sculpture. Also in Cologne.

Konrad MEUSCHEL, Kaiserpl 5 (653428).
Old and rare books, especially on Goethe; prints. Open 1000–1200, 1530–1830; appointment always advisable.

ROHRSCHEID GmbH, Am Hof 28 (opposite University) (631281/3).
Important stock of 15th/19th-century books on history, topography, German literature, illustrated books, incunabula, old maps, views. Open 0830–1830.

Hanno SCHREYER, Heerstr 53 (638268).
Topographical prints, paintings, old maps, town views, fine old books, drawings.

Bremen

Dealers
GRAPHISCHES   KABINETT-KUNSTHANDEL   (Wolfgang Werner), Rembertistr 1a (327478).
German expressionists, paintings, graphics, watercolours. Open 1000–1300, 1530–1830; appointment always advisable.

Berthold GREVE, Mathildenstr 28–9 (73838).
Antiques, paintings, furniture, porcelain, silver, glass. Open 0800–1800; also by appointment.

Georg W. RUDEMESSER (Margarete Rudemesser), Am Wall 150 (324143).
Porcelain, paintings.

SCHROEDER & LEISEWITZ, Carl-Schurz-Str 39 (344083).
18th-century English furniture, silver, jewellery, paintings. Open 1000–1300, 1600–1800; also by appointment (always advisable).

Friedrich TRUJEN, Parkstr 83 (341847).
Books.

Cologne

Dealers
Kunsthaus BINHOLD, Hohe Str 96 (214222).
Old masters, modern-master paintings, antiques.

Georg FAHRBACH, Neumarkt 1 (211373/4).
Large general stock of antiques.

Walter FRIEDRICH, Deutzes Freiheit 103 (813494).
Antiques and objets d'art. Open Mon.–Fri. 1000–1300, 1500–1800; Sat. 1000–1400; appointment always necessary. Restorations.

Eberhard GIESE, Komödienstr 34 (215655).
Antiques, furniture, old masters.

GOYERT, Hahnenstr 18 (211730).
Original old and modern prints and reproductions. Restorations.

HALM (Egon P. Halm), Komödienstr 15 (232339).
Antiques, paintings, coins, jewellery. Open 1000–1800; appointment always necessary.

Otto HART, Zeughausstr 26 (215576).
Antique furniture, porcelain, faience, tapestries.

Franz HEUSER, St Apernstr 14–18 (214637).
Antiques.

Galerie Theo HILL, Schildergasse 107 (212972).
Old and modern drawings, prints, watercolours.

Bernhard von HUNERBEIN, Friesenstr 4 (216814).
Antique clocks, silver, Sheffield plate.

H. G. KLEIN, St Apernstr 2 (cnr of Breitestr) (217596).
Good stock of high-quality 18th century silver, pictures, faience,
sculpture, glass, prints. Also in Bonn.

Antonio KRINGS, Richmodstrasse 27 (216980).
Faience, antiques.

Wilhelm KUTSCH, Deichmannhaus, Bahnhofsvonpl (211820).
Old and rare books, prints, maps, antiques. Open Mon.–Fri.
0900–1830; Sat. 0900–1400; appointments always advisable.

Elfriede LANGELOH, Komödienstr 47 (211394; private 237344).
18th-century German porcelain.

Güther LEISTEN, In der Höhle 6 (nr Höhle Station) (232747).
Rare books, drawings, etchings.

L. N. MALMEDE GmbH, Schildergasse 107 (211488).
Important stock of old masters and primitive paintings, early
works of art, furniture, fine tapestries.

Hans MISCHELL, Komodienstr 44 (244703).
Porcelain specialist.

Alfred Otto MULLER, Schildergasse 107 (231513).
19th/20th-century pictures.

OFFERMANN-SCHMITZ, Colonia-Hochhaus (*39th floor*), An der Schanz 2 (*7603871*).
Chinese and Japanese art, especially swords, netsuke, prints. By appointment only.

J. G. RUST, St Apernstr 44 (*241844*).
Arms, militaria.

SCHULZ Buch und Kunstantiquariat, Apostelnstr 20 (*216823; private 428697*).
Old and secondhand books, old graphics, works of art.

Auctions

ANGERSBACH & Co., Steinfeldergasse 6–8 (*213002*).

KUNSTHAUS AM MUSEUM (Carola van Ham), Drususgasse 1–5 (*238137*).
Carola van Ham is a leading expert on jugendstil.

Kunsthaus LEMPERTZ, Neumarkt 3 (*210251*).
Highly important auctions of antiques, sculpture, paintings, tapestries, Oriental works of art and ceramics. Separate department for modern works of art. 7–8 sales yearly (announced in the *Burlington Magazine* of London).

VENATOR KG, St Apernstr 56–62 (*232962; private 431007*).
Folklore items, antiquities, rare books, maps and prints always in stock.

Düsseldorf

Dealers
Anita *ALBRECHT,* Königsallee 14–16 (*entrance in Schadowstr*) (*321836*).
Silver, antique jewellery.

A. & L. BODENHEIM, Prinz-Georg-Strasse 15 (*492126*).
Fine stock of Oriental carpets, 15th/18th-century tapestries. Also in West Berlin.

BOSS & GOPFERT, Steinstr 2 (21326).
Antique furniture, silver, tapestries, etc.

Galerie EBERT, Am Heiligenhauschen 5 (54905).
General antiques.

Dr Rainer HORSTMANN, Kaiser-Wilhelm-Ring 39 (571348).
German expressionist paintings.

Dr Walter KIMPEL, Höhestr 47 (17332).
Coins, medals.

Claus LINCKE, Königsallee 96 (329257).
Prints, drawings, maps, views, engravings, modern lithographs.

Hans MARCUS, Grabenstr 11a (321140).
Old maps and prints, drawings, etchings, lithographs, finely-illustrated books. Also in Amsterdam.

Margit MAYER, Königsallee 56 (323046).
18th/19th-century English furniture, antiques, silver.

Galerie G. PAFFRATH, Königsallee 46 (326405).
19th/20th-century paintings; specialist in the Düsseldorf school.
Open Mon.–Fri. 0900–1800; Sat. 0900–1300; also by appointment (always advisable).

Maria RUTZ, Königsallee 28, Ko-Center (17785).
General stock of antiques, including glass, jewellery, silver, porcelain; specialist in Greek and Russian icons. Open 0930–1830.

Walter SCHON, Oststr 36 (357414).
General antiques.

Hans TROJANSKI, Blumenstr 11 (17904).
Old masters, modern prints, drawings, sculpture, Far East works of art. Open 0900–1830.

VALENTA Kunstgalerie, Kaiser-Wilhelm-Ring 34 (56432, 347486).
Old and 19th-century paintings.

H. VOGEL, Benrather Str 7 and Bilkerstr 5 (13269).
Antique clocks, scientific instruments.

Auctions
CHRISTIE'S, Alt Pempelfort 11a (364212).
Based in London.

PONGS, Bismarckstr 22 (13960).

SCHELMA, Luegpl 3 (336217).

SCHENK, Kolnerstr 30 (16403).

STEINBUCHL, Sternstr 14 (443422).

Frankfurt am Main

Dealers
Alfred ANDREAE, Römerberg 34 (281740).
Fine antique furniture, pewter, china, sculpture, decorative items.
Open 0900–1300, 1400–1800.

Erich BIENERT, Dompl 10 (288980).
Fine 18th-century furniture, porcelain, faience, decorative items.

E. BOHLANDER, Weckmarkt 7 (nr Cathedral) (288225).
General antiques, paintings.

Siegfried BRUMME, Braubachstr 34 (287263).
Antiquarian books, prints, maps. Also in Mainz.

CHRISTOF, Löher Str 2 (611099).
Arms, militaria, antiques.

Joseph FACH, Fahrgasse 8 (287761; private 515533).

Fine stock of prints, illustrated books, drawings, paintings, small antiques. Open Mon.–Fri. 0900–1300, 1500–1830; Sat. 0900–1400; appointment advisable.

FRANKFURTER Bücherstube, Börsenstr 2-4 (281494, 287465).
Old and rare books, illustrated books, maps, views, decorative prints.

FRANKFURTER Münzhandlung, Freiherr-von-Stein-Str 9 (727420).
Coins, medals.

Wilhelm HENRICH, Schumannstr 57 (772328).
Antiques, glass.

Ute HESS, Braubachstr 28 (284293).
Antiques, faience, coins.

Michael KEGELMANN, Saalgasse 3 (288418).
18th-century German furniture, glass, ceramics, clocks, carpets.

MAGAZIN 1900–1935, Glauburgstr 83 (554031).
Small furniture, glass, silver, paintings and lithographs of 1900–35.

Saeed MOTAMED, Johanna-Melber-Weg 16 (617903).
Important specialist in Persian art; large stock of ceramics, bronze, glass, miniatures, textiles, jewellery, silver.

Johann NUMBERGER, Berliner Str 39 (285687).
Old weapons. Open Mon.–Fri. 1000–1300, 1500–1800; Sat. 1000–1400.

Heinz PIEROTH, Fahrgasse 23 (284282; private 623675).
Specialist in early sculpture; fine silver, furniture. Open 1000–1300, 1500–1800; also by appointment (always advisable).

M. & D. ROOS, Neue Mainzerstr 2 (287223).
Meissen specialist.

Friedrich RUTTMANN, Fahrgasse 17-19 (nr Cathedral) (285019).
General antiques, especially furniture, brass, drug jars.

Carl SCHNEIDER, Börsenpl 13-15 (556726).
Antique furniture, pewter, paintings, faience, sculpture, etc.

J. P. SCHNEIDER Jr, Rossmarkt 23 (282406).
Paintings, especially 19th-century.

Hans & Else STOR, Fahrgasse 9 (616171).
Arms, militaria. Open 1000–1300, 1500–1830.

Wilhelm THEIS, Domstr 4 (454231).
Furniture, pewter.

TRESOR DE LIVRES, Darmstadter Landstr 119-25 (682551).
Old and rare books, engravings. Open 0800–1700; appointment always advisable.

Deborah ULREICH, Goethepl (284922).
Antique jewellery.

Robert VATER, Börsenpl 2 (287138).
Porcelain, faience.

Julia WEGENER, Börsenpl 13–15 (285925).
Fine antique furniture, faience, silver, etc.

Markets
Flea market (Flohmarkt) Schifferbunken, Chifferstr.
Open Sat. 0900–1400.

Auctions
Hans Georg DEHIO, Feldbergstr 29 (721052).
Antiques, art.

Hamburg

Dealers
Walter ANDRAEAS Jr, Wischhofstieg 5 (6019283).
Specializes in military books (international) and the study of weapons. Customers and visitors collected from hotel.

Gertrud Iris BERGER, Finkenäu 30 (2202504).
Chinese and Japanese prints. Open by appointment.

Ernst BLASS, Hohe Bleichen 26 (346050).
German arms and armour.

Galerie Hans BROCKSTEDT, Magdalenenstr 11 (4104091).
Pictures, graphics, objets d'art, jugendstil.

Das BUCHERKABINETT, Poststr 14-16 (343236).
Old and rare books on all subjects, autographs, manuscripts, old maps, views. Auctions

Jean HERMSEN & Co., Poststr 36 (345171).
Antique oak furniture, pewter, china, small items. Open Mon.–Fri. 0900–1800; Sat. 1000–1300.

HEUSER & Co., Oberstr 80 (442337).
Art of 1850–1900, porcelain, faience, silver, glass, bronze, sculpture, etchings, Jugendstil. Open 0900–1300, 1500–1800; appointment always advisable.

F. K. H. HUELSMANN, Hohe Bleichen 15 (342017).
Important stock of antiques, furniture, porcelain, silver, glass. Open 0900–1800.

Felix Roman JAGIELSKI, Poststr 37-9 (343712).
General antiques, ethnographical items, furniture, china, glass, some firearms.

Monika JOSEPH, Elbchaussee 2, 11 and 12 (385868, 343597; private 8801889).
European antique furniture, jugendstil. Open 0900–1300, 1400–1800.

E. KOEPPE & Co., Gänsemarkt 29 (352815).
Fine porcelain, faience, silver, antique furniture.

Adolf MEYER & Co., Hohe Bleichen 23 (342670).
Antique furniture, tapestries, bronze, fine silver, porcelain, bibelots, etc. Open Mon.–Fri. 0900–1300, 1400–1800; Sat. 1000–1300.

Anne MICHAELSEN, Neue-ABC-Str 10 (345020).
General antiques, paintings.

Karl MODSCHIEDLER, ABC Str 7 (342060).
Pewter, copper, brass, glass, porcelain, jewellery.

K. & M. REITZ, ABC Str 50 (353382).
General antiques, clocks.

Markets
Flea market (Flohmarkt), Fischmarkt.
Open 1st Sat. of every month in summer.

Auctions
Das BUCHERKABINETT, Poststr 14-16 (344219, 340385, 342893).
See 'Dealers'. Sales regularly.

Dr Ernst HAUSWEDELL, Pöseldorfer Weg 1 (448366).
15th-20th-century, valuable books, autographs, pictures, prints, drawings etc. Sales twice yearly in spring and autumn.

C. F. SCHLUTER, Ballindamm 14 and Grosse Theaterstr 42 (347948/ 347443).
Antique furniture, paintings, Oriental carpets.

Hanover

Dealers
Erich BECKMANN, Georgstr 48 (323074).
17th/19th-century pictures, icons, jewellery. Open Mon.–Fri. 0830–1830; Sat. 0830–1330.

Lilo DEGENER, Hindenburgstr 33 (812068).
Antiques, sculpture, porcelain, silver.

Uwe FRIEDLEBEN, Kramerstr 8 (25289).
Antique furniture, porcelain, glass.

Galerie KOCH, Theaterstr 15 (322006).
Antiques, paintings, sculpture, carpets, tapestries. Open Mon.–Fri. 0900–1800, Sat. 0900–1400.

Galerie Christoph KUHL, Kaiser-Wilhelm-Str 1 (523751).
19th/20th-century graphics, paintings, sculpture, books, maps, glass, pewter, ceramics, folk art.

Walter LOWE, Königstr 54 (20990; private 05137 3863).
German furniture, porcelain, silver. Also in West Berlin.

Hermann MOOSHAGE, Burgstr 33 (12073; private 650502).
General antiques. Open Mon.–Fri. 0900–1800; Sat. 0900–1400.

Robert A. MUELLER, Hebbelstr 7 (691517).
Antiquarian books on all subjects.

Kunstsalon Harald SAAL, Friedrichswall 13 (328770; private 312770).
Baroque furniture, 18th-century German porcelain and glass. Open 1000–1330, 1500–1900.

Rainer ZEITZ. Friedrichswall 19 (324507)
Venetian glass, majolica, Continental silver, renaissance and baroque sculpture. Appointment necessary.

Mainz

Dealers
Siegfried BRUMME, Kirchgarten 19 (21074).
Antiquarian books, prints, maps. Also in Frankfurt.

Munich

Dealers
Hermann BEISLER, Ottostr 3b (555634).
Maps, prints, books on topography and German literature.

Julius BOHLER, Briennerstr 25 (555229).
Fine old masters, works of art, sculpture. Open 0900–1300, 1430–1800; appointment always advisable.

Galerie CARROLL, (Peter Proschel), Residenzstr 21 (299282).
French furniture, bronze, objets d'art, pictures, 18th-century antiques. Open 0930–1800; appointment always necessary.

FISCHER-BOHLER (Karl Fischer), Residenzstr 10 (222583).
18th-century antiques, including furniture, faience and silver.

Hellmuth GARTENSCHLAGER (J. Barry), Ottostr 6 (552871).
Silver, jewellery.

Galerie GEBHARDT, Ottostr 6/1 (552475).
Old masters and 19th/20th-century paintings, especially the
German school. Open Mon.–Fri. 0900–1800; Sat. 0900–1200;
appointment always necessary.

Galerie GUNZENHAUSER (Graphisches Kabinett) (Dr Alfred
Gunzenhauser), Turkenstr 23 (cnr of Theresienstr) (282319).
Expressionist and post-impressionist paintings, drawings and
original prints. Open Mon.–Fri. 1000–1300, 1430–1800; Sat.
1000–1300; appointment always advisable.

Heinrich HAUSER, Schellingstr 17 (281159).
Antiquarian books, prints, maps, some 15th- and 20th-century
paintings.

H. HUGENDUBEL, Salvatorpl 2 (226646).
Old and rare books, Bavarica prints, maps, collectors' and
scientific works.

Carl JAGEMANN, Residenzstr 3 (225493).
Antique watches and clocks. Open 0900–1300, 1400–1800.

K. H. KASTNER, Ottostr 3b (553596).
Specialist in antique clocks.

Galerie Wolfgang KETTERER, Prinzregentstr 60 (472083).
Modern art, jugendstil. Open Mon.–Fri. 0800–1300, 1400–1730;
Sat. 0900–1300.

Erika KIRMSE, Barerstr 2 (594469).
General antiques, coins. Open 0900–1800.

Rudolf KITTEL, Radlsteg 1 (222981; private 561128).
German antiques. Open 1000–1800.

Graf KLENAU OHG, Maximilianstr 32 (222282).
Orders, decorations, militaria, antique weapons, early coins.
Open 0800–1700; appointment always advisable. Auctions.

Karl & Maria KOCH, Ottostr 6 (597189).
Antiques, furniture, porcelain, carpets, silver, jewellery.

B. KOESTLER (Ernst Barkemeyer), Maximilianstr 28 (221508).
Paintings, mainly 19th-century.

Anna Karolina KUNTZE, Ottostr 11 (554591).
Antiques, paintings, furniture, porcelain, silver,

Liselotte KUPFER, Brennenstr 5 (241490).
Silver, jewellery, curiosities.

Oskar LABINER, Fernand-Miller-Pl 3 (593916).
18th-century porcelain, 17th/18th-century silver, gold, other
antiques.

Ludwig MORY, Marienpl 8 (224542).
Pewter. Open Mon.–Fri. 0900–1800; Sat. 0900–1400.
Restorations.

August MULLER, Maximilianpl 20 (226470).
Views, maps, prints.

Galerie Ilas NEUFERT, Oskar-von-Miller-Ring 2.
Icons. Open Mon.–Fri. 0900–1300, 1430–1800; Sat. by
appointment.

Walter OESTERLE, Ottostr 6/4 (555193).
China, glass, silver, other antiques.

Ludwig PACHTNER, Maximiliansthr 6 (221909).
Antiques, German porcelain, glass.

*PESCOLLER-KUNSTRING (Erwin Pescoller), Briennerstr 4 and
Maximilianstr 14 (281532, 282485, 469347).*
Very large stock of Dresden and Meissen porcelain; silver,
sculpture, paintings.

Konrad RIGGAUER, Lilienstr 11-13 (443779).
16th/19th-century drawings.

H. M. RITTER, Prannerstr 5 (226481).
Fine stock of Continental period silver and baroque furniture.

Dr Th. & E. ROSE, Zentnerstr 44 (373439).
Glass.

Hermann ROTH, Ottostr 3a (557810).
Antiques, pewter, china.

Helmut SCHALLER, Prannerstr 5 (224593).
Antique clocks, watches, Jugendstil.

Xaver SCHEIDWIMMER, Ottostr 3 (594979; private 797545).
Old masters of German, French, Italian and Dutch schools. Open
0900–1800.

Dr Helmut SELING, Oskar-von-Miller-Ring 31 (284865).
Fine stock of antique silver and gold.

Dr H. W. SPEER, Pfisterstr 7 (227730).
Objets d'art, sculpture, silver, porcelain, jewellery, pewter,
copper.

Galerie STANGL (Otto Stangl), Briennerstr 11 (299911).
20th-century pictures, prints, sculptures.

Dr Konrad STRAUSS, Bauerstr 38/1 (371724).
Specialist in porcelain and faience. Open Mon.–Fri. 0900–1700;
appointment always advisable.

Albert Rich STURM, Ottostr 6 (593811; private 165583).
19th-century paintings and antiques.

WAFFEN BAVARIA, Karlspl 8 (555913/555683).
Weapons of all kinds. Open 0900–1830.

Markets and fairs
Flea market fair, Maria-Hilfpl.
Three times yearly on 1 May, 25 July and 17 Oct.

Antique fair.
Yearly in 2nd fortnight in Oct.

Auctions
HARTUNG & KARL, Karolinenpl 5a (283024).
Books, autographs.

Graf KLENAU OHG, Maximilianstr 32 (222282).
See 'Dealers'. 12 sales yearly.

NEUMEISTER KG, Briennerstr 14 (283011).
Antiques, silver, glass, sculpture, paintings, pottery, Oriental carpets, tapestries, antique furniture, Eastern art. Six sales yearly in March, May, June, Sept. Oct. and Dec.

Hugo RUEF, Gabelsbergerstr 28 (522750).
Antiques, paintings, furniture, Oriental carpets, sculpture, antiquities. Three or four sales yearly in spring, summer and autumn.

Stuttgart

Dealers
Kunsthaus Walter BUHLER, Wagenburgstr 4 (240507).
19th-century and modern paintings, old and modern graphics, small sculptures. Open Mon.–Fri. 0900–1300, 1400–1800; Sat. 0900–1300; appointment always advisable.

Hermann COMBE, Wilhelmsbau, Kleine Königstr 8 (290875).
Antiques, paintings, jewellery. Auctions.

FELGER.
Books.

Otto GREINER, Kronprinzstr 20 (297562).
Art, antiques. Auctions.

KOEHLER & VOLCKMAR.
Books.

H. H. KRICHELDORF, Bolzstr 4/11 (293229).
Classical bronzes and pottery; specialist in Greek and Roman coins.

MULLER & GRAFF, Calwerstr 54 (294174).
Books.

Dr Fritz NAGEL (Kunst und Auktionhaus), Breitscheidstr 127 (632560).
General antiques including paintings, furniture, carpets, arms, porcelain and watches. Open 0830–1800. Auctions.

Fritz NEIDHARDT, Königstr 20/4 (223320).
18th/19th-century fine illustrated books, prints.

Friedrich PLESSING, Owentorstr 48
Books.

Frank RUZEK, Tonstr 17 (245611).
Antiques, works of art.

M. Bauer SCHATZINSEL & Sohn (Fr. C. Eckard), Königstr 1 (296482).
Japanese and Chinese works of art, porcelain, pictures. Open Mon.–Fri. 0900–1830; Sat. 0830–1400.

STUTTGARTER Antiquariat, Rathenaustr 21 (224402).
Specialist in German 1st editions, 16th-century books and incunabula. Auctions.

Galerie VALENTIEN, Königsbau (292709).
19th/20th-century art.

Reinhard WEHRLE, Am Kräherwald 171 (628191).
Carpets, 19th/20th-century pictures.

Auctions
Hermann COMBE, Wilhelmsbau, Kleine Königstr 8 (290875).
See 'Dealers'.

Otto GREINER, Kronprinzstr 20 (297562).
See 'Dealers'.

Dr Fritz NAGEL (Kunst und Auktionhaus), Breitscheidstr 127 (632560).
See 'Dealers'. Four sales yearly.

STUTTGARTER Antiquariat, Rathenaustr 21 (224402).
See 'Dealers'.

West Berlin

Dealers

Irmgard & Wolfgang BARTEL, Eisenacher Str 117 (2162790).
Oriental carpets, German furniture, glass, silver, porcelain. Also
in Bad Godesberg.

*Galerie Gerda BASSENGE, Kurfürstendamm 206 (913883) and Erdener
Str 5a (8861932).*
Books, engravings. Auctions.

A. & L. BODENHEIM, Budapesterstr 40-4 (2611691).
Fine stock of Oriental carpets, 15th/18th-century tapestries. Also
in Düsseldorf.

CREDE, Eisenacher Str 108 (2164110).
Oriental art, jugendstil.

M. DURLICH, Keithstr 5 (243660).
Silver, furniture, paintings, porcelain.

Alphonse FLASCHAAR.
Firearms, antique weapons.

JORDAN & GOGOLIN, Motzstr 28 (2117728).
Paintings, militaria, ship models.

JUNG, Keithstr 8 (2116957).
Prints, porcelain, general antiques.

Axel KETTNER, Ansbacher Str 43-5 (2117121).
16th/20th-century paintings, drawings, furniture, porcelain, antiques. Open Mon.–Fri. 1100–1830; Sat. 1100–1400; appointment always advisable.

Fritz KITZING, Keithstr 19 (243780) and Manfred-von-Richthofen Str 218 (696091).
General antiques, 19th-century paintings.

Herbert KLEWER, Viktoria-Luise-Pl 12a (2114302).
Antique furniture, paintings, porcelain, faience.

Peter KRAUSE, Fasenenstr 30 (8817251).
Antique furniture, porcelain, silver, decorative objects.

KUNST-SALON, Kurfürstendamm 203-4 (8814597).
Antiques, porcelain, jewellery.

Walter LOWE, Bleibtreustr 48 (8833762).
German furniture, porcelain, silver. Also in Hanover.

Dietrich MENZ, Kleiststr 37 (2166750).
Arms, militaria, medals. Open 0900–1830.

NANTE, Bleibtreustr 41 (8835926; private 8864855).
Illustrated books, long-case clocks, furniture, crystal, bronze, *Alt Berlin,* bric-à-brac of the 1920s–30s (e.g. old 78 records, photographs, magazines, ephemera). Open 1000–1800 (appointment always advisable).

OLDENBURG, Bergstr 13 and Keithstr 12 (both 7923533).
19th-century paintings, furniture, silver, glass, porcelain, general (Bergstr); pictures, sculpture, contemporary masters (Keithstr).

PROPLYAEN-KUNSTHANDLUNG GmbH, Lietzenburgerstr 102 (911436).
Paintings, pewter, faience, furniture, etc.

Horst Alex RITTERSHOFER, Meinekestr 3 (8814306).
Books.

SCHLIEPHAKE & VOLKER, Lutherstr 15 (240235).
Arms, militaria.

Lothar SCHONKNECHT, Kalckreuthstr 3 (244193).
Porcelain, faience, furniture, paintings, silver, jewellery.

Dr Alfred SPECHT, Keithstr 18 (2116970).
Old masters.

Leo SPIK, Kurfürstendamm 66 (8836170/9).
Paintings, furniture, tapestries, carpets. Auctions.

Galerie SPRINGER Berlin, (Rudolf J. Springer), Fasenenstr 13 (3139088; private 845863).
Modern art, 20th-century books. Open Mon.–Fri. 1500–1800; Sat. 1000–1300; appointment always advisable.

Carl WEGNER, Martin-Luther-Str 113 (7822491).
Antiquarian books on social sciences, theatre, topography; also autographs, maps, views. Open Mon.–Fri. 0900–1830; Sat. 0900–1400.

Wilhelm WEICK, Eisenacher Str 10 (247500).
Antiques, paintings, Berlin porcelain.

Hans YOKOHAMA, Keithstr 10 (243135).
Large stock of Meissen and Dresden porcelain.

Markets and fairs
Flea market (Flohmarkt), in disused underground station in Nöllendorfpl.
Open Sun.

Coin fair
Yearly.

Auctions
Galerie Gerda BASSENGE, Kurfürstendamm 206 (913883) and Erdener Str 5a (8861932).
See 'Dealers'.

Leo SPIK, Kurfüstendamm 66 (8836170/9).
See 'Dealers'.

Museums

Bonn

BEETHOVEN HAUS, Bonngasse 20.
The composer's birthplace.

CITY ART COLLECTION, Rathausgasse 5.
18th/20th-century German paintings.

Cologne

KUNSTGEWERBEMUSEUM, Eigelsteintorburg.
Bohemian glass, pottery (German faience in particular).

ROMAN-GERMANIC MUSEUM, Zeughaus.
World-famous collection of Roman glass.

Darmstadt

PORCELAIN MUSEUM.

Dortmund

GESCHICHTLICHES MUSEUM, Ritterhausstr 34.
Roman gold coins.

Düsseldorf

GOETHE MUSEUM, Jägerhofstr 1.
Manuscripts, 1st editions, sculpture and medals connected with
the writer.

HETJENS MUSEUM, Palais Nesselrode, Schulstr 4.
Ceramics from the Stone Age to the present.

SCHLOSS JAGERHOF, Jacobistr 2.
One of the biggest collections of early Meissen in the world.

Essen

GERMAN POSTER MUSEUM, Steelerstr 29.
International posters from the 19th century onwards.

Frankfurt

GOETHE HAUS, Grosser Hirschgraben 23.
Goethe's birthplace; collection of manuscripts and paintings.

MUSEUM FUR KUNSTHANDWERK, Schaumainkai 29.
18th-century furniture, porcelain, glass, silver and textiles.

Hamburg

HAMBURG HISTORICAL MUSEUM, Holstenwall 24.
History of the port of Hamburg and its shipping.

KUNSTHALLE, Glockengiessewall 1.
Important collections of sculpture, graphic arts, coins and 18th/
20th-century paintings.

MUSEUM FUR KUNST UND GEWERBE.
19th-century Meissen ware, German stoneware, Nymphenburg
porcelain.

Munich

ALTE PINAKOTHEK.
Not to be missed with its magnificent collection of 14th/18th-
century European paintings.

BAVARIAN STATE LIBRARY, Ludwigstr 23.
Incunabula, 1st editions, illuminated medieval books.

BAYERISCHES (BAVARIAN) MUSEUM, Prinzregentstr 3.
Medieval art, miniatures, German stoneware, the largest collection of early German sculpture in the Federal Republic, tapestries, 16th-century armour, fine wood-carvings.

CITY MUSEUM.
Biedermeier furniture.

HAUS DER KUNST, Prinzregentstr 1.
19th/20th-century art, especially German.

SCHACKGALERIE, Prinzregentstr 9.
Late 19th-century German paintings.

SCHLOSS NYMPHENBURG.
Museum of Nymphenburg porcelain; fine rococo interiors.

STATE GRAPHIC COLLECTION, Meiserstr 10/1.
Drawings and prints from the late gothic period to the present.

Stuttgart

AUTOMOBILE MUSEUM, Mercedes-Benz works.
Contains the world's oldest motorcycle.

LANDESGEWERBEMUSEUM.
German stoneware pottery.

West Berlin

BAUHAUS ARCHIVE, Schlossstr 1 (3072045).

KUNSTGEWERBEMUSEUM (Arts and Crafts Museum).
Bohemian glass, early silver.

MUSEUMS IN DAHLEM, Arnimallee 23.
The Cabinet of Engravings has 23 000 drawings from the 15th–18th centuries, 350 000 prints and engravings and 5 000 illustrated books, mainly of the 15th and 16th centuries. It is one

of the largest graphic collections in Europe. Among the drawings are 125 by Durer, 50 by Brueghel the Elder, more than 150 by Rembrandt and 27 illustrations by Botticelli for Dante's *Divine Comedy*. Closed Mon.

MUSICAL INSTRUMENTS MUSEUM, Bundesalle 1-12 (8817835).
16th/20th-century European musical instruments.

SCHLOSS CHARLOTTENBURG, Luisenpl.
Roman and Trojan antiquities, a famous collection of Berlin porcelain and of model soldiers belonging to Wegely, founder of the Berlin Porcelain Factory.

Wuppertal

CLOCK MUSEUM.

Further reading

Cushion J. P. *The Pocket Book of German Ceramic Marks* (London: Faber, 1965)
Ducret, S., *German Porcelain and Faience* (London, 1962)
Morley-Fletcher, Hugo, *Meissen* (London: Barrie & Jenkins, 1971)
Savage, George, *Eighteenth-century German Porcelain* (London: Spring Books, 1968)

Fine ebony veneered rack-striking bracket clock by Thomas Tompion of London, the supreme English clockmaker. It was sold at Christie's in 1973 for £19,950

5
Great Britain

Introduction

England

England is the acknowledged treasure house of the world for art and antiques, but the market is an extremely complicated and delicate mechanism which few collectors can hope to understand without years of study. As much as 85 per cent of the British antique trade is carried on between dealers, who naturally know to a fine margin exactly what the buying and selling rates are at any one time. Obviously it is difficult for collectors to penetrate the chain at the most advantageous point, though this does not mean that there are no bargains to be found. There are a few short-cuts. For instance, the knowledgeable can find bargains at London's Bermondsey Market, when dealers from all over south-east England gather before 6 a.m. on a Friday to pick over one another's stock. Goods move fast and later in the morning the best Bermondsey pickings are on sale in Bond Street and the Home Counties—with considerably marked-up price tickets.

Price levels are delicately tuned all over the country. It is cheaper to buy in the London suburbs than in the centre, but not necessarily cheaper in the country—it very much depends on the goods and the dealer's knowledge. It's no good expecting giveaway prices in an unprepossessing antique shop in an obscure Cornish village; the owner is quite likely to have the latest Christie and Sotheby catalogues and price lists in his office and to be keenly aware of the market. But it is very much a matter of playing the field, and through travelling it can be profitable as well as enjoyable to back personal fancies against local taste. Items of local interest always fetch more in their own area; for example an early map of Sussex costs more in Brighton than in Newcastle and a 19th-century print of Tyneside shipping more in Newcastle than in Brighton. However, a commemorative pottery mug of Queen Victoria's coronation may be cheaper in a Midlands town than in London, the ceramics centre of Britain.

A word of warning about country auctions: although they often look as if they should be full of bargains, the custom of 'the ring'—now largely stamped out in London following exposure by the *Sunday Times* in the 1960s—still flourishes in some country areas. It is a perfectly legal (but frustrating for outsiders) ploy by which local dealers unite to bid for a certain piece, then dispose of it among themselves. Country-house sales are also notorious for artificially-induced values, though here it is usually the atmosphere and glamour of the setting which leads sensible people to make wild bids.

As a general rule, London is the centre for almost everything. The antique market is much more centralized in Britain than, say, France or the Federal Republic of Germany. Even in the specialized field of Scottish silver the leading dealer—How of Edinburgh—has a London address. London rather than Leeds is the place to go for Leeds creamware, and London rather than Newcastle for the 18th-century enamelled glass decorated by the Beilby family of Newcastle. On the other hand, serious collectors of clocks should visit Tetbury (Gloucestershire) to see the outstanding stock of dealer Meyrick Nielsen.

For sound historical reasons there is hardly a field of antiques or works of art in which collectors, cannot choose and buy more advantageously in Britain than in any other country. For a start, Britain's vast reservoirs of art treasures have not been plundered or dispersed through invasion or a major war on its own territory. Aristocrats doing the Grand Tour brought back huge quantities of works of art, and shrewd milords sent empty wagons to Paris after the Revolution to buy up French treasures on the cheap. The prosperous merchants of Victorian times salted away their spare assets in silver, Sheffield plate, jewellery and sporting pictures, and much still survives intact in family houses around the country—especially in Scotland, a still largely untapped source of family heirlooms.

One striking development of the last decade in the British art market has been the growth of what may be called 'national-heritage' buying, which has brought crowds of European and

Japanese dealers to the London salerooms to buy back Dutch marquetry, French ormolu, Meissen porcelain, Japanese swords and all kinds of other items brought home triumphantly in former times by acquisitive British travellers. London is still the world's undisputed art marketplace, with the advantage that foreign buyers are not charged value added tax, though there has been disquiet in the London fine-art world—fearing a loss of international custom—since the 'Big Two' salerooms, Sotheby's and Christie's, imposed a buyer's commission of 10 per cent in addition to the customary 10 per cent for the vendor. From time to time alarmed complaints are heard that Britain is being drained of antiques by foreign buyers, as when a Brighton dealer advertises regular container-loads to the Continent or Richard Booth in Hay-on-Wye (Powys) talks of despatching bulk shipments of books to Sydney or San Francisco. In fact, as many shiploads as are exported come back: Phillips, the third most important London auction house, imports a load every six weeks from the USA for sale in Britain.

The collector in Britain still has an embarrassment of riches to choose from, in a range of sources that stretches from thriving London street markets like Bermondsey and the Portobello Road (which is by no means devoid of bargains despite the year-round tourists) to the great Bond Street dealers and fine-art salerooms, and from country specialists like Wallis & Wallis in Lewes (Sussex), who deal exclusively in militaria, to rewarding small personally run shops like Aboyne Antiques in Aboyne (Aberdeenshire) whose proprietress is well connected in local society and has an enviable entrée to the treasures of Scottish country homes. In remote country districts like Northumbria there are local village auctions and markets where genuine bargains can be found. And even in the august London salerooms most trade is in the under-£200 bracket; pictures are sold at prices from £10 upwards, and the volume of goods through the cheaper end of the market is such that even the saleroom experts make mistakes from which sharp-eyed collectors can benefit.

Members of the British Antiques Dealers' Association (BADA), the trade's strict governing body, are required to have had at least three years' experience (though it is not uncommon for it to be more like two centuries) and to be vouched for by an existing member. Items on sale at leading antique fairs like London's Grosvenor House and Chelsea will have been thoroughly vetted and the participating dealers will usually be among the top specialists in their field.

Among the obvious attractions of Britain are English, Irish and Scottish silver and glass, English and Welsh porcelain, the products of the great London gunsmiths and mapmakers, and the rich fields of English pewter, watercolours, clocks and—though this may be outside the logistical scope of most travellers—English furniture. However, Britain also offers the world's finest collecting opportunities in a myriad of lesser specialities, including autographs and manuscripts, photographs and postcards, treen, model steam engines, bookplates, fairings, scientific instruments, posters, old advertisements, old typewriters and sewing machines, model soldiers, 18th/19th-century English enamels, ephemera, fire-marks and even pot lids.

The collection boom in Britain has been so great in the last 10 years and has spread so rapidly to embrace items of what seems the day before yesterday, that sometimes it seems doubtful if there is anything which ranks as totally uncollectable. Whatever it is, someone somewhere will probably pay good money for it. The boom has been partly because of inflation—tangible assets being more satisfactory than money—partly because the US customs have relaxed the definition of an antique to anything 100 years old or more, and partly because of Britain's capital gains tax which affected items worth more than £1000. All these boosted the cheaper end of the market, while the top end burgeoned under the feverish publicity of more and more record prices in the salerooms. Expanding with the new trend, both the major salerooms in London grew offshoots to handle items from the Victorian period up to the 1930s and even beyond; Sotheby's Belgravia has sold a 1950s jukebox for a considerable sum, not to mention several boxes of Christmas crackers of uncertain age. Even the grand Grosvenor House Antiques Fair in London now accepts items from the 1930s—previously it strictly defined an antique as pre-1830.

No doubt all collectors would like a time machine, to whisk them back 35 years when a fine-quality Ming Palace dish could be bought for £20, or even 12 years ago when a pair of fine English duelling pistols could be had for £25, only a hundredth of today's price. But extraordinary finds still happen, even in the antiques trade itself; for instance, there is the dealer who paid another dealer £35 for a bowl which turned out to be Ming— he sold it for £20 000 and bought himself a Rolls-Royce with half the profit.

Scotland

Although there is hardly a corner of England that has not been combed for antiques in the last 30 years, Scotland remains a largely untapped source, especially in its great family houses. The contents of these establishments have been less dispersed than in the south, but this is gradually changing—perhaps under the threat of a wealth tax or because of inflation. It is significant that both Christie's and Sotheby's in London also have active agents in Scotland and that Sotheby's Belgravia has held several sales at Gleneagles Hotel. Recently London's Phillips moved in and took over Dowell's, the old-established Edinburgh auction house; it is now known as Phillips in Scotland and holds weekly sales. The last great source of British antiques is about to be opened up.

Obviously plenty of English antiques and works of art are to be found in Scotland, but Scottish artists and craftsmen were also outstanding in many areas, including firearms and other weapons, books, coins, glass, jewellery, paintings, pewter, pottery, silver, snuff mulls and treen.

Wales

Wales today is a somewhat arid hunting-ground for antiques, most of the best indigenous items having been thoroughly cleaned out by London dealers, who still scour Cardiff antique shops regularly twice a week. Swansea and Nantgarw porcelain are the two great Welsh specialities but good examples are more likely to be found in London than in Swansea or Cardiff, which in any case do not boast anything like the same number of antique shops as, say, Glasgow or Edinburgh.

Welsh antiques as such are thin on the ground anyway: basically they come down to Swansea and Nantgarw porcelain, Swansea cottage pottery (also hard to find nowadays), Welsh oak furniture such as dressers, and the famous carved wooden Welsh love spoons which were the traditional symbol of betrothal. Most of the latter which are seen today are modern, however.

The paucity of antique shops in Wales as compared to Scotland may stem partly from the lack in Wales, traditionally a poor country with few landed gentry, of the large country houses and castles which are still in family hands north of the Tweed. But there is a growing interest in antiques among young people in Wales; more and more are setting up as antique dealers, and an antique market held twice a week in Cardiff city centre is a recent innovation which may stimulate new opportunities for collectors in Wales.

Specialities

Advertisements

Old advertisements, many of tin, draw collectors to a shop called Dodo Design in London.

Autographs and Manuscripts

Autographs and manuscripts from the whole field of English literature and history can be chosen from at rare-book dealers like Maggs and Sotheran in London and Wilson in Witney (Oxfordshire).

Books

Britain is the antiquarian book centre of the world, even if London's Charing Cross Road and Bloomsbury are shadows of their former glory with some of the best shops closed or driven out by redevelopment. No matter what the speciality, somewhere in Britain can be found a prime source for it. Fisher Nautical in Brighton, primarily a mail-order business though callers are welcome, has what is probably Europe's largest stock of nautical books and periodicals, and the Meridian Bookshop in London is another with this speciality. Block in London has an unrivalled theatre collection. Booth in Hay-on-Wye (Powys) not only has a vast choice of topographical books on Wales, England and Scotland but also claims to run the world's biggest bookshop, with nearly 1 million volumes. Altogether he has seven shops in Hay-on-Wye and plans to turn this quiet town into one vast book emporium. He buys in bulk and likes to sell in bulk as well, but browsers are welcome. Some claim to have found great bargains there, but the sheer volume of stock may prove too overwhelming for those who are not determined book hunters.

Edinburgh has always been an important publishing centre and it is today the best city after London for book collectors, with antiquarian and secondhand booksellers scattered plentifully throughout the 18th-century 'New Town'. The Edinburgh Bookshop, which is primarily a new bookshop but has its antiquarian stock beautifully arranged at the back as in a private living-room, sometimes has fine miniature books; it also deals in fine bindings, Scottish genealogy and history and natural history. Another Edinburgh dealer, Thin, now mainly deals in new stock, but has five basement rooms of antiquarian and secondhand books specializing in Scotland, Americana and hand-illustrated works. In Glasgow, Smith of St Vincent Street has a large stock of antiquarian books relating to Scotland.

Recent years have seen an upsurge in investment-collecting, particularly of natural-history books with fine illustrations—indeed, of all colour-plate books. Private-press books have a keen following; the works of William Morris's Kelmscott Press and C. H. St John Hornby's Ashendene Press are scarce and pricey, but there are many lovely works being produced today by one or two artist-craftsmen operating a hand-press in a back room. Rota in London is a leading specialist in private-press books, and occasionally Sotheby's holds a sale of them at Chancery Lane in London.

Victorian novels and early detective stories are avidly collected, and fortunes have been made by people who shrewdly got in on the ground floor and collected the first books printed on such subjects as medical science, the internal combustion engine and even television. The trick—perhaps impossible now—is to find a field as yet unexplored, or unexploited. In the more erudite reaches of book-collecting, first editions of the 17th and 18th centuries are extremely hard to find, as is poetry, though Victorian poets are still underrated. The works of Victorian authors such as Dickens and Thackeray, originally issued in magazine parts, were printed in vast editions, so that their first editions are worth only tiny sums in relation to their reputation.

Bookplates

Bookplates are a very underrated field and cheap to collect. Some antiquarian bookshop stock them, for example Traylen in Guildford.

Bronze

English romantic bronzes of the late 19th century are now a focus of interest after decades of neglect; Sotheby's Belgravia in London is a good hunting-ground for these attractive pieces. Eminent men such as Sir Alfred Gilbert (of 'Eros' fame in London's Piccadilly Circus), Sir George Frampton (who sculpted 'Peter Pan' in London's Kensington Gardens), Lord Leighton the painter and Sir Bertram Mackennal all did small statuettes, hand-finished and numbered in truly limited editions. But it is not unknown for one to turn up at a fraction of its value on a Portobello Road stall in London. A nose for the real thing and knowledge of the artist's work, in this as in so many other fields, can pay a handsome dividend.

Clocks, Watches and Barometers

English clocks are of the greatest technical interest to collectors: the years 1660–1750 marked England's supremacy in the field, with one mechanical refinement coming after another, such as rack-striking, repeat mechanisms and improved escapements. The king of English clockmakers was Thomas Tompion (1638–1713): other distinguished 17th-century makers include Knibb, Quare, Graham, Mudge and East. Long-case clocks declined after 1750 except in some provincial areas. Bracket clocks and 19th-century carriage clocks have risen steeply in price since 1970, top makers of early 19th-century carriage clocks including Dent, Grant and Frodsham. Antique clocks were prone to alterations by the Victorians—many were given new dials and cases or changed from a short to a long pendulum. Enamelled and engraved dials are more sought after than painted ones and, in general, the smaller any type of clock, the more expensive. In contrast to the general rule that leading specialist dealers are in London, serious clock collectors go to dealer Nielsen in Tetbury (Gloucestershire) for Britain's finest selection.

Frequently stocked by clock specialists are barometers—a very

English instrument given the national preoccupation with the fickle island weather. The golden age of the barometer was the 18th century and first half of the 19th century. The typical early form was the 'stick' barometer, succeeded by the wheel type with a large dial and pointer. The best 18th-century examples were in walnut, mahogany, ebony or other fine woods, with silvered plates or dials. Master clockmakers such as Tompion occasionally made barometers—these are now museum pieces.

Coins and Medals

A new breed of coin investor has appeared in the last few years, trying to keep two jumps ahead of inflation with 'portfolios' mixing numismatic and gold bullion coins. In British salerooms, Scottish gold coins issued in the reigns of James V and James VI have recently been pacemakers in the numismatic market, with some pieces fetching amounts in the £30 000 bracket. The Scottish coinage as a whole is an interesting one, both silver and gold, and early silver pennies are not yet prohibitively expensive—but London is the centre to buy. English silver coins have been advancing strongly also (one oddity of George III's long reign was that it produced so many gold issues that it is noted for the relative scarcity of its silver). Japanese collectors have been buying heavily into English crowns—in 1973/74 the Cromwell Crown of 1658 in *fleur du coin* (uncirculated) condition multiplied in value seven times. Anglo-Saxon hammered silver pennies, struck in 70 different centres, are still moderately priced and worth seeking out.

British campaign medals are a prolific collecting field, perhaps because Britain has been involved in so many colourful wars. The Waterloo Medal of 1815 was the first issued to all officers and men taking part in a campaign. Gallantry awards are more recent, ranging from the Distinguished Conduct Medal of 1854 to the George Cross of 1940. The Victoria Cross, the supreme award for gallantry, now fetches several thousands of pounds, depending on the story behind it. The dedicated British medal collector can trace the recipient's naval or military career through the muster lists and medal rolls in the Public Record Office.

Enamels

English enamels of the 18th and 19th centuries are much prized.

Halcyon Days in London sells modern recreations of Battersea and Bilston enamels as well as the antique originals.

Ephemera

Ephemera, that is printed oddments like trade cards, tickets, old letterheads, Christmas cards and other trivia which express the transient spirit of an age, fascinate some collectors. An Ephemera Society has recently been formed for them.

Fairings

Fairings, the crude pottery groups once given away as prizes in country fairs, now fetch four-figure sums. Phillips in London holds periodic sales.

Firearms and Antique Weapons

Duelling pistols and sporting guns crowned the British gun maker's art, and English firms such as Holland and Holland and James Purdy have been making sporting guns for the last 250 years. London had most of the top makers: Joseph and John Manton, the Swiss-born Durs Egg, Robert Wogdon, John Twigg, H. W. Mortimer and Henry Nock. Birmingham, where most of the fine flintlocks were made, was noted for Westley Richards. Duellers always came in pairs, one for each opponent, and in a polished wooden case complete with all fitments such as powder flask and bullet mould.

Scottish pistols from the 1630s onwards are a romantic and decorative subject. Many early firearms were destroyed when the government outlawed Highland arms and traditional dress following the Jacobite risings of 1715 and 1745. Many of the finest later pieces came from Doune (Perthshire). Scottish pistols were not as mechanically fine as the best English ones, often being put together from bits of other weapons, but they were some of the most graceful firearms ever made, especially those from the 1730s and 1740s. A major characteristic is that they were usually made of all-steel or steel and brass, even the stock, which ended in an elegant shape such as the fishtail, heart or double scroll; Celtic motifs in the decoration and thistle-shaped muzzles were other distinctive features. Makers included Thomas Cadell, first to introduce the craft of pistol-making to Doune in 1646, the two Murdochs, John Christie and James Innes. Scottish pistols were usually made in pairs, with different locks for the right and left hands. Pairs of duelling pistols were, however, not so much in demand in Scotland as in England and Ireland. The percussion system of firing was invented by an eccentric Scottish cleric, the Rev. Alexander Forsyth, in 1805–07, but steel flintlock pistols continued to be made well into the 19th century for dress purposes.

Duelling pistols have been a great growth area of collecting; whereas 10 years or so ago a pair by a famous maker could often go for a mere £25 in a country sale, now the price would be up a hundredfold. Weapons by the Mantons and Egg are particularly prized. Percussion pistols are about two-thirds the price of flintlocks, but some shrewd dealers are already salting them away—their day will undoubtedly come.

Among Scottish edged weapons are found the Highland claymore and big two-handed broadsword. Some swords were spuriously marked with the name of Andrea Ferrara. Curiously enough, most Scottish arms are found in England now.

Firemarks

Firemarks are a recent collecting boom, apparently sparked off by a couple of articles in *The Times* and *The Antique Collector*. They are the small metal plaques once placed on buildings to indicate that they were insured against fire.

Glass

In the 17th century George Ravenscroft perfected a clear lead crystal of English materials which was better than the Venetian formula, and by 1695 there were 47 glass factories producing flint glass. Large amounts were exported, particularly to the Netherlands and Scandinavia for engraving. English style drinking-glasses ousted the *façon de Venise* glass in the 18th century when the wonderful array of baluster, air-twist and colour-twist glasses was developed. Stourbridge and Newcastle were important glass-making centres; Newcastle was noted for engraving and enamelling, especially for the enamel work of the Beilby family. Jacobite glasses commemorating the Stuart claim to the Scottish throne, are perennially popular, as are 'privateer' glasses, usually inscribed with the slogan 'Success to' the ship concerned.

The 1745 Excise Act, which taxed glass by weight, influenced the whole style of English glass; it became lighter and more shallowly cut, while glass makers who wanted to continue making the heavy style moved to Ireland. The glass from Nailsea—a glass factory near Bristol which turned out oddities such as shepherds' crooks, bells and walking sticks in a glass characterized by coloured loops and stripes—was exempt from the Excise Act, as was bottle glass. Bristol glass (not made solely in Bristol) was typically deep blue, but also came in amethyst, green and, more rarely, ruby; the most valuable comes from the second half of the 18th century. However, genuine Bristol glass is not easy to find; much carrying that name actually comes from Czechoslovakia. By the 19th century, cheaper pressed glass had superseded cut crystal in the mass market and many decanters were made of this.

The Scottish glass industry was established at Wemyss in 1610, but in the late 17th and 18th centuries Leith, near Edinburgh, became noted first for bottle glass and subsequently wine glasses and apothecary vessels. In the late 18th and 19th centuries fine-cut and engraved crystal was produced by the Verreville glass factory in Glasgow. Edinburgh and Leith Flint Glass Works became Webb's Crystal in 1921, producing mainly undecorated tableware and drawn-stem wine glasses. Moncrieff's Glass Works at Perth (still in production) made glasses and pharmaceutical wares; an Alloa glass factory made bottles and Nailsea-type wares in streaked bottle glass. Fine stipple-engraving was also practised in Scotland, with glasses engraved with seals and family coats of arms.

Bottle-collecting is a fast-growing hobby in Britain. Real enthusiasts stake out forgotten Victorian rubbish tips which they excavate for treasures. Some of the original 'seal' bottles used in the days before wine decanters can still be found at reasonable prices, in all parts of the country from Inverness to Cornwall. There is also a bottle stall in the Portobello Road market in London.

Jewellery

There has been a boom in Victorian jewellery in Britain and some of the semiprecious stones such as alexandrites, aquamarines, peridots and the rare green garnets are particularly in demand. Opals are cheaper in London than in Australia, their country of origin. Pearls have never quite recovered from the market collapse when cultured pearls came in; they are not advised for investment. Chinese buyers are snapping up jade in London, the rich emerald colour being the most highly prized. Georgian and Regency jewellery (pre-1830) is probably a better investment than Victorian now because prices have not risen so fast. These pieces are hard to find because so much was broken up and incorporated into later pieces, but there are still a number of Georgian rings to be picked up at antique fairs. Beware of paying too low a price—if the setting is irrevocably worn the stones may drop out.

Rings are the most popular of Victorian jewellery, followed by bracelets, earrings and necklaces. Good Victorian cameos (the rarest being carved in amethyst) are very desirable and Cameo Corner in London is probably the best place to find them, along with other pieces of early jewellery. The black-and-gold mourning jewellery of the 19th century is now being collected. Some mourning brooches, typical of the Victorian approach to death, contained elaborate designs made from the hair of the dead person; the more elaborate the design, the better.

Tassie glass-paste medallions were a Scottish speciality. James Tassie (1735–99) was a Scottish engraver and modeller of cameos who developed a method of moulding finely-ground and heated glass. He used opaque white and coloured glass paste to reproduce cameos and engraved gems. He was especially noted for large profile-portrait medallions.

The London street markets are a good source of jewellery for the knowledgeable: more than half the stalls on the Portobello Road deal in jewellery. One of these specializes in watch-chain seals, which make a very attractive and easily portable subject for collecting; the earliest classical pieces are oddly enough, less popular than the ornate Victorian seals.

Miniatures

Portrait miniatures, the luxurious forerunners of the family photograph album, have been linked with the English court ever since Hans Holbein introduced the art to England in the reign of Henry VIII. Miniature-painting continued until the invention of the daguerrotype in 1841. Elizabeth I amassed a fine collection and Charles I had his favourite paintings copied in miniature to take on his travels. James I required all his courtiers to wear a miniature with the royal portrait, which accounts for the large number of that monarch's portraits still around. Oliver Cromwell sold off many of the royal treasures, but Charles II bought a considerable number back, and the present Queen occasionally buys back pieces that were formerly in the royal collections. Many noble old families also have splendid collections.

In Europe the art of miniature painting really began with Holbein, only 13 of whose miniatures are known to exist. One outstanding English name was Nicholas Hilliard, jeweller and painter to Elizabeth I; his work shows an unmistakable jeweller's eye, with brilliance and detail in costuming. Samuel Cooper, John Hoskins, John Smart, Richard Cosway, George Engleheart and Andrew Plimer were other top miniaturists, and by the middle of the 18th century England was pre-eminent in the art. Typical of the 18th century was the oval gilt frame with a lock of the sitter's hair in the back of the case. Paintings on ivory were always post-1700 and the earliest frames were round and made of turned wood A common fake is the miniature in an oblong ivory 'piano key' frame which doesn't fit any period. Oil-on-copper miniatures are cheaper than others as some find them rather dull, but can reveal their richness with clever lighting; these date from the 16th century to about 1720.

Model Soldiers

Model soldiers are avidly collected, though 50 per cent of the quarterly sales at Phillips in London go to foreign buyers.

Model Steam Engines

Model steam engines of ships, locomotives and industrial engines are popular. Ship-building yards always made two scale 'builder's models' of each liner or cargo steamer they turned out, plus half-models, also desirable to collectors. Minns in London is the leading expert.

Paintings

For paintings under the £500 mark the late 19th and 20th

centuries are the best bet. Much of the market for Victorian paintings became overheated in 1973 and some extraordinarily inflated prices were paid. Only the economic recession of the next three years cooled prices off, but there are still opportunities among the less fashionable names of that prolific period. However, 19th-century watercolours have largely remained a depressed area.

The collecting of watercolours, a very English art form, only really got going about 1960 after a boom in Victorian times. In the late 1950s a Copley Fielding landscape could have been bought for £10 which would now be in the upper hundreds. Some artists are greatly prized, such as J. M. W. Turner, his contemporary Thomas Girtin and Richard Parkes Bonington in particular. Girtin died young in 1802 and Turner later remarked: 'If Tom had lived, I should have starved.' Colour is valued, and the grey and sepia-toned washes of the 18th century are in consequence underrated. Perhaps the finest selection of watercolours in England is to be found at Stanhope Shelton Pictures in Monks Eleigh (Suffolk).

As a general rule, portraits and figures are unpopular watercolour subjects for collectors, except for Rowlandson and Birket Foster; also lacking in public appeal, in either watercolour or oil, are stormy seascapes (calm waters are the thing, preferably lit by the setting sun), cows in meadows and those dour Victorian still-lifes of dead birds and game. Sporting pictures, ineffably English, have a (perhaps artificially) high market value, and names like Herring, Ferneley, Stubbs and Alken can be approached by most collectors only through the medium of the engraving (see 'Prints and maps').

Scottish painters contributed much to the mainstream of British art, though many early ones found it necessary to follow Dr Samuel Johnson's 'high road to England' to make a living. William Aikman (1682–1731) was the first to do so, but Allan Ramsay (1713–84) returned to Edinburgh after the statutory spell in London and Rome, there to become the foremost portrait painter of his time. Robert Strange, the first of the Scottish engravers, and Gavin Hamilton were others who had to go to Europe to be recognized. Alexander Runciman, however, gained the Mastership of the Trustees' Academy, which established Edinburgh's reputation as an artistic teaching centre. The first Scottish artist to be internationally recognized was Sir Henry

Raeburn (1756–1823), who became president of the Royal Scottish Academy as well as a Royal Academician in London.

The romanticizing of the Scottish past which typified much of the 19th century, thanks to Sir Walter Scott's historical novels, found many painters to express it, among them William Allan, Andrew Geddes and Sir David Wilkie. There were also Sir Francis Grant, who specialized in hunting scenes, William Dyce and John Milne Donald, a forerunner of the impressionists.

Donald worked in Glasgow and it was this roaring industrial city which surprisingly produced Scotland's most notable contribution to modern art history: the Glasgow school. Founder members of this group, characterized by its bold expressive handling of colour and paint, included W. Y. Macgregor, James Guthrie, Alexander Roche, Arthur Melville, Thomas Mille Dow and John Lavery, who as Sir John Lavery later became a fashionable Royal Academy painter in London. Some experts feel the Glasgow school is still considerably undervalued in salerooms. Another son of Glasgow whose contribution to early 20th-century art from architecture to watercolours was seminal was Charles Rennie Mackintosh. The School of Art which bears his stamp throughout its design is a 'must' for every visitor to Glasgow.

Other notable Scottish artists included John MacWhirter (1839–1911), whose attractive watercolours, many of Italian landscapes, have risen strongly in popularity since the early 1960s, and Sir William MacTaggart (1835–1910), who brilliantly interpreted light and atmosphere in an impressionistic style. His work was almost unknown outside Scotland until 1935.

London salerooms, particularly Phillips, Bonham's, Sotheby's Belgravia and Christie's South Kensington, offer a huge turnover each week of inexpensive paintings from as little as £10 upwards.

Pewter

Early British pewter, made of Derbyshire lead and Cornish tin, had a soft lustre quite different from that of Continental makes. The London Pewterers' Company laid it down by charter in 1348 that fine pewter should be made of an alloy of copper and tin with the copper added to the tin 'as much of its own nature it will take'. It was later established as 112 lb (49.8 kg) of tin to 26 lb (11.8 kg) of copper, but 18th-century fine pewter usually contained 112 lb (49.8 kg) of tin to 6–7 lb (2.7–3.2 kg) of antimony.

Some pewter pieces are actually rarer than silver of the same period because so much was melted down or thrown away. The 17th century was the golden age, but many pieces from this time were not marked despite a ruling of 1503 making punch marks compulsory. Still scorned in Britain is the lighter Britannia Metal (not to be confused with the high-quality Britannia Standard silver), made in the 19th century from 90 per cent tin and 10 per cent antimony and spun, not cast. US collectors do not despise it, however, and it will probably come into demand as the supply of old pewter dwindles.

The characteristic Scottish pewter article was the 'tappit-hen' measure which at first designated the Scottish pint—3 imperial pints (1.7 litres) in volume—but later covered any measure for ale or spirit so long as the form was tall and slim with a cylindrical base and concave middle section. These are attractive to collectors but have dramatically risen in price in recent years. Typical Scottish measure shapes included the early pot-bellied type (1680–1740), the pear-shaped style (early 19th century) and the thistle-shaped type (1800–30). The latter was banned by weights-and-measures inspectors because it tended to leave some liquid in the bowl when it was tipped, and few such measures survive.

Dealers outside London include Bolan in Moreton-in-Marsh (Gloucestershire) and Keil in Cheltenham.

Photographs and Postcards

Photographs and postcards fetch rapidly-appreciating prices for the best examples, but there is still the chance of a discovery in a battered cardboard box in some seaside junk shop.

Porcelain

There were about 16 principal British factories, each of which has its devoted body of collectors. Finest of all was Chelsea, the first to develop soft-paste porcelain in the mid 18th century. Chelsea ware divides into four periods according to the marks used. The 'red anchor' (1752–58) pieces are the most popular with collectors today, but red-anchor marks also occur on other types of porcelain—the Chelsea mark is small and hard to find. Chelsea red-anchor figures were some of the loveliest ever made. Other marks were the 'incised triangle' (1743–50) whose pieces are rarely found outside museums, 'raised anchor' (1750–52) whose pieces showed definite Meissen influence, and 'gold anchor' (1760–69) whose pieces were much more lush and more elaborately decorated. Chelsea's blue-and-white ware, made in the 1750s, is particularly rare; it sometimes carried a blue-anchor mark.

Blue-and-white ware, inspired by the Chinese porcelain imported by the East India Co. was made for household use by the Bow factory in the East End of London, as well as plain and coloured figures. The best period was 1752–60; later the modelling became crude.

Lowestoft porcelain has a faithful following. A local clay was found which encouraged the emulation of Meissen and Chinese ware. Production was mostly tableware, much of it blue-and-white. Odd small pieces marked 'A Trifle from Lowestoft' are collected—they were forerunners of the much later Goss souvenir china—as are the unique 'birth plaques' made for children and the small figures of swans, cats, dogs and sheep. The plaques and animals are rare.

More blue-and-white was made at Longton Hall factory (Staffordshire), founded in the 1740s. So were figures such as the Four Seasons, typical of nearly all British factories at this period. The marks were, variously, crossed LLs, a J crossed with an L, a reversed swastika, a cross and single letters.

Production at Derby began in 1750, specializing in figures and expensive tableware. Andrew Planché, one of the founders, made highly sought-after figures—up to 50 different types are known. The factory was taken over by William Duesbury in 1756–86 when it turned out scores of less highly-regarded figures, mostly of national heroes. The biscuit figures of the late 18th and early 19th centuries are, however, some of the most beautiful productions of this factory. Some patterns were made for years and dating becomes a matter of studying body and glaze. Derby ware of 1775–1800 was noted for its brilliant painting of landscapes, seascapes, flowers and birds. Characteristic of this factory were the four 'patch marks' like thumbprints on the base where the piece was held for firing in the kiln. Purple, blue and crimson marks indicate manufacture before 1800; later the famous crown and crossed batons and a D were marked in red.

The only great British factory of the 18th century still in

production today is Worcester, founded in 1751. For collectors, the cream of its output came in the early years to 1776, when the rococo style flowered. This period, presided over by Dr John Wall, is known as the Dr Wall Period or First Period Worcester. The blue-and-white ware of this period is among the finest in Europe. Worcester porcelain was later decorated in dramatic colours such as turquoise, yellow, pea-green, claret and a 'scale' blue with a fish-scale effect; these are highly prized. Gilding was made from honey mixed with gold, producing a particularly soft effect. The Worcester porcelain factory was also the first to use transfer-printing. After the death of Dr Wall came the Flight Davies or Middle Period (1776–93) when rather undistinguished blue-and-white ware was made. This was succeeded by the Flight and Barr Period (1793–1840) when quality once again improved. The world's best collection of old Worcester porcelain is in the city of Worcester itself; set up in 1789 and later bought by a member of the Lea and Perrins Worcester Sauce family, it is open to the public. Preston's in Bolton is a leading specialist in First Period Worcester.

There has often been confusion over whether certain ware was Middle Period Worcester or produced at the rival Caughley (pronounced Carfley) factory in Shropshire during 1772–1812. This factory concentrated on blue-and-white transfer-printed porcelain, tea services being its biggest line.

Coalport, Liverpool, Plymouth, Bristol and New Hall (Staffordshire) were other leading factories of the second half of the 18th century, Plymouth porcelain being the first true hard-paste porcelain made in Britain. Outstanding, however, was the Welsh porcelain made at Nantgarw and Swansea for a period in the early 19th century. Both types are avidly collected in Wales itself, though their classical restraint is an acquired taste for some. Nantgarw porcelain (made in 1813–19) was pure white with a rich glaze and delicate translucence; Swansea porcelain was sturdier and slightly cloudier and had a greenish tinge. Nantgarw ware was marked with the full name; Swansea ware was marked sometimes by 'Dillwyn and Co.' or a trident symbol. Hutchings in Newport (Gwent) is a specialist in these wares.

Spode, Minton, Rockingham and Copeland complete the roster of leading porcelain names. In 1846 Copeland and Garrett was the first firm to market Parian ware, a whiter and more marble-textured version of the 18th-century Derby biscuit porcelain. It was first known as 'statuary porcelain' and early busts are extremely scarce. Other makers soon rushed into the market. It was the Minton factory which chose the name Parian (after the marble-producing island Paros), and the medium was at its peak employed by 50 potters turning out portrait busts, figures and, to a lesser extent, tableware. Belleek in Ireland made a particularly attractive, glistening white version. At the cheaper end of the market, Robinson and Leadbeater produced a vast range of portrait busts in various sizes; these always had square bases and were usually marked R and L. Small busts are still fairly cheap, but not as worth collecting as the larger pieces.

Posters

Posters are marvellously evocative of a vigorous commercial era. Britain has its own tradition, quite different from the art deco style of France or the art nouveau one of the Low Countries. Lord's Gallery in London is a good source.

Pot Lids

Pot lids, the decorated tops of Victorian commercial containers for such household goods as fishpaste and hair-pomade, are keenly collected. Rare examples can fetch over £400. Phillips in London holds periodic sales.

Pottery

Lead-glazed earthenware still survives from the 14th and 15th centuries. Tin-glazed earthenware, English Delft ware, was made from the beginning of the 16th century, starting with Malling jugs, to the 18th century. Centres of manufacture included Bristol, Lambeth, Liverpool, Wincanton, Glasgow and Dublin. Ming porcelain was copied at Lambeth in the late 17th century.

By the 18th century Staffordshire had become the main centre of English pottery, though important sources included Leeds and Liverpool. Among potters producing cream-coloured earthen-ware and salt-glazed ware were Astbury, Heath, the Wood family, Turner, Palmer and Rollins. It was Josiah Wedgwood who refined cream-coloured earthenware into what was marketed first as creamware and later as pearlware. Transfer-printing, developed in the late 18th century, transformed the appearance of creamware and by the end of that century it had largely replaced tin-glazed ware in Europe. (Creamware is still relatively inexpensive but collectors should beware of reproductions.) Wedgwood also made decorative stoneware, black basalt ware (used strikingly for urns and portrait busts) and his characteristic embossed jasper ware.

Scottish transfer-printed pottery is a relatively unexplored field about which little has been written. All the major Scottish potteries were situated around the Clyde and Forth estuaries, the largest centre being Glasgow. Potteries here included the Delftfield works (the earliest factory); the Verreville Pottery (sold several times and finally ending up in the ownership of the Cochran family) which introduced durable domestic stoneware; the Britannia (also founded by Cochran) which was devoted largely to export to the USA and Canada, the pottery being decorated with views of those countries; the North British Pottery; the Victoria Pottery in Pollokshaws; the Glasgow Pottery which also made fine hand-painted china, Parian ware and terracotta; the Annfield pottery; and in Greenock the Clyde Pottery and Greenock (later Ladyburn) Pottery.

Lustreware is a typically British product which 20 or so years ago was hardly collected at all. Developed in Staffordshire about 1790, its metallic sheen was obtained by applying a thin film of dissolved gold or platinum; different body colours resulted according to the colour of the pottery ground. Gold on brown or black produced a coppery lustre; on white or cream it usually turned out pink. Yellow is particularly sought after by collectors. Platinum produced a silver lustre; silver 'resist' lustreware with a canary yellow background is rare and very collectable. This was made by covering parts of the surface with a greasy substance before the metallic wash was applied. Around 1810–15 the Wedgwood factory made a mottled pink lustre known as 'moonlight'. Lustreware was produced at Leeds but large quantities were made also in Sunderland—there were many jugs commemorating the famous Iron Bridge over the River Wear—and Newcastle and Swansea were other centres. Lustreware was also made in the Victorian period but the most valuable pieces date from the early 19th century. Much of the original ware was unmarked, which makes it difficult to date, and there are modern reproductions.

Another interesting 19th-century development was ironstone china, patented by C. J. Mason in 1813. The clay was supposedly mixed with iron slag, making the pottery extremely durable; it could also be handsomely decorated. The leading expert in England on Mason's Ironstone, Parian and 19th-century ware in general is Geoffrey Godden in Worthing (Sussex). He has written and edited many books on pottery and porcelain and his shop offers collectors a permanent reference display as well as periodic special exhibitions.

Wemyss ware, an art pottery produced in Kirkcaldy from the 1880s to the end of the 1920s, was a brilliant boldly-decorated ware now much in demand by Scottish collectors. Some was designed for household use, such as toilet sets, inkstands, candlesticks or biscuit jars, but the makers also specialized in whimsical-looking animals: pigs and cats painted with bold shamrocks were favourites for the US export market. Decoration leaned heavily towards flowers and fruit, big pink roses being a favourite theme. At one time so fashionable that it was sold by Thomas Goode of Mayfair in London, Wemyss ware is now mostly found in Scotland, at fairly high prices because of the local demand. Mrs. Iris Fox in West Bow, Edinburgh, is a leading collector and specialist dealer.

Commemorative ware forms a huge collecting field. It began to appear in large quantities around 1780, when mass production was introduced into ceramic manufacture. The combination of this and the invention of transfer-printing caused the boom in commemoratives which reached its heyday in Victoria's reign. Royalty has always been the most popular subject, but naval themes and Nelson in particular run a close second, followed by military, political and industrial subjects. The earliest royal commemorative piece was a Delft mug made for Charles II's coronation, but there are plenty of George III items around at prices from £100. The one royalty piece every collector wants is a Victorian coronation mug, and the cost of one may well be less in the Midlands than in London. Some Victorian pieces are reproductions of earlier ones; dating must rely on style and shape.

Minor pottery fields offering scope for collectors include Staffordshire portrait figures, a popular Victorian art form (the chief maker was Sampson Smith in Longton, mark SS), and Toby jugs, made by many manufacturers from the late 18th century—the series by F. Carruthers Gould modelling First World War leaders is particularly sought after.

Prints and Maps

After the Second World War nobody wanted to buy etchings, and marvellous parcels of Whistlers and Sickerts went for almost nothing in the salerooms. The reason apparently was that after years of drabness and blackout no one wanted black-and-white pictures on their walls—colour was all-important. Things are different now, but fine British draughtsmen like D. Y. Cameron, Sir Muirhead Bone and Sir Frank Brangwyn are still underrated in the market. A collector often has the chance of picking up an etching by a famous painter—Augustus John, for instance—at a fraction of the price of a watercolour or oil by the same artist. A first-state Whistler (the artist's first concept, before alterations) is now very expensive, but many atmospheric Whistlers can be had for less than £100.

Mezzotints, produced by the 18th-century process which made pictures with gradations of tone available to a mass market, are just reviving in popularity, although high prices are now paid for works by such famous mezzotint artists as Richard Earlom and Robert Laurie. Sporting prints, usually done in aquatint after the paintings of Herring, Alken and Pollard, are commanding much higher prices than a few years ago.

The English tradition in map-making is very important; Saxton and Speed were the greatest names. Christopher Saxton completed the first collection of detailed county maps with the authority and backing of Elizabeth I, but these rarely come on the market. The maps and atlases of John Speed, a Cheshire tailor, are more common but now fetch many thousands of pounds. Another outstanding name was John Ogilby who devised the first road maps. In the early 19th century incredibly-detailed steel-engraved maps were made by the Greenwood brothers in the one-inch county series; these are a good investment, as are any 19th-century Ordnance Survey maps. Counties have a fashion rating: for example, Northamptonshire and Bedfordshire count only half the value of Sussex, Lancashire or Cheshire.

Paper made before 1750 can be detected by its impressed

watermark, from wires set well apart in the trays. Baynton-Williams, the Map House and Weinreb & Douwma are leading London dealers in prints and maps, while P. J. Radford in Sheffield Park (Sussex) has a huge mail-order business. The Parker Gallery in Albemarle Street is an old established and reputable dealer specializing in topographical and military prints.

Scientific instruments

Scientific instruments were a considerable British craft. The best dealers are Davidson and Wynter in London.

Sheffield Plate

A Sheffield cutler named Thomas Bolsover accidentally fused some copper with silver in a furnace and created Sheffield plate, ideally suited to meet the aspirations of the Victorian middle class who could not quite rise to silver to display their wealth. It was usually made in hollow-ware because of the problems of concealing the copper at the edges of flatware, which inevitably became eroded with use. Popular items were tea trays, salvers, tea and coffee pots, candelabra, wine coolers, entrée dishes and argyles (an ingenious double-lined pot for keeping gravy warm). Among the most successful manufacturers were S. Roberts the Younger (Sheffield) and M. Boulton (Birmingham), followed in the 19th century by the royal silversmiths, Rundell, Bridge & Rundell, who employed distinguished artists. Sheffield plate was generally unmarked, though Boulton and Roberts did mark their ware. In 1840 the more flexible method of electroplating was invented by Elkington of Birmingham and by 1880 the manufacture of Sheffield plate had almost died out.

Silver

Recent years have seen a great deal of investment collecting in English silver, though people are more wary since the Georgian silver market collapsed in 1969/70 on account of too many investors trying to sell at the same time. Georgian silver has only just achieved its pre-crash levels, but in the meantime Victorian silver has become immensely popular—for use as well as aesthetic pleasure—and values in this field have gone up steeply.

English silver has a particularly long lineage though little medieval plate survives, having been largely destroyed in the Reformation and the Civil War, except for college and guild plate. The largest collection of Tudor and Jacobean plate, ironically enough, is in the Kremlin in Moscow—testimony to the grandiose largesse of former centuries to foreign statesmen and institutions. Until 1650 the chief stylistic influence on English silver was German, which was succeeded by Dutch and then French styles. With the Restoration the aristocracy and rising wealth of the middle classes caused vast quantities of plate to be commissioned, and functional pieces such as tea and coffee pots came in with the introduction of those beverages in the late 17th century. By 1730 the rococo style was well established, the finest exponent being the Huguenot Paul de Lamerie, but it was soon superseded by the neoclassical Adam style. Plainer designs lent themselves well to the mass production techniques of the industrial revolution and invention of Sheffield plate (see 'Sheffield Plate').

The great prestige name of 18th-century English silver was Hester Bateman, whose mark increases the value of a piece two or three times. Born in 1709 she took over her husband John's business in 1760; her early work was in spoons and forks and she also made attractive wine labels. She worked in a neoclassical style with a characteristic beaded edge. There are an estimated 11 000 Hester Bateman pieces in existence. Eventually her sons John and Peter, her grandson William and John's widow Ann continued the business.

Not much Scottish silver survives earlier than the 18th century, but this period was rich in distinctive forms including: the near-spherical 'bullet' teapot; the 'quaich' or drinking-bowl with flat handles either side (miniature quaiches, 2–3 in (5–7.5 cm) across, were made at Inverness and are rare collector's pieces); the bannock rack, a large type of toast rack to hold the breakfast bannocks of oatmeal; and the thistle cup, made from the late 17th century, which had a slightly bulging body in the form of a thistle. Some notable 18th-century makers were William Scott (Dundee), Edward Lothian, Patrick Robertson and Charles Blair (Edinburgh) and Coline Allan and George Walker (Aberdeen). Edinburgh was the main centre for Scottish silver manufacture.

Most leading English Victorian silversmiths worked for commercial firms, notably J. S. Hunt of Hunt & Roskell (successors to the business established by the great Regency maker Paul Storr) and Robert Garrard, whose name still flourishes over the Crown jewellers in Regent St. Other London makers of note were Barnard, Joseph Angell with his distinctive angular style, Charles Fox, Rawlings & Brown and J. C. Edington. An odd man out among Victorian makers was Christopher Dresser, who designed modernistic functional pieces foreshadowing the Bauhaus style of the 1920s.

The 19th-century romantic revival initiated by Sir Walter Scott had its effect on Scottish silver. A distinctively neobaronial flavour developed, well matched to the interiors of those turreted mansions built for the commercial magnates of the time. Makers of the 19th century included Ferguson and McBean (Inverness), William Marshall (Edinburgh) and Robert Gray and Son (Glasgow). Among small pieces, two types of brooch were typically Scottish: the circular plaid brooch (Victorian examples are often set with cairngorms or other semiprecious stones) and the heart-shaped 'luckenbooth' brooches, usually made for betrothals and called after the locked booths which used to surround St Giles's Cathedral in Edinburgh.

Around the turn of this century, much distinguished work was done for the London firm of Liberty by makers such as C. R. Ashbee and Omar Ramsden, who worked on into the 1930s. Their pieces are highly sought after and have risen in value as a result of the Victoria and Albert Museum's exhibition of Liberty ware in 1975.

Hallmarking in England was instituted in 1300—a leopard's head punch; in 1363 came the maker's mark, in 1478 the date letter, in 1544 the sterling mark, and in 1784–1890 the sovereign's head or duty mark. Scottish hallmarking dates from the 16th century in Glasgow, though the maker's mark was first used in Edinburgh in 1485; in 1759 the thistle became the standard sterling mark. Assay offices were set up in York, Newcastle, Norwich, Bristol, Salisbury, Lincoln, Birmingham and Sheffield, and several Scottish towns had their own assay marks up to 1836, when it was laid down that all Scottish silver should be assayed in Edinburgh, Glasgow or London. The Glasgow assay office only closed in 1964. Attribution of London marks before 1697 is difficult because a fire in the assay office destroyed a parchment with all the maker's names. In 1697, following the establishment of the new high-silver-content Britannia standard, makers had to re-register their marks.

English silver spoons are a popular collecting theme which makes it possible to assemble a representative selection of styles and periods without spending a fortune. Apostle spoons, given as christening presents from Tudor to Carolean times, are the rarities here but are also the most widely faked. Scottish spoons offer the chance to collect the rarer assay marks from small towns like Montrose, Elgin, Wick, Tain and Banff.

Outside London, leading silver dealers include Bruford in Exeter (especially spoons), Porter in Bournemouth (also strong on antique spoons), Bracher & Sydenham in Reading, Preston's in Bolton, Koopman in Manchester, and Mallory in Bath. The leading dealer in Scottish silver, How of Edinburgh, is actually based in London.

Good collections of Scottish silver can be seen at the Aberdeen Art Gallery and Museum, the Royal Scottish Museum and National Museum of Antiquities of Scotland in Edinburgh, and the Glasgow Art Gallery and Museum.

Snuff Boxes and Snuff Mulls

Snuff originated in Britain around 1680 and snuff boxes were made in the 18th and 19th centuries in silver, gold, enamel, ivory and lacquer, tortoiseshell and base metals. Gold boxes were rarely signed, from 1714 to 1760 were mainly oval and chased with classical decoration, but after 1720 also often had miniatures on the lids. Rectangular shapes were popular from 1760 to 1815, with French influence in the enamel and four-colour gold decoration. Engine-turning replaced enamelling in 1800. Silver boxes were properly hallmarked but wear has often rubbed the marks away. Birmingham in the 19th century was a centre of silver- and gold-box production and the much-sought-after enamel boxes were made here as well as in Bilston and Liverpool. Silver-plated boxes were made in the late 1750s in Sheffield and lacquered metal boxes in Pontypridd and Birmingham from 1738 onwards.

Victorian snuff boxes are mostly regarded as inferior in workmanship to earlier models, though the products of makers such as Samuel Pemberton, Joseph Wilmore and Nathaniel Mills fetch a premium. Collectors usually aim for a speciality such as Staffordshire, agate or 'castletop' boxes (with a chased view of a stately home or coat of arms), but on the whole English boxes are nothing as elegant as the enamel boxes of France and Switzerland or the Russian jewel-encrusted examples.

Snuff mulls, a speciality of Scotland, were often bizarre-looking snuff containers for both table and pocket use. They were made in the late 18th and early 19th centuries of horn, ivory, shell, deer's hoof, etc., mounted with silver or pewter and sometimes set with semiprecious stones. Some took the form of animals. Two makers who signed their ware were Constantine and Durie.

Treen

Treen were small wooden articles made for domestic and decorative purposes. The treen made of Scottish sycamore wood in Mauchline (Ayrshire), among other places, were decorated with transfer-printed views, portraits and other subjects, always in black on the plain wooden ground. The commonest were snuff boxes, needle cases, pill boxes, trinket boxes and the like. Flat circular boxes for holding stamps had a postage stamp replica on the lid and date from the 1840s; soon after the introduction of the Penny Post; they are rare.

The great Pinto Collection of treen can be seen at the Birmingham City Museum and Art Gallery. Leading dealers include Toller in Eton (Berkshire).

The trade

An extremely informative magazine is the *Antique Dealer and Collector's Guide,* which has a useful column of news on sales in Europe. Its approach is more popular and more broadly based than that of *Apollo,* which, however, manages to blend scholarship with a very readable style, particularly in the editorials, and the *Connoisseur,* latterly edited by art deco specialist Bevis Hillier. The illustrious *Burlington Magazine* is for scholars and specialists and comes out quarterly; the others are monthly publications. On a popular level, the monthly *Antique Collector* is well worth buying, especially for its regional surveys of antiques and prices around Britain.

Aberdeen

Dealers

John BELL, 56-8 Bridge St (24828).
Four storeys of fine furniture, silver, glass, china, Sheffield plate.
Member of BADA.

TREASURE HOUSE (E. C. &. W. G. Edwards), 16 Holburn St (20219).
Small furniture, china, silver; specializes in Georgian and
Victorian periods. Closed Wed. and Sat. afternoons.

William YOUNG, 1 Belmont St (53757/8).
Fine stock of antique furniture and works of art. Member of
BADA.

Aboyne

Dealers

ABOYNE ANTIQUES (Mrs Carmen Smith, Station Sq).
English and Scottish ware, predominantly 18th/19th-century silver, porcelain and 18th-century furniture—all reasonably priced.

Bath

Dealers

MALLORY. 1-4 Bridge St and 5 Old Bond St (24147).
Silver.

Birmingham

Dealers

ALLEGRO Antiques (Mrs A. W. Johnston), 293 Broad St (643 6275; private 458 3493).
General antiques, Victoriana. Open 1000–1630; closed Sun.,
Wed. and Sat. afternoons.

The ANTIQUE GUN Shop (Derek Roland Lord), 1240 Pershore Rd, Stirchley (458 3946).
16th/20th-century arms and armour. Open 0915-1715; closed
Sun. and Wed. afternoons.

DAMASCUS Antiques (Miss M. H. Rowlands) (777 1153).
18th/19th-century furniture, Georgian and Victorian jewellery.
Open 1000–1830; closed Sun. and Wed. afternoons.

D. & M. DAVID Ltd, 3 Livery St (236 1304).
Pre-1850 furniture and silver, pre-1880 pictures and miniatures.
Open Mon.–Fri. 0900–1300, 1400–1700. Restoration of silver,
pictures and furniture. Member of BADA.

*Perry GREAVES Ltd, 2–4 The Priory, Queensway (236 9297) and 1
Corporation St (643 5479).*
English silver, old Sheffield plate, jewellery. Open Mon.–Sat.
0900–1730. Member of BADA.

NATHAN & Co., 32 Corporation St (643 5225/0575).
Silver, jewellery. Open 0900–1700; closed Sat. afternoon.
Restorations.

*Westley RICHARDS & Co Ltd, Grange Rd, Bournbrook (472 1701).
(about 3½ miles from city centre, off A38 road).*
Antique weapons and curios of 1700–1900. Open Sun.–Fri.
0900–1230, 1330–1700. Restoration of modern shotguns and
rifles.

*STRATFORD House Antiques Ltd, St Martin's Lane, Broad St (643
2057).*
Toys, treen, small pictures, copper, brass. Open Mon.–Sat.
1000–1730.

*TILLEY'S Antiques (S. A. Alpren), 2 Springfield Rd, Moseley (777
8168).*
Furniture, porcelain, glass, silver, maps, prints, clocks. Open
1000–1800.

Douglas YOUNG, 762 Pershore Rd, Selby Park (473 3448).
17th/19th-century English, Dutch and Victorian oil-paintings.
Appointment necessary.

Markets
*BIRMINGHAM THURSDAY ANTIQUE FAIR, 141 Bromsgrove St
(692 1414).*

Arms, militaria, furniture, porcelain, silver, jewellery, Victoriana, glass, clocks. 25 stalls. Open Thur. 1000–2100.

Auctions
PHILLIPS IN KNOWLE, Solihull (6151).
An offshoot of Phillips in London. Sales weekly.

Bournemouth

Dealers
R. E. PORTER, 2-4 Post Office Rd (24289).
Silver, especially antique spoons.

Brighton

Dealers
Alan ADRIAN, 51 Upper North St (25277).
18th/19th-century furniture, clocks (carriage, long-case, bracket), marine instruments, brass. Open Mon.–Wed. and Fri.–Sat. 1000–1730. Restorations.

Richard ALEXANDER, 3 Nile St (27344).
Specialist in post-1500 Oriental items; antiquities, collectors' items of all periods. Open Fri.–Wed. 1000–1300, 1400–1600.

BAY TREE House (Maurice Lovett), 19 Middle St (24688).
17th/19th-century scientific marine instruments. Open Mon.–Sat. 0930–1730.

Margaret CADMAN, 25 Ship St (29627).
English pottery and porcelain, enamels, jewellery, furniture. Open Mon.–Sat. 0900–1715. Member of BADA. Exhibitor at Grosvenor House Antique Fair in London.

The CLOCK Shop, 9 Ship St (24362).
Pre-1900 clocks and watches. Open Mon.–Fri. 0900–1300, 1400–1900; Sat. 0900–1300, 1400–1530. Restoration of antique clock movements.

Denys COWELL, 60 Middle St (26758).
Large stock of early oak and mahogany; Chinese porcelain, paintings, silver, objets d'art. Open 0930–1730; closed Sun., and Sat. afternoon. Member of BADA.

FISHER NAUTICAL, 88 Gloucester Rd (687480).
Probably Europe's largest stock of nautical books covering everything from dinghies to warships to passenger liners; shipping magazines. Holds publishing rights for reprints of Lloyds' Register back to 1760. Mail order.

HARE & ELYARD, 48 Market St (735205).
Glass, early china, scent bottles, small silver boxes. Open Mon. and Wed.–Sat. 0930–1600.

David HAWKINS, 4 Frederick Pl (27409, 21009).
China, clocks, bronze, comprehensive stock of Victorian and Edwardian furniture. Open 0830–1700; closed Sun., and Sat. afternoon. Weekly deliveries to the Continent and container-packing facilities.

HOLLEYMAN & TREACHER Ltd, 21a Duke St (28007).
Large and varied stock of secondhand and antiquarian books. Good collection of 19th-century topographical prints. Open Mon.–Sat. 0930–1730.

KINGSBURY Antiques, 59 Ship St (28058).
Old Sheffield plate, silver, glass, porcelain, objets d'art. Open Mon.–Sat. 0900–1700.

MAGPIE House Antiques, 27 Kemp St (683892).
Early Staffordshire figures and Victorian portrait figures of 1790–1900, pot lids, fairings, Doulton pottery. commemoratives of 1830–1937, Worcester porcelain, brass, Tunbridge ware. Open 0930–1730; closed Sun., and Wed. afternoon.

The ORIGINAL PIANOLA Shop (Mrs Mary Belton), 102a North Rd (67197).
Unique collection of reconditioned pianolas; original and modern piano rolls, horned gramophones. Open 0900–1730; also by appointment.

PAVILION Antiques, 8 Little East St (27949).
Pre-1840 English furniture, pre-1900 English watercolours, small Oriental wares. Open Mon.–Sat. 0930–1300, 1415–1730. Restoration of small furniture, papier-mâché and small antiques.

Molly RENDELL, 15 Ship St Gardens (26919).
19th-century paintings and watercolours, 18th/19th-century rugs, 19th-century Oriental ware. Open Tues.–Wed. and Fri.–Sat. 1100–1300, 1400–1800; Mon and Thur. 1100–1300. Restoration of paintings and watercolours.

Frank SEMUS, 9 Boyce St (28883).
Walnut, mahogany and oak; military furniture, ironstone services, brass, copper. Open Mon.–Fri. 0900–1230, 1330–1600; Sat. 0900–1230.

SHERATON House, 7 Brighton Pl (24590).
18th/19th-century furniture, 17th/19th-century bronzes, pewter. Open Mon.–Sat. 1000–1800.

Barbara SMITH, 39-40 Meeting House Lane (25123).
Silver and silver plate including reasonably-priced small items and single spoons; coins, stamps. Open Mon.–Wed. and Fri.–Sat. 1000–1630.

E. & D. TAPSELL & Sons, 18 and 59 Middle St (28341) and 10 Ship St Gardens.
English, Continental and Oriental porcelain; antique furniture, long-case clocks, military antiques, scientific instruments.

TUDOR-HART Antiques, 19 Bond St (64435).
Georgian and Regency furniture, 18th/19th-century English china and pottery, lacquer, silhouettes, objets d'art. Open 1000–1730; closed Thur. afternoon. Restorations.

VICTORIANA, 31 Meeting House Lane (26591).
Jewellery, china, pottery, some Parian ware busts, copper, kitchen moulds. Open Mon.–Sat. 0930–1730.

WITCH BALL Antiques, 48 Meeting House Lane (26618).
18th/19th-century engravings, maps, cartoons and prints. Open Mon.–Sat. 1030–1800.

C. WOODCOCK, 44 Meeting House Lane (28509).
Jewellery, pictures, violins. Open Mon.–Wed. and Fri.–Sat. 1000–1700.

YELLOW LANTERN Antiques, 34 and 65b Holland Rd, Hove (71572).
Large stock of French and Regency furniture, French clocks and ormolu, Continental porcelain 1820–60. Open Mon.–Fri. 0900–1300, 1415–1730; Sat. 0900–1300. Restorations.

Bristol

Dealers

Adrian BURCHALL, 15 Charlotte St, Park St (24717).
Bracket clocks of 1800–50, wall clocks of 1810–50, long-case clocks of 1770–1820. Open most days 0930–1730; appointment advisable. Restoration of English clock movements and dials.

David COOPPER, 76 Alma Rd (34583).
Furniture of 1650–1840, silver, plate general antiques. Open Mon.–Fri. 0900–1300, 1330–1730; Sat. 0900–1300.

Derek CORNWELL, 14 The Mall (39566).
18th/19th-century furniture, 19th-century paintings (mainly English), post-1850 works of art. Open Mon.–Fri. 0900–1300, 1415–1800; Sat. 0900–1300. Occasional restorations.

F. G. & H. M. COX Ltd, 66 Park Row (24837).
Jewellery, silver, 18th/19th-century glass including Bristol glass. Open 1000–1730; closed Sun., and Sat. afternoon.

Christopher DAVIS & Co., 38 Princess Victoria St, Clifton (38537).
English clocks of 1680–1830. Open Mon.–Tues. and Thur.–Fri. 1000–1300, 1400–1730; Wed. and Sat. 1000–1300. Restorations.

FROST & REED Ltd, 10 Clare St (552525).
17th/19th-century paintings, watercolours and prints. Closed Sun.

HAMMERTON Antiques Ltd, 4 The Mall, Clifton (30501).
Antiquarian maps, prints. Open Mon.–Fri. 1000–1800; Sat. 1000–1630. Member of BADA.

Elizabeth JENKINS, 52 Cotham Hill (33553).
Silver and Sheffield plate of 1780–1900; antique, Victorian and Edwardian glass; oak coffers and other furniture. Open 1015–1730; closed Wed. afternoon.

The OLD LANTERN Antiques, 20 Cotham Hill (34397).
Silver, plate, clocks, watches, jewellery, glass; specializes in Georgian and Victorian periods. Open Mon.–Sat. 1030–1830.

POTTERS, 14 Park Row (22551).
Coins (Roman to present), silver (George II to George V), glass of 1750-1870. Open Mon.–Sat. 1030–1730.

QUINNEY'S Antiques, 54 Park Row (23555) and 17 The Mall (35877).
Silver, guns, militaria, glass, porcelain. Open 1000–1730; closed Sun., and Sat. afternoon.

Markets
CANONS MARSH MARKET, Anchor Rd (behind the Cathedral).
Silver, jewellery, china, furniture, coins. Open Sat. 0800–1300.

Cardiff

Dealers
ANTIQUES UNLIMITED, 78 Cowbridge Rd East, Canton (31235).
(About ½ mile from Cardiff Castle on the A48 road).
Large stock of Victoriana and Edwardiana; pottery, glass, militaria, jewellery. Closed Sun.

BROADWAY Antiques, 185 Broadway, Roath (24470).
Furniture, Victoriana, glass, pewter, copper, brass, paintings, silver. Closed Wed. afternoon.

W. D. GITTINS & Sons, 129 Albany Rd, Roath Park (35847).
Good selection of furniture, china, silver, plate, copper, brass, bric-à-brac. Closed Sun. and Wed.

MILES Antiques, 151 Albany Rd (31485).
General antiques, Victoriana. Closed Wed. afternoon.

OWEN'S Antiques, 82 Salisbury Rd (32440) and 1 Wharton St (36369).
General 18th/19th-century antiques. Closed Sun. and Wed.

PHILP & Son, 77 Kimberley Rd (43826).
English and Continental furniture of 1600–1850; metalware of
1600–1850; pottery, porcelain, paintings, prints, objets d'art and
silver of 1700–1900. Closed Sun. Author of books on furniture and
pottery. Member of BADA.

Paul WAGNER, 2d Wellfield Rd (35446).
18th/19th-century furniture, paintings, china, glass, copper,
brass, small silver. Closed Wed. afternoon.

Markets
Antique market, Mill Lane.
Open Thur. and Sat.

Cheltenham

Dealers
H. W. KEIL, 131 Promenade (22509).
Pewter.

Edinburgh

Dealers
Alexander ADAMSON, 12 Randolph Pl (225 7310).
18th- and early 19th-century furniture, porcelain and silver.
Closed Sat. after 1200. Restoration of furniture.

H. CHERNACK, 85-7 Rose St (225 3038).
Silver, jewellery. Closed Sat. after 1200.

*CIRCA 1800, 8 Deanhaugh St, Stockbridge (332 5171) and 63 Thistle St
(225 1879).*
19th-century furniture, copper, brass, oil lamps. Restoration of
paintings, weapons and furniture.

Paul COUTS, 101-7 West Bow (225 3238).
Large stock of period furniture of 1650–1820, ormolu, paintings.
Closed Sat. after 1200. Restoration of fine period furniture.

Eric DAVIDSON, 4 Grassmarket (225 5815).
18th/19th-century furniture, oil-paintings, porcelain and silver. Closed Sat. after 1200.

The EDINBURGH Bookshop, 57 George St (225 4495).
Antiquarian books.

Mrs Iris FOX, West Bow.
Leading collector and specialist dealer in Wemyss ware.

GOING FOR A SONG, 37 Thistle St (225 6350) and 16 Dundas St.
Victoriana, clocks, 18th/19th-century Scottish paintings and prints. Open Sat. to 2000.

GORDON & GORDON, 10 Randolph Pl (225 1960).
Large furniture, paintings, antique silver. Closed Sat. after 1200.

GRANT Prints and Maps Ltd, 77 Dundas St (556-5380).
Scottish topographical prints of 1790–1870, maps, original Scottish landscapes. Closed Sat. after 1200.

LETHAM Antiques, 45 Cumberland St (556 6565).
Late 18th-century to mid 19th-century furniture, paintings of 1850–1940, jewellery, glass, silver, porcelain, metalware, pottery.

D. LETHAM, 74 Thistle St (225 7399).
General 17th/18th-century antiques. Closed Sat. after 1200. Member of BADA.

LINTON Antiques, 95 West Bow (226 6946).
18th/19th-century pictures, glass, bronze, art nouveau, prints, ephemera. Closed Sat. after 1200.

Janet G. LUMSDEN, 51a George St (225 2911).
18th/19th-century English porcelain, English glass, jade carvings, snuff boxes. Closed Sat. afternoon.

P. McVEIGH, 98 West Bow and 16a Johnston Terrace (226 7460).
General antiques, silver, early earthenware, pictures, curios, weapons.

John O. NELSON, 22-4 Victoria St (225 4413).
Antiquarian maps and prints.

Robert NOTMAN, 116-18 Canongate (556 5605).
Furniture, Sheffield plate, silver, porcelain, pewter, copper, brass.

Alan RANKIN, 72 Dundas St (556 3705).
Small stock of 18th-century Scottish books, prints and maps.
Appointment necessary.

James SCOTT, 43 Dundas St (556 8260).
Antique curios, silver, jewellery, small furniture, unusual items.
Closed Thur. afternoon.

Daniel SHACKLETON, 74 Thistle St (226 5713).
Paintings, watercolours, prints.

Douglas STRONG, 52 Thistle St (225 4330).
Georgian furniture, 18th-century porcelain, 18th/19th-century
clocks. Closed Sat. afternoon.

Jan STRUTHER, 13 Randolph Pl (225 7985).
English ceramics (especially Delft), glass, treen, silver, English
furniture. Closed Sat. afternoon. Member of BADA.

James THIN, 53-9 South Bridge (556 6743).
Antiquarian and secondhand books. Closed Sat. after 1200.

WHYTOCK & REID, Sunbury House, Belford Mews (226 4911).
18th- and early 19th-century English and Continental furniture,
Eastern rugs. Closed Sat. afternoon. Restoration of furniture and
rugs.

WILDMAN Bros, 54 Hanover St (225 6754).
Silver, Sheffield plate, porcelain, glass, jewellery. Closed Sat.
afternoon.

Auctions
PHILLIPS IN SCOTLAND, 65 George St (225 2266).
An offshoot of Phillips in London. Sales weekly.

SOTHEBY'S BELGRAVIA, Gleneagles Hotel.
Based in London. Sales yearly on last weekend in Aug.

Markets
GRASSMARKET Fair, 12-16 Grassmarket (Robert Maxtone Graham).
Antique and collector's market with about 70 stalls, housed in a converted dairy. Open Thurs., Fri. and Sat, with Mon. – Sat. opening during the Edinburgh Festival.

Eton

Dealers
Charles & Jane TOLLER, 51 High St (62058).
Treen, 17th/18th-century furniture, pewter, delft, brass, copper, needlework.

Exeter

Dealers
William BRUFORD, Bedford St (54901).
Silver, especially spoons.

Glasgow

Dealers
Jean MEGAHY, 481 Great Western Rd (334 1315).
General small antiques, small furniture, silver, porcelain, glass, objets d'art. Closed Sat. afternoon.

MOFFAT, Muirhead & Co., 132-6 Blythswood St (332 2115).
Large stock of furniture, silver, weapons, china. Closed Sat. afternoon. Restoration of furniture. Member of BADA.

John SMITH & Son (Glasgow) Ltd, 57-61 St Vincent St (221 7472).
Secondhand and antiquarian books. Closed Sat. afternoon.

STONE, 176 Buchanan St (332 2856).
General antiques, Victoriana, bric-à-brac, Chinese and Persian carpets.

THORNTON TAYLOR Antiques, 2 Fernleigh Rd (637 7749).
Wide range of porcelain of 1750–1850; Georgian and Victorian jewellery, glass, silver, Chinese hardstones. Closed Sun., and Mon. afternoon.

S. WINESTONE & Son, 10 Sandyford Pl, Sauchiehall St (221 6924).
General 17th/18th-century antiques. Closed weekends.

Sandy YOUNG, 8-14 Otago St (339 4832).
18th- and early 19th-century antiques and fine arts. Closed Sat. afternoon.

Guildford

Dealers
TRAYLEN, Castle House, 50 Quarry St (72424).
Antiquarian books, bookplates.

Harrogate

Dealers
Robert AAGAARD, 2 Montpellier Gardens (65201).
Furniture and porcelain of 1700–1820. Closed Sun. Restoration of furniture. Member of BADA.

The ATTIC, 7 Station Parade (68669).
18th/19th-century prints and furniture, oak, brass, copper. Closed Sun. and Wed.

BARNARD Gallery, 1 Crown Pl (3190).
Old maps and prints, watercolours. Closed Sun. and Wed. Restorations. Member of BADA.

A. M. BEEVERS, 1 Montpellier Gardens (4285).
English furniture, porcelain, silver, glass. Closed Sun., Mon and Wed. afternoons.

W. F. GREENWOOD & Sons, 3 Crown Pl (4467).
Furniture of 1660–1830, pottery and porcelain of 1740–1830, silver, jewellery. Closed Sun. and Wed. afternoons.

E. M. HARDY, 16 Montpellier Parade (4493).
General antiques, Victoriana. Closed Sun. and Wed. afternoons.
Member of BADA.

Araxie LOVE, 35-7 Swan Rd (61161).
18th-century walnut and mahogany furniture, 18th- and early
19th-century porcelain. Member of BADA.

Charles LUMB & Son, 34 Montpellier Parade (3776).
18th-century furniture. Closed Sun. and Wed. afternoons.
Member of BADA.

OMAR (Harrogate) Ltd, 8-10 Crescent Rd (3675).
Persian, Turkish and Caucasian rugs and carpets. Closed Sun.
and Wed. afternoons. Restorations.

W. WADDINGHAM, 10 Royal Parade (65797).
17th/18th-century furniture, Chinese porcelain, paintings.
Closed Sun. and Wed. afternoons. Member of BADA.

Christopher WARNER, 15 Princes St (3617).
Jewellery of 1740–1860, silver of 1720–1850. Closed Sun. and
Wed. afternoon. Restorations.

N. WILSON, 19-21 Cold Bath Rd (68718).
Furniture, English and Oriental porcelain, 18th/19th-century
glass. Closed Sun. and Wed. Member of BADA.

Hay-on-Wye
Dealers
Richard BOOTH.
Vast stock of books, bought and sold in bulk as well as singly,
comprising nearly 1 million volumes in seven shops, including
large choice of topographical books on Wales, England and
Scotland.

Leeds
Dealers
CHARM Antiques, 31 Great George St (27718).
16th/19th-century maps and prints, Victorian jewellery, china, silver. Open 1030–1700; closed Sun., and Wed. and Sat afternoons.

Gerald C. DIMERY, 154 Shadwell Lane, Moortown (682777).
English furniture, porcelain, pottery, brass, copper, pewter. Open daily usually.

J. FEATHER, 120 Gledhow Valley Rd (684915).
Antique furniture, glass, porcelain, pottery, silver. Open Mon.–Fri. 0930–1730.

Nat GAUNT, 70 North St (28847).
Porcelain, pottery, coloured glass, jug and basin sets, Royal Worcester, Wedgwood. Open Mon.–Sat. 0900–1730.

Auctions
PHILLIPS IN HEPPER HOUSE, East Parade (40029).
An offshoot of Phillips in London. Sales weekly.

Leicester

Dealers
D'OFFAY Gallery, 91 London Rd (59567).
19th-century oil-paintings (especially sporting subjects), barometers, 18th/19th-century furniture. Open Mon.–Fri. 1000–1300, 1430–1730; Sat. 1000–1300. Restorations of oil-paintings.

J. GREEN & Son, 22 Melton Rd (61495).
18th/19th-century English furniture; china, oil-paintings and silver of all periods. Open Mon.–Fri. 0900–1300, 1400–1730; Sat. 0900–1300.

Walter MOORES & Son, 89 Wellington St (24416).
General antiques of 1680–1820, 17th/19th-century furniture. Open Mon.–Sat, 0830–1830.

OVENALL Antiques, 146b London Rd (57382).
English pottery and English, Oriental and Continental porcelain—all pre-1870. Open 0930–1800; closed Sun., and Sat. afternoon.

Elizabeth WALLACE, 93 Wellington St (26253).
Pottery, porcelain, Georgian and Victorian silver, Victorian curios. Open Mon.–Fri. 1000–1700.

WITHERS of Leicester, 142a London Rd (58739).
17th/19th-century furniture, 18th/19th-century china, Victorian oil-paintings. Open Mon.–Wed. and Fri. 0900–1230, 1400–1730; Thur. and Sat. 0900–1230.

Lewes

Dealers
WALLIS & WALLIS, 210 High St (3131).
Militaria, auctions.

Liverpool

Dealers
BOODLE & DUNTHORNE Ltd, 35 Lord St (227 2525).
18th/19th-century silver, old clocks, Sheffield plate. Open Mon.–Sat. 0900–1730. Restorations of silver.

BOYDELL Galleries, 15 Castle St (236 3256).
18th/20th-century paintings, drawings and watercolours. Closed weekends. Restorations and framing.

FEATHER, 14 Upper Duke St (709 1380).
Oil-paintings (especially shipping and country scenes), general antiques, Victoriana. Closed Sun.

LEONARD of Liverpool, 69 Bold St (709 8462)
Large stock of furniture of 1700–1840; pottery, porcelain, silver, paintings. Open 1000–1730; closed Sat. afternoon.

OLIVIA'S Antiques, 16 Rodney St (709 7740).
Silver, pocket watches, clocks (long-case and carriage), paintings, Dresden and Basque figures, glass, bronze. Open Mon.–Fri. 0930–1730; Sat. 0930–1630.

PRYOR & Son, 110 London Rd (709 1361).
Jewellery, carved stones and jade, Georgian and Victorian silver, porcelain, coins, clocks, paintings. Closed Sun., and Wed. afternoon.

Pat STONE Antiques, 12 South John St (236 1696).
18th/19th-century furniture, pottery, porcelain, glass, English and Continental plate and silver, oil-paintings, watercolours, prints, maps. Open Mon.–Tues. and Thur.–Sat. 0930–1730.

London

Dealers in Arms and Armour
Peter DALE, 11-12 Royal Opera Arcade, Pall Mall, S.W1 (930 3695).
16th- and 19th-century firearms, 14th/19th-century edged weapons. Closed weekends.

FAIRCLOUGH (Arms) Ltd, 25 Conduit St, W1 (493 3946).
Antique weapons, Japanese swords.

P. C. L. GERMAN, 125 Edgware Rd, W2 (723 9342).
15th/19th-century arms and armour, metalware. Closed weekends.

See also Lee under **Clocks and Watches** below.

Dealers in Bronze
Robert O'CONNOR, 19 Crawford St, W1 (935 1245).
12th/18th-century bronzes, Italian and majolica pottery, oak furniture. Closed weekends.

David PEEL & Co Ltd, 2 Carlos Pl, W1 (493 3161).
16th/18th-century bronzes. Closed weekends.

SLADMORE GALLERY, 32 Bruton Pl, W1 (499 0365).
Large stock of bronze animal sculpture; specialist in French animalier school. Restorations.

Dealers to see also: Arts and Crafts of China, Horan ('Antiquities and Oriental art'); Block ('Furniture'); Bloom, Christie ('Silver and pewter'); Duncan-Smith, Under Two Flags ('Other').

Dealers in Clocks and Watches
CAMERER CUSS & Co., 54-6 New Oxford St, WC1 (636 8968).
Clocks of 1600–1910, watches of 1600–1930. Closed weekends.
Restorations.

GRAUS Antiques, 125 New Bond St, W1 (629 6680).
Watches, clocks, silver, objets d'art. Closed weekends.

E. HOLLANDER, 80 Fulham Rd, SW3 (589 7239).
Antique long-case and bracket clocks; 18th/19th-century silver,
plate and barometers. Closed weekends. Restorations. Member
of BADA.

Ronald A. LEE, 1-9 Bruton Pl, W1 (629 5600, 499 5266).
Clocks, furniture, pictures, arms and armour. Closed weekends.
Member of BADA.

Dealers to see also: Mallett ('Furniture'); Barrett, Garrard
('Jewellery and objets d'art'); Bloom ('Silver and pewter');
Duncan-Smith ('Other').

Dealers in Coins and Medals
BALDWIN & Sons Ltd, 11 Adelphi Terrace, WC2 (930 6879, 839 1310).
Coins, medals, decorations. Closed weekends. Member of BADA.

COINS AND ANTIQUITIES Ltd, 76 New Bond St, W1 (629 9835).
Closed weekends.

Richard LOBEL, Cavendish Court, 11-15 Wigmore St, W1 (636 1188)
Investment specialist in numismatic and bullion coins.

B. A. SEABY, 11 Margaret St, W1 (580 3677).
Classical to modern coins, banknotes, medals, decorations,
numismatic books. Closed weekends.

SPINK & Son, 5-7 King St SW1 (930 7888).
Large stock of coins of all periods to Victorian; medals,
numismatic books.

Stewart WARD, 64 Great Portland St, W1 (636 7601).
English hammered and milled silver, Roman coins, medallions.

Dealers in Furniture

ALEXANDER & BERENDT Ltd, 1a Davies St, W1 (499 4775).
17th/18th-century French furniture. Closed Sun., and Sat. afternoon.

ARK Antiques, 285 Upper St, W1 (226 4571).
Victoriana, Georgian and oak furniture. Open 1000–1800; closed Sun., and Thur. afternoon.

Sidney J. BLOCK, 12 Hinde St, Manchester Sq, W1 (935 9482).
English and Continental furniture, porcelain, bronze, ormolu, glass. Closed weekends.

BRODIE & KENT, 112 Crawford St, W1 (486 1502).
18th/19th-century English and French furniture, oil-paintings. Closed weekends.

Tobias JELLINEK, 66b Kensington Church St, W8 (727 5980).
Specialist in 17th-century English oak. Closed Sun. Member of BADA.

MALLETT & Son, 40 New Bond St, W1 (499 7411) and 2 Davies St, W1 (629 2444).
Fine stock of English furniture of 1690–1835, clocks (New Bond St); Continental furniture, clocks (Davies St). Closed weekends. Member of BADA.

F. PARTRIDGE & Sons Ltd, 144-6 New Bond St, W1 (629 0834).
English and French 18th-century furniture, English and Continental silver, English and Italian paintings. Closed weekends.

Dealers to see also: O'Connor ('Bronze'); Vandekar ('Glass'); Dumez-Onof ('Paintings and sculpture'); All About Antiques, Bayswater Antiques Market ('Other'). Lee ('Clocks and watches').

Dealers in Glass

DENTON Antiques, 87 Marylebone High St, W1 (935 5831).
Specialist in chandeliers and cut glass.

Howard PHILLIPS, 11a Henrietta Pl, W1 (580 9844).
Pre-1830 glass. Closed weekends. Member of BADA.

J. & E. VANDEKAR, 138 Brompton Rd, SW3 (589 8481).
Pre-1830 English, Continental and Oriental glass; porcelain, pottery, furniture. Member of BADA.

Dealers to see also: Moss ('Oriental art'); Block ('Furniture').

Dealers in Jewellery and Objets d'art
C. BARRETT & CO., 51 Burlington Arcade, W1 (493 2570).
Oriental ivory, jade, coral, carvings, watches, Russian enamels, silver. Restorations.

CAMEO CORNER Ltd, 26 Museum St, WC1 (637 0981/2).
Ancient to art nouveau jewellery. Closed weekends (but open Sat. in Dec). Restorations. Member of BADA.

COLLINGWOOD, 46 Conduit St W1 (734 2656).
Jewellery, Georgian silver. Closed weekends. Restorations. Member of BADA.

GARRARD & Co. Ltd, 112 Regent St, W1 (734 7020).
Large stock of silver, clocks and jewellery. Restorations. Member of BADA.

M. HAKIM, 4 Royal Arcade, Old Bond St, W1 (629 2643).
Objets d'art, jewellery, snuff boxes, English enamels. Closed weekends. Restorations. Member of BADA.

HANCOCKS & Co, 1 Burlington Gardens, W1 (493 8904).
Jewellery, silver. Closed weekends. Restorations.

HARVEY & GORE, 4 Burlington Gardens, W1 (493 2714).
Jewellery, silver, antique paste. Closed weekends. Restorations. Member of BADA.

HENNELL Ltd, 1 Davies St, Berkeley Sq, W1 (499 3011).
Jewellery, silver; one of the oldest-established firms—240 years in the trade. Closed weekends. Restorations. Member of BADA.

Richard OGDEN, 28-9 Burlington Arcade, W1 (493 9136).
Especially good selection of antique rings. Closed Sat. after 1200.
Member of BADA.

WARTSKI Ltd, 138 Regent St, W1 (734 2794/2038).
Fine antique jewellery, silver, snuff boxes; the leading specialist in
Fabergé. Restorations. Member of BADA.

Dealers to see also: Pinacotheca ('Oriental art'); Graus Antiques
('Clocks and watches'); Bloom, Lavender, McAleer, Phillips
('Silver and pewter'); Green's Antique Galleries ('Other').

Dealers in Oriental art
ARTS AND CRAFTS OF CHINA, 89 Baker St W1 (935 4576).
Porcelain, ivories, hardstones, bronze. Closed Sat. afternoon.

BLUETT & Sons, 48 Davies St W.1 (629 3397/4018).
Closed weekends. Member of BADA.

John CRICHTON, 34 Brook St W1 (629 7926).
Specialist in Chinese and Japanese porcelain, mainly pre-18th
century. Closed weekends. Member of BADA.

ESKENAZI Ltd, 166 Piccadilly, W1 (493 5464).
Early Chinese ceramics, Japanese netsuke. Closed weekends.
Member of BADA.

Helen GLATZ, 91 and 102 York St, W1 (723 2888).
15th/18th-century Chinese porcelain. Closed weekends. Member
of BADA.

H. R. HANCOCK, 37 Bury St SW1 (930 6670).
Chinese porcelain; 200 years in the trade. Closed weekends.
Restorations.

George HORAN, 28 St Christopher's Pl, W1 (622 5968).
Fine old Chinese porcelain and pottery, Japanese porcelain,
netsuke, jades, bronze.

Alexander JURAN, 74 New Bond St, W1 (629 2550, 493 4484).
Oriental rugs, carpets and tapestries. Closed weekends. Member of BADA.

Hugh M. MOSS, 12 Bruton St, W1 (499 5625).
Large stock of Oriental art, especially Chinese snuff bottles. Closed Sat. after 1200. Member of BADA.

Sydney L. MOSS, 51 Brook St, W1 (629 4670).
Large stock of Chinese antiques of 1500 BC to 1800 AD, Japanese netsuke, Persian pottery, Roman glass. Closed weekends. Member of BADA.

PINACOTHECA Ltd, 26 St Christopher's Pl, W1 (486 1887).
Early Chinese porcelain, objets d'art; Greek, Roman and Egyptian antiquities. Closed weekends.

Dealers to see also: Fairclough (Arms) ('Arms and armour'); Barrett ('Jewellery and objets d'art'); Kauffmann ('Paintings and sculpture'); Berkeley Galleries, Franses of Piccadilly ('Other').

Dealers in Paintings and Sculpture
Arthur ACKERMANN & Son, 3 Old Bond St, W1 (493 3288).
English sporting pictures and prints. Closed weekends.

Thomas AGNEW & Sons Ltd, 43 Old Bond St, W1 and 3 Albemarle St, W1 (629 6176).
Large stock of paintings, drawings, watercolours and engravings of all schools. Closed Sun., and Sat. afternoon. Member of BADA.

ARCADE Gallery Ltd, 28 Old Bond St, W1 (493 1879).
Classical sculpture of 1000 BC to 500 AD, 9th/18th-century Middle Eastern and African sculpture, 15th/19th-century European paintings and sculpture. Closed Sun.

BROD Gallery, 24 St James's St, SW1 (839 3871).
Dutch 17th-century and Flemish paintings, drawings and watercolours of all periods. Member of BADA.

CHILTERN Art Gallery, 10 Chiltern St, W1 (455 8003).
16th/19th-century paintings, drawings, watercolours. Open
Mon.–Fri. 1400–1800; Sat 1100–1430. Restorations.

CLARGES Gallery, 5 Clarges St, W1 (629 3715).
19th/20th-century watercolours and drawings. Closed weekends.

P. & D. COLNAGHI, 14 Old Bond St, W1 (493 1943).
Large stock of English paintings and drawings, old masters and
prints. Closed weekends.

D'OFFAY Gallery, 9 Dering St, W1 (629 1578).
English paintings, drawings and sculpture of 1890–1940. Closed
weekends.

Michel DUMEZ-ONOF, 109 Mount St, W1 (499 6648).
Greek and Roman sculpture, works of art, Gothic and Renaissance furniture. Closed weekends. Restorations. Member of BADA.

FORES Ltd, 123 New Bond St, W1, (629 5319).
17th/20th-century British sporting pictures. Closed weekends.
Restorations.

Richard GREEN, 36 Dover St, W1 (493 7997).
19th-century paintings, old masters, sporting subjects. Member
of BADA.

GROSVENOR Gallery, 48 South Molton St, W1 (629 0891).
General stock of paintings (especially 20th-century oils), watercolours, lithographs, sculpture. Open Mon.–Fri. 1000–1800.

HEIM Gallery, 59 Jermyn St, SW1 (493 0688).
Old masters, sculpture. Also in Paris.

LEGGATT Bros, 30 St James's St, SW1 (930 3772).
Large stock of 18th/19th-century oil-paintings. Closed weekends.
Restorations.

Arthur KAUFFMANN, 21 Grafton St, W1 (235 4120).
Paintings, medieval sculpture, Oriental works of art. Closed
weekends. Member of BADA.

LEFEVRE Gallery, 30 Bruton St, W1 (629 2250).
Impressionist paintings.

LEGER Galleries, 13 Old Bond St, W1 (629 3538).
Old masters, early English watercolours. Closed weekends, but open Sat. during exhibitions. Restorations. Member of BADA.

LEICESTER Galleries, 22a Cork St, W1 (437 8995).
19th/20th-century paintings and drawings, sculpture. Restorations.

MAAS Gallery (Jeremy Maas), 15a Clifford St, W1 (734 2302).
English paintings, drawings and watercolours of 1750–1930. Jeremy Maas is author of *Victorian Painters*.

MARK Gallery, 9 Porchester Pl, W2 (262 4906).
Russian icons, old masters.

MARLBOROUGH Fine Art, 39 Old Bond St, W1 and 6 Albemarle St, W1 (629 5161).
19th/20th-century paintings.

O'HANA Gallery, 13 Carlos Pl, W1 (499 1562).
19th/20th-century paintings and sculpture. Closed Sat. after 1200.

The PARKER Gallery, 2 Albemarle St, W1 (499 5906).
Very old-established gallery (225 years) specializing in maritime and military prints and paintings, historical prints and old ship models. Restorations. Member of BADA.

W. H. PATTERSON, 19 Albemarle St, W1 (629 1910).
18th/19th-century old master oil-paintings. Closed Sat. after 1200. Restorations. Member of BADA.

Frank T. SABIN, 4 New Bond St, W1 (499 5553).
18th/19th-century engravings and drawings. Closed weekends. Member of BADA.

Arthur TOOTH & Sons, 31 Bruton St, W1 (499 6741).
French impressionists and post-impressionists, contemporary artists. Member of BADA.

WADDINGTON Galleries, 2 and 34 Cork St, W1 (439 1866).
Large stock of paintings and watercolours (Dufy, Picasso, Dubuffet, Matisse, Leger), abstracts.

WILDENSTEIN & Co Ltd, 147 New Bond St, W1 (629 0602).
Large stock of old masters, impressionist paintings, drawings and pictures.

TRYON Gallery, 41 Dover St, W1 (493 5161).
Sporting and natural-history pictures and prints. Closed weekends. Restorations.

Dealers to see also. Brodie & Kent, Partridge ('Furniture'); Ede, All About Antiques, Lee ('Other').

Dealers in Prints and Maps
R. H. BAYNTON-WILLIAMS, 18 Lowndes St, SW1 (235 6595/6).
Old maps and prints. Member of BADA. Author of *Investing in Maps*.

The MAP House, 54 Beauchamp Pl, SW3 (589 4325).
Antique maps, Closed weekends. Restorations.

WEINREB & DOUWMA Ltd, 93 Great Russell St, WC1 (636 4895).
Maps, engravings, atlases to late 19th century.

Dealers to see also: Ackermann, Agnew, Colnaghi, Parker Gallery, Sabin, Tryon Gallery ('Paintings and sculpture'); Edwards ('Rare books'); Under Two Flags ('Other').

Dealers in Rare Books
Jon ASH, 18 Cullum St (off Fenchurch St) EC3 (626 2665).
The only secondhand bookshop in the heart of the City; quite strong on travel, transport and topography.

Andrew BLOCK, 20 Barter St, WC1 (405 9660).
Amazing stock of theatre books and memorabilia, presided over by an octogenarian character who seems to have been to every

notable first night of the century, and who knows the whereabouts of every book in his cluttered building.

CHANCERY LANE Bookshop (Mr Nolan), Chichester Rents (off Chancery Lane), WC2(405 0635).
Specializes in books of Irish interest.

DAWSONS of Pall Mall, 16 Pall Mall, SW1(930 2515).
Large stock of antiquarian books, especially English literature and the history of science; colour-plate books. Closed weekends. Restorations.

Francis EDWARDS, 83 Marylebone High St, W1(935 9221).
Large stock of rare books, especially travel, military and naval history and transport; atlases, illuminated manuscripts, incunabula.

H. M. FLETCHER, 27 Cecil Court, WC2(836 2865).
Large stock of secondhand books, 95 per cent of them pre-1850.

HERALDRY TODAY, Beauchamp Pl, SW3(584 1656).
Specialist in heraldry and genealogy.

MAGGS Bros Ltd, 50 Berkeley Sq, W1(499 2051).
Famous old firm of rare-book dealers; manuscripts, autograph letters. Closed weekends. Member of BADA.

MARCHMONT Bookshop, 39 Burton St, WC1(387 7989).
Displaced from its original Bloomsbury location by re-development, this has a notable stock of antiquarian books.

MERIDIAN Bookshop, 7 Nelson Road, Greenwich, SE10(858 7211).
Specialist in nautical books and periodicals.

PICCADILLY Rare Books, 2-4 Princes Arcade, Piccadilly, W1(734 3840).
Very centrally-located attractive shop specializing in British topography, travel and genealogy.

Bernard QUARITCH, 5-8 Lower John St, Golden Sq, W1(734 0562).
Old-established rare-book sellers, formerly in Grafton St (off Bond St) but moved because of redevelopment. Closed weekends.

Bertram ROTA, 4-6 Savile Row (off Sackville St), W1 (734 3860).
Specialist in modern 1st editions, private-press books.

Henry SOTHERAN, 2-5 Sackville St, W1 (734 1150).
The oldest-established of the West End booksellers. Comprehensive stock of rare books, fine bindings and prints; autographed letters. Closed weekends.

Harold T. STOREY, 3 Cecil Court, WC2 (836 3777).
Specialist in naval history and travel.

Thomas THORP, 47 Holborn Viaduct, EC1 (353 8332).
Old-established firm formerly in Albemarle St. Large stock of antiquarian and general secondhand books; specialities English law and angling. Closed weekends.

TRAVIS & EMERY, 16 Cecil Court, WC2 (240 2129).
Specialist in musical literature and scores.

WILDY & Sons, Lincoln's Inn Archway, Carey St, WC2 (242 5778).
Largest specialist stock of books on law and criminology.

Dealers to see also: Pleasures of Past Times, Under Two Flags ('Other').

Dealers in Silver and Pewter
Paul BENNETT, 75 George St, W1 (935 1555).
Large stock of Georgian and modern silver; Sheffield plate. Closed weekends.

N. BLOOM & Sons Ltd (Ian Harris), 40-1 Conduit St, W1 (629 5060).
Antique and Victorian silver and jewellery; Russian enamels, animalier bronzes, carriage clocks. Closed weekends. Restoration of silver and jewellery. Member of BADA. Ian Harris is author of *The Price Guide to Antique Silver* and *The Price Guide to Victorian Silver*.

J. H. BOURDON-SMITH, 24 and 25a Conduit St, W1 (629 0434, 499 3072).
Old silver of 1680–1830, Victorian and modern silver. Closed weekends. Restorations. Member of BADA.

CARRINGTON & Co., 130 Regent St, W1 (734 3727).
Large stock of Georgian and Victorian silver. Open Mon.–Fri.
0900–1800; Sat. 0900–1700. Restorations.

J. CHRISTIE, 26 Burlington Arcade, W1 (629 3070).
18th-century silver, animalier bronzes. Member of BADA.

HEMING & Co., 28 Conduit St, W1 (629 4289).
Silver of 1700 onwards, especially birds and animals. Closed
weekends. Restorations. Member of BADA.

*HOW of Edinburgh (Mrs G. F. P. How), 2-3 Pickering Pl, St James's,
SW1 (930 7140).*
Britain's leading dealer in Scottish silver; stock chiefly pre–1800.
Closed weekends. Restorations.

Simon KAYE, 1b Albermarle St, W1 (493 7658).
Large stock of Georgian silver; Sheffield plate. Closed weekends.
Restorations. Member of BADA.

D. S. LAVENDER, 63 South Molton St, W1 (629 1782)
Silver, jewellery, miniatures, snuff boxes. Closed weekends.
Member of BADA.

*LANGFORDS Silver Galleries, 11 Charterhouse St, EC1 (405 6401, 242
5506).*
Silver and plate with emphasis on Victoriana.

M. McALEER, 1a St Christopher's Pl, W1 (486 1171).
An interesting collection of small silver, Irish and Scottish silver,
Victorian jewellery. Closed weekends, but open on Sat.
by appointment.

MARKS Antiques Ltd, 49 Curzon St, W1 (499 1788).
Silver, Sheffield plate. Closed Sat. afternoon. Restorations.

Richard MUNDEY, 19 Chiltern St, W1 (935 5613).
Pewter specialist. Closed weekends.

The PEWTER CENTRE, 87a Abingdon Road, W8 (937 4118).
Antique pewter. Restorations.

S. J. PHILLIPS, 139 New Bond St, W1 (629 6261).
Large stock of silver, jewellery, gold boxes, miniatures. Closed weekends. Restorations. Member of BADA.

David RICHARDS, 10-12 Cavendish St, W1 (935 3206).
Large stock of antique and Victorian silver, old Sheffield plate, Victorian plate. Closed weekends. Restorations.

S. J. SHRUBSOLE, 43 Museum St, WC1 (405 2712).
Late 17th/mid 19th-century silver, old Sheffield plate. Closed weekends. Restorations. Member of BADA.

Dealers to see also: Graus Antiques, Hollander ('Clocks and watches'); Partridge ('Furniture'); Barrett, Collingwood, Garrard, Hancocks, Harvey & Gore, Hennell, Wartski ('Jewellery and objets d'art'); Duncan-Smith, Green's Antique Galleries ('Other').
See also: Bond St Silver Galleries, Cutler St Silver Market, London Silver Vaults ('Markets and other antique centres').

Other Dealers

ALL ABOUT ANTIQUES, 68 Marylebone High St, W1 (935 5859).
General antiques, furniture, paintings, porcelain. Restoration of upholstery.

BAYLY'S Gallery, 8 Prince's Arcade, Piccadilly, W1 (754 0180).
Staffordshire china, fairings, prints, inexpensive pictures, old music covers.

BAYSWATER ANTIQUES MARKET (Mrs R. McKay Martin), 122 Bayswater Rd W2 (229 0051).
Period furniture, brass, porcelain, bric-à-brac. Open Mon.–Wed. and Fri 1000–1800; Sun. 1100–1800.

J. & A. BEARE Ltd, 179 Wardour St, W1 (437 1449).
Violins, cellos, bows. Closed Sat. Member of BADA.

BENARDOUT & BENARDOUT, 7 Thurloe Pl, SW7 (584 7658).
Carpets, rugs, tapestries. Restorations. Member of BADA.

BERKELEY Galleries, 20 Davies St, W1 (629 2450).
Antiquities, Far Eastern and primitive art. Closed weekends.

The BUTTON QUEEN, 25 St Christopher's Pl, W1 (935 1505).
Specialist in 19th-century and modern buttons, buckles and cuff links. Open Mon.–Fri. 1000–1800.

Arthur DAVIDSON, 179 New Bond St, W1 (930 6687).
17th/19th-century scientific instruments, curiosities, early furniture. Closed weekends.

DODO, 185 Westbourne Grove (nr Portobello Rd) (229 8243).
Old advertisements, many of tin. Open Tues.–Sat 1000–1800.

A. R. DUNCAN-SMITH, 97 Wigmore St, W1 (935 7421).
Porcelain, clocks, marble, silver, plate, ivories, bronze. Closed weekends.

Charles EDE Ltd, 37 Brook St, W1 (494 4944).
Greek, Roman and Egyptian antiquities. Closed weekends. Member of BADA.

FRANSES of Piccadilly, 169 Piccadilly, W1 (629 1935/2434).
European and Oriental carpets, especially Persian. Closed weekends. Restorations.

Stanley GIBBONS, 391 and 395 Strand, WC2 (836 9707).
Large stock of rare stamps; banknotes, coins. Closed Sat. after 1200. Auctions.

GREEN'S Antique Galleries, 117 Kensington Church St, W8 (229 9618).
18th-century to contemporary jewellery, automata, dolls, china, silver. Closed Sun., and Thur. afternoon.

HALCYON DAYS, 14 Brook St, W1 (499 5784).
18th/19th-century English enamels, modern recreations of Battersea and Bilston enamels. Open Mon.–Fri. 0915-1730.

W. E. HILL & Sons, 140 New Bond St, W1 (629 2175).
Antique stringed instruments. Closed Sun. Member of BADA.

LORDS Gallery, 26 Wellington Rd (nr the cricket ground), NW8 (722 4444).
Posters.

Jonathan MINNS, 1a Hollywood Rd. SW10(352 5248).
Leading expert in model steam engines. Consultant to Christie's (auctions).

PLEASURES OF PAST TIMES (David Drummond), 11 Cecil Court, WC2(836 1142).
Fascinating small shop run by an actor, stocking old theatrical books, children's books with fine bindings, playbills, postcards and ephemera. Closed 1415–1515.

Carol Ann STANTON, stalls in 109 Portobello Rd, Camden Passage and The Antique Hypermarket.
Dolls, miniature furniture, toys.

UNDER TWO FLAGS, 4 St Christopher's Pl, W1(935 6934).
Toy soldiers, old military books and prints, porcelain, bronze.

Harriet WYNTER, 352 King's Rd, SW3(352 6494).
Scientific instruments.

Dealers to see also: those listed in Bond St Silver Galleries, Camden Passage Antiques Centre and Portobello Rd ('Markets and other antique centres').

Markets and other antique centres

The ANTIQUE HYPERMARKET, 26-40 Kensington High St, W8 (937 6911/8888).
Distinctive building with Greek-style caryatids containing three floors and 100 stands of specialists in furniture, clocks, jewellery, Oriental art, old masters and porcelain. Most stands open Mon.–Sat. 1000–1745.

The ANTIQUE SUPERMARKET, 3-5 Barrett St, W1.
Comprehensive antique market with 80 stalls, specializing mainly in Victoriana, small silver items and jewellery. Open Mon.–Wed. and Fri. 1000–1800; Thur. 1000–1900; Sat. 1000–1700.

Great Britain

ANTIQUARIUS ANTIQUE MARKET, 153 King's Rd, SW3 (351 1145, 352 4739/4690).
Large market with 200 stalls, many dealing in jewellery. Open Mon.–Sat. 1000–1800.

BERMONDSEY MARKET, Long Lane, SE1.
Comprising the main street market of 270 stalls on a large open space (New Caledonian Market, end of Long Lane) and the covered market of over 150 stalls in a converted factory (Bermondsey Antique Market, 251-5 Long Lane). Wide range of antiques with the accent on Victoriana, especially silver, ceramics and furniture. Open (officially) Fri. 0700–1800; closed Christmas Day. However, this is where the dealers buy, and the early birds catch the bargains; in practice, all the action is over by 0900 and habitués arrive as early as 0500 to pick over the first goods on the stalls. In winter it's a good idea to do the open market first, then seek shelter in the covered market when the feet grow numb on the cobblestones. Prices reasonable, but one can sometimes do as well on Portobello Road.
How to get there. Underground (Northern Line) to Borough, then a walk down Long Lane; or underground (Northern Line) or main-line train to London Bridge, then a 10-minute walk down Bermondsey St.

BOND ST ANTIQUE CENTRE, 124 New Bond St, W1 (629 1819).
Jewellery, silver, pictures, miniatures, prints, etc. 44 dealers.

BOND ST SILVER GALLERIES, 111-12 New Bond St, W1.
Several dealers in silver and Sheffield plate, including:
Angel & Kaye (493 5178).
Arthur Black (493 6184).
Henry Black Ltd (493 5551).

CAMDEN PASSAGE ANTIQUES CENTRE, Camden Passage (off Upper St behind the Angel, Islington), N1.
50 shops and 30 boutiques including specialists such as:
C. K. Chiu—art nouveau and art deco;
Strike One—clocks of many types;
and a number of dealers in Staffordshire and commemorative pottery. Open Mon.–Fri. 1030–1730. Also a street market with 70 stalls, open Wed. and Sat.

CHELSEA ANTIQUE MARKET, 245a and 253 King's Rd, SW3 (stallholders' phone 352 9695/0449/1424).
General antiques. Over 100 dealers. Open Mon.–Sat. 1000–1800.

CUTLER ST SILVER MARKET, Cutler St, E1.
Small street market specializing in silver, also jewellery, coins, stamps. Open Sun. 0800–1200. Dealers buy here, which means reasonable prices but sharp competition for collectors.

How to get there. Underground to Liverpool St (Circle, Central and Metropolitan Lines) or Aldgate (Circle and Metropolitan Lines), then a 5-minute walk along Houndsditch.

LONDON SILVER VAULTS, 53-65 Chancery Lane, WC2 (242 3844).
Underground complex of 25 dealers offering a large and varied selection of silver and plate.

PORTOBELLO ROAD, Notting Hill Gate, W11.
Famous street market which is now a considerable tourist attraction, which means overcrowding and inflated prices, especially in summer. However, it *is* still possible to find reasonably-priced items—even bargains—especially in winter and early in the day. Collectors should concentrate on the stretch between Westbourne Grove and Colville Terrace where most of the serious antiques are to be found. There are several covered markets (arcades) on the left and in all there are about 2000 stalls and shops trading in antiques on this old street. Main opening hours 0830–1730, but many stalls close at 1630 in winter. Some of the specialist dealers worth a visit include:
on Portobello Rd—Trad (no. 67), decorative brasswork including ship's relics; pewter, copper; Judy Fox (no. 81), English Studio pottery of 1870–1920—and a nearby stall specializes in bottles; Graham Webb (no. 93), musical boxes; Geoffrey Van (no. 107), rare 16th-century furniture, polychrome statues, Hispano-Moresque ceramics.
Antique Arcade, 109 Portobello Rd—Carol Ann Stanton (stall), dolls, miniature furniture, toys—also has stalls in Camden Passage and The Antique Hypermarket.
Collectors' Corner—stalls 3, 4, 5, 6, 8, Staffordshire and Studio pottery, 18th-century porcelain; stall 7, pewter, brass.
Dolphin Antiques—upstairs stall, records of the 1920s.
Harris's Arcade—stall 20, medals.

Portobello Antique Arcade—stalls at entrance 3, large stock of arms and militaria.

Portobello Silver Galleries, 82a Portobello Rd.

Portwine Arcade, 175 Portobello Rd and Elgin Terrace—stall 4, 19th-century and early medical instruments.

Red Lion—stall 52, Japanese prints; stall 72, camera specialist.

Roger's Antique Arcade—stalls at Kensington Park Rd end, art glass, Wedgwood china.

Shepherd's Antique Arcade—stall 10, silver (also sells in Bermondsey Market) Mrs Collins (stall 25), art nouveau.

Weaver Arcade—many stalls specializing in silver.

Westbourne Antique Arcade, 113 Portobello Rd and 283 Westbourne Grove—stalls at Westbourne Grove end, specializing in jewellery; Mr Satsuma (stall 5), Japanese Satsuma pottery; Commemorative Corner (stall 13, Portobello Rd end), commemorative pottery.

Arcade, 284 Westbourne Grove—stall 16, marine prints and watercolours.

How to get there. Underground to Notting Hill Gate (Central, Circle and District Lines), then a short walk along Pembridge Rd to the top of Portobello Rd. Buses 7, 15 and 52 stop nearby; buses 12, 27, 28, 31 and 88 stop within a 5-minute walk at Notting Hill Gate.

Fairs

ANTIQUARIAN BOOK FAIR.

Yearly in June, Europa Hotel.

CHELSEA ANTIQUES FAIR.

A top antique fair, with all items authenticated. Held twice yearly, Chelsea Town Hall, spring and autumn.

GROSVENOR HOUSE ANTIQUE FAIR.

Leading antique fair at which all items have been thoroughly vetted and the dealers are usually top specialists in their field—includes items up to 1930s. Yearly, June.

Auctions

BONHAM'S, Montpelier St, Knightsbridge, SW7 (584 9161) and 75 Burnaby St, Chelsea, SW10 (352 0466).

Sales at Montpelier St Tues.–Fri., 1100:

Tues.—silver (fortnightly); wine (monthly); jewellery (periodically); 20th-century paintings and graphics (bimonthly); Wed.—watercolours, prints (fortnightly); books, arms, militaria, 'bygones' (periodically); Thur.—furniture, oil-paintings (weekly); Oriental carpets and rugs (monthly); Fri.—porcelain (weekly); clocks, watches (periodically).

See the *Daily Telegraph, The Times* and art magazines for announcements.

Sales at Burnaby St Tues. and Thur., 1030:

Tues.—furniture (weekly);

Thur.—modern carpets and rugs (monthly).

CHRISTIE'S, 8 King St, St James's, SW1 (839 9060).

210-year-old fine-art saleroom. Sales Mon.–Fri., 1100:

Mon.—ceramics, Oriental works of art;

Tues.—objets d'art, prints, drawings, watercolours, coins, antiquities, glass, modern pictures;

Wed.—silver, jewellery, arms, books;

Thur.—furniture, musical instruments, wine;

Fri.—pictures.

See the *Daily Telegraph* (Mon.), *The Times* (Tues.), the *Financial Times* (Sat.) and art magazines for announcements.

CHRISTIE'S SOUTH KENSINGTON, 85 Old Brompton Rd, SW7 (581 2231).

A recent offshoot of the parent in St James's, dealing with items of lesser provenance and antiquity. Among collectables handled here are fans, Victorian paintings, phonographs, marine and military prints, car mascots and uniforms. Sales Mon.–Fri., 1100.

PHILLIPS, Blenstock House, 7 Blenheim St (off New Bond St and Oxford St), W1 (629 6602) and Hayes Pl (off Lisson Grove), Marylebone, NW1 (723 1118).

This 'no. 3' in London's fine-art auction league has increased its turnover spectacularly in the last few years, helped by the fact that it does not—as Christie's and Sotheby's controversially decided to do—impose a 10 per cent buyer's commission. The quality of Phillips's goods has also gone up and the range has been diversified. Sales at Blenheim St Mon.–Wed. and Fri., 1100:

Mon.—antique furniture, Persian rugs, pictures, works of art;

Tues.—Continental and decorative furniture, Oriental rugs, objets d'art, clocks, bronze (weekly); jewellery, books (periodically);
Wed.—ceramics, glass;
Fri.—silver, plate.
There are also monthly sales of pot lids, fairings, Baxter prints and Stevengraphs and intermittent sales of lead soldiers, lace, art nouveau and Oriental art. See the *Daily Telegraph* (Mon.) and *The Times* (Tues.) for announcements.

At Hayes Place, Phillips hold more down-market weekly sales of household goods at which interesting items of furniture, brass, objet d'art, paintings and curiosities can be picked up in a job lot. Sales Thur, 1000.

Phillips incorporates Glendining, the well-known coin auctioneer. Phillips in Scotland (Edinburgh), Phillips in Knowle (Birmingham) and Phillips in Hepper House (Leeds) are offshoots.

SOTHEBY & Co., 34-5 New Bond St, W1 (493 8080) and Hodgson's Rooms, 115 Chancery Lane, WC2 (405 7238).
Sales at New Bond St Mon.–Fri., 1100:
Mon.—books (weekly); antiquities, armour;
Tues.— books (weekly); glass (monthly), Chinese and other porcelain, arms, armour (periodically);
Wed.—pictures (weekly); coins (periodically);
Thur.—silver, drawings, prints (weekly; jewellery, coins (periodically);
Fri.—furniture, carpets (weekly).
See the *Daily Telegraph* (Mon.), *The Times* (Tues.), the *Financial Times* (Sat.) and art magazines for announcements.

Some of Sotheby's book sales are held at New Bond St, others at Chancery Lane.

SOTHEBY'S BELGRAVIA, 19 Motcomb St, SW1 (235 4311).
Specializes in Victoriana and Edwardiana and works of art up to 1930. Sales Tues.–Thur., 1100:
Tues.—pictures, prints;
Wed.—furniture, works of art;
Thur.—porcelain, silver.
Sales devoted to art nouveau, art deco and the popular 'Collectors' Sales' taking in anything from cigarette cards to old sewing machines and typewriters are held periodically.

The Belgravia catalogues are particularly informative and well illustrated—reference works in themselves for fields still largely unmapped.

Stamp auctions
Stanley GIBBONS, 391 Strand, WC2 (836 9707).
See 'Other dealers'.

H. R. HARMER, 41 New Bond St, W1 (629 0218/0377).
Sales fortnightly, beginning Mon. afternoon, except mid July to end Sept.

Robson LOWE, 50 Pall Mall, SW1 (839 4034).
About 80 sales yearly.

Manchester

Dealers
ANTIQUES AND FINE ARTS (Prestwich Ltd), 399 Bury New Rd, Prestwich (773 1827).
Victorian and Georgian furniture and antiques, early walnut and oak. Open Mon.—Tues. and Thur.–Sat. 0903–1300, 1400–1800; Wed. 0930–1300.

The ARMOURER'S Shop, 61 Bridge St (834 6038).
Militaria, arms and armour post–1600; reference books. Open Mon.–Sat. 1030–1700.

J. F. BLOOD & Sons, 99 Wilmslow Rd (224 2446).
Specializes in period 1850–1914; pottery, china, glass, watercolours, prints, oil-paintings; books of all periods. Open Sun.–Tues. and Thur.–Fri. 1030–1730; Wed. 1100–1700; Sat. 1030–1700.

CATHEDRAL Antiques and Galleries, 74 Victoria St (773 3110).
Continental porcelain, early Meissen, English porcelain, paintings. Open Mon.–Sat. 1030–1630.

The CONNOISSEUR, 528 Wilmslow Rd, Withington (445 2504).
18th/19th-century English and French furniture, 19th-century

Sèvres and Meissen porcelain, 18th/19th-century paintings. Open Tues. and Thur.–Sun. 1000–1300, 1430–1830; Mon. 1430–1830.

DENISON Antiques, 373-85 Bury New Rd, Prestwich (773 2339).
Large stock of general antiques, silver, glass, brass and works of art. Closed Sun.

FULDA Gallery, 60 Victoria St (834 8532).
Small stock of oils and watercolours of 1700–1900. Open Mon.–Fri. 1330–1730; Sun. 1030–1300.

KOOPMAN & Son Ltd, 4 John Dalton St (834 2420, 9036).
Silver, jewellery, porcelain, objets d'art. Open Mon.–Fri. 1000–1700.

LAPWING Antiques, 24 and 103 Lapwing Lane, West Didsbury (445 2889/8340).
English pottery and porcelain pre–1850, English glass pre-1800.

LAWNDORE Ltd, 33 King St West (834 3675).
19th-century porcelain, 18th/19th-century jewellery and silver, Victorian paintings. Open 0930–1730; closed Sun., and Sat. afternoon.

ST JAMES Antiques, 41 South King's St (834 9632).
Specialist in antique jewellery. Closed Sun.

Markets
BUTTER LANE ANTIQUE CENTRE, 40 King St West (834 1809).
Mainly Victoriana, Edwardiana, bric-à-brac, costumes, silver, brass, pewter. About 20 regular stalls. Open Mon.—Sat. 1030–1730.

Monks Eleigh

Dealers
STANHOPE SHELTON PICTURES.
Fine stock of watercolours.

Moreton-in-Marsh

Dealers

George BOLAN, Creswyke House, High St. (50751).
Pewter.

Newcastle

Dealers

FENWICK Ltd (Roger Freer Antiques), Northumberland St. (25100).
General 18th/19th-century English antiques, reproduction silver plate, brass, copper, jewellery. Open Mon.–Wed. and Fri.–Sat. 0900–1730, Thur. 0900–1930. Restorations of furniture, jewellery, silver and pictures.

E. L. HATTAM, 134 Westgate Rd (24459).
Large stock of silver and silver plate (late Georgian and Victorian), china, Victorian and modern jewellery. Open 0930–1700; closed Sun., and Wed. afternoon.

REID & Sons Ltd, 23 Blackett St (21366)
Specialist in silver. Closed Sun., and Sat. afternoon.

S. & R. ANTIQUES, 13 High Bridge, Bigg Market (26739). (In city centre, 5 minutes from station.)
Victorian jewellery, silver. Open Tues.–Sat. 0900–1700.

WESTGATE Antiques (J. Seery), 283 Westgate Rd (24951) and 244 Jesmond Rd (81069).
Furniture, paintings, china, porcelain, silver, clocks. Open Mon.–Sat. 1000–1630.

Newport

Dealers

D. S. HUTCHINGS, 210 Chepstow Rd (71944).
Specialist in Nantgarw and Swansea porcelain.

Nottingham

Dealers

E. M. CHESHIRE, 15-17 Mansfield Rd (43160).
17th-century oak, 18th-century mahogany, brass, copper, treen.

COLLECTORS' CORNER (C. R. Iliffe), 96 Hucknall Rd (65686).
Small antiques, coloured glass, Staffordshire figures, pewter,
brass, pottery, porcelain, coins. Open 1030–1730; closed Sun.,
and Thur. afternoon.

M. KEMP, 89 Derby Rd (47055).
Victorian jewellery, Georgian and Victorian silver, Victorian
china. Open Mon.–Wed. and Fri.–Sat. 0915–1300, 1400–1730.
Restorations of china, silver and jewellery.

LANGALE Ltd, 213 Mansfield Rd (44764).
Copper, brass, pewter, china, porcelain (18th- and 20th-century);
prints, maps (17th- and 19th century); silver, plate, curios, glass
(19th/20th-century).

Michael D. LONG, 173 Mansfield Rd (44137).
Militaria, arms. Open Mon.–Sat. 0930–1730.

NOTTINGHAM Antique Market, 93-5 Derby Rd (48167).
Large general stock of antiques, Victoriana and bric-à-brac.
Open Mon. Thur. and Sat. 1000–1700; Fri. 1000–2200.

Thomas TURNER, 265 Mansfield Rd (45333).
18th/19th-century English and Continental furniture, paintings,
watercolours and works of art. Open Tues.–Wed. and Fri.
1030–1700; Sat. morning.

VICTORIANA, 24 Heathcoat St (52059).
Victorian items, oil-paintings, general antiques. Open Mon.–Sat.
1000–1730.

Reading

Dealers
BRACHER & SYDENHAM, 26 Queen Victoria St (53724)
Silver.

Rugby

Auctions
WARWICK & WARWICK, Graphic House, 35-7 Albert St (5430, 76063).
Stamps.

Sheffield

Dealers
ARTESQUE, 886 Eccleshall Rd (60576).
Silver, plate, china, brass, copper, small furniture. Open
Tues.–Wed. and Fri.–Sat. 0930–1800.

L. R. BAMFORD, 361 Eccleshall Rd (65888).
Victoriana, bric-à-brac. Open 1000–1730; closed Thur.
afternoon.

G. W. FORD & Son, 288-92 Glossop Rd (22082).
Large stock of furniture, porcelain, silver and plate, all of
1750–1830; paintings. Open Mon.–Fri. 0830–1800; Sat. morning
after 0900. Restoration of furniture. Member of BADA.

HINSON, 679 Eccleshall Rd (65927).
18th/19th-century oil paintings and watercolours. Open
0900–1730. Restorations.

JACKSONS of Sheffield, 223 Abbeydale Rd (52101).
18th-century furniture and silver, pictures. Open 0900–1730;
closed Sun., and Thur. and Sat. afternoons.

JAMESON & Co., 257 Glossop Rd (23846).
Large stock of pre-1820 furniture; glass, china, weapons. Open
Mon.–Wed. and Fri.–Sat. 0930–1330, 1400–1745. Restoration of
furniture.

JOSE, 405 Eccleshall Rd (62214).
Victorian furniture, silver and china; Georgian antiques; Oriental
porcelain, netsuke, ivories and paintings. Open Mon.–Wed. and
Fri.–Sat. 1000–1800.

OLIVANT & Son, 277 Eccleshall Rd (61539).
General antiques. Open 0930–1800; closed Sun., and Thur.
afternoon.

Sheffield Park

Dealers
P. J. RADFORD.
Prints, maps. Large mail-order business.

Swansea

Dealers
M. GRIFFITHS, 30a Dillwyn St (54241).
Vintage cars and their restoration, Victorian metalware and
china, coins, clocks, paintings, weapons. Closed Sun., and Thur.
afternoon.

R. HUGHES, 13 Dillwyn St (56673).
18th/19th-century furniture, oil-paintings, clocks, porcelain,
pewter, glass, objets d'art. Closed Sun. and Thur., and Mon.
morning.

Ron MACKAY, 213 Oxford St (53393) and 3 St Helen's Rd (42366).
Large stock of antique clocks, watches, jewellery, china, glass,
silver, plate and Victoriana. Closed Sun., and Thur. afternoon.

T. W. PRICE, 93 St Helen's Rd (41690).
General antiques, porcelain, pottery, Victorian furniture.

Tetbury

Dealers
Meyrick NIELSEN, Avon House, Market Pl (52201).
Britain's finest selection of clocks. Member of BADA.

Witney

Dealers
John WILSON.
Autographs and manuscripts.

Worthing

Dealers
Geoffrey GODDEN, 19 Crescent Rd (35958).
Leading specialist in pottery and porcelain, including ironstone, Parian and 19th-century ware in general. Permanent reference display; periodic special exhibitions. Author and editor of many books on pottery and porcelain.

York

Dealers
GATE ANTIQUES, 51 Goodramgate (Donald Butler) (27035).
Victorian furniture, brass and copper; china and pottery 1800–1900. Open daily except Sunday, 0930–1700.

W. F. GREENWOOD and Sons Ltd, 37 Stonegate (23864).
Large stock of furniture 1660–1830; pottery and porcelain, 1740–1830; silver and jewellery, 1720–1830. Open daily except Sundays and Wednesday p.m. 0900–12.45, 1400–1750. Member of BADA.

Henry HARDCASTLE Ltd, 51 Stonegate (23401).
Period English silver and plate, some jewellery. Open Monday–Saturday. 0900–1730; closed Wednesday p.m. Member of BADA.

Robert MORRISON and Son, 131 The Mount (55394)
Large stock of furniture; oil paintings, general antiques. Open Monday–Friday 0900–1730; closed Sunday afternoon. Member of BADA.

TIFFANY ANTIQUES, 2 Boroughbridge Road (71353).
Furniture, pictures, porcelain, glass, pewter, silver, bronze. Open

Monday–Friday 0900–1800 and by special appointment at weekends. Restoration of pictures.

Museums

An excellent guide to all Britain's museums and art galleries is the British Tourist Authority's *Museums and Art Galleries* (yearly).

Aberdeen

ABERDEEN ART GALLERY AND MUSEUM.
Good collection of Scottish silver.

Birmingham

ASSAY OFFICE, Newhall St.
Silverware, coins, tokens, medals; library dealing with gold and silver manufacture, which includes several thousand letters by Matthew Boulton, the leading maker of Sheffield plate.

BIRMINGHAM CITY MUSEUM AND ART GALLERY, Congreve St.
Fine collection of old masters and English watercolours, including the famous pre-Raphaelite painting *The Last of England* by Ford Madox Brown; ceramics, silver, Pinto Collection of treen.

MUSEUM OF SCIENCE AND INDUSTRY, Newhall St.
Collections devoted to general industrial and scientific interest, including small arms and scientific instruments.

Brighton

BRIGHTON MUSEUM AND ART GALLERY.
Excellent collections of surrealist paintings, watercolours, art nouveau and art deco; Willett Collection of English pottery and porcelain. Open Mon.–Fri. 1000–1800.

ROYAL PAVILION.
George IV's dazzling seaside palace, a treasure-house of Regency furnishings.

Bristol

CITY ART GALLERY, Queen's Rd.
Emphasis on English and Oriental ceramics. Open Mon.–Fri. 1000–1730.

Dudley

BRIERLEY HILL GLASS MUSEUM, Moon St.
Unique collection of international glass; fine reference library. Open Mon.–Tues. and Thur.–Fri. 1400–1700.

STOURBRIDGE GLASS COLLECTION, Mary Stevens Park, Stourbridge.
Superb collection of local glass in this centre of British glass-making.

Edinburgh

HUNTLY HOUSE, 142 Canongate.
Important collections of Edinburgh silver, glass and Scottish pottery. Open Mon.–Fri. 1000–1700.

MUSEUM OF CHILDHOOD, 38 High St.
All aspects of childhood from toys to education. Open Mon.–Fri. 1000–1700.

NATIONAL MUSEUM OF ANTIQUITIES OF SCOTLAND, Queen St.
Scottish arts and crafts from the Stone Age to the present, including Scottish coins, medals and silver and Highland weapons. Open Mon.–Fri. 1000–1700.

ROYAL SCOTTISH MUSEUM.
Good collection of Scottish silver.

SCOTTISH NATIONAL GALLERY OF MODERN ART, *Royal Botanic Garden.*
Modern Scottish paintings.

SCOTTISH UNITED SERVICES MUSEUM, *Crown Sq.*
Scottish military uniforms, medals, arms and equipment.

Glasgow

ART GALLERY AND MUSEUM, *Kelvingrove.*
Famous for its galleries of 16th/20th-century British painting; the Scott Collection of arms and armour containing 15th-century Milanese armour; the Whitelaw Collection of Scottish arms; engineering exhibits especially relating to the sea and ship-building, with a fine collection of ship models including the *Queen Mary*; good collection of Scottish silver.

Leeds

CITY ART GALLERY.
Paintings, silver, extensive collection of Leeds and Staffordshire pottery.

Leicester

LEICESTERSHIRE MUSEUM AND ART GALLERY, *New Walk.*
17th/20th-century English ceramics, English silver, 19th/20th century French paintings, unique collection of German expressionists.

Liverpool

HORNBY LIBRARY, *William Brown St.*
Prints, manuscripts, rare books on the art of printing and the book, autographs, private-press books.

WALKER ART GALLERY, William Brown St.
Notable collection of European paintings, including a representative choice of the English school from Holbein onwards, paintings by the Liverpool school, pre-Raphaelites and late Victorian works.

London

The following are only a tiny selection of London museums, a rich field which caters for almost every collecting instinct, from relics of Dickens, Keats and Samuel Johnson in their own houses to the history of medicine at the Wellcome Institute.

BRITISH MUSEUM.
Comprehensive collections of antiquities, prints, drawings, coins and medals—not to be missed.

COURTAULD INSTITUTE, Woburn Sq.
Important collection of impressionists and post-impressionists.

GOLDSMITH'S HALL, Foster Lane, EC2.
Fine collection of antique plate, largest British collection of modern silver and jewellery.

HORNIMAN MUSEUM, London Rd, Forest Hill, SE23.
Large collection of musical instruments.

IMPERIAL WAR MUSEUM, Lambeth Rd, SE1.
All aspects of the two world wars—not to be missed by militaria, medal and arms collectors.

KODAK MUSEUM, Wealdstone, Harrow.
History of photography and cinematography.

LEIGHTON HOUSE ART GALLERY AND MUSEUM, 12 Holland Park Rd, W14.
Permanent exhibition of high Victorian art with rooms in period decoration, including a famous 'Arab Hall' done out in applied tiles.

MARTINWARE POTTERY COLLECTION, Public Library, *Osterley Park Rd, Southall.*
Large collection of Martinware—characterful bird and caricature pieces.

MUSICAL MUSEUM, Kew Bridge.
Unique collection of automatic pianos, organs and music boxes.

NATIONAL ARMY MUSEUM, Royal Hospital Rd, Chelsea.
History of British and colonial forces 1485–1914.

NATIONAL GALLERY.
Concentrates on the European masters, with a representative selection of British painters from Hogarth to Turner.

NATIONAL MARITIME MUSEUM, Romney Road, Greenwich, SE10(858 4422).
Britain's maritime history illustrated comprehensively with paintings, prints, ship models, relics of distinguished sailors; fine collection of manuscripts; large library with reference section.

NATIONAL POSTAL MUSEUM, King Edward Street, EC1 (432 3851).
Definitive collection of British postal stamps; Universal Postal Union collection of the whole world since 1878; philatelic archives of stamp printers Thomas de la Rue covering issues of 200 countries 1855–1965.

PERCIVAL DAVID FOUNDATION OF CHINESE ART, 53 Gordon Sq, WC1.
Famous for its Chinese ceramics and Library on Chinese art.

PUBLIC RECORD OFFICE AND MUSEUM, Chancery Lane WC2.
More a reference tool for scholars than a museum, but includes such national treasures as the Domesday Book, the signatures of kings and queens, Shakespeare, Milton and Guy Fawkes, and the log of Nelson's *Victory.* The Army and Navy Muster Rolls are indispensable sources for tracing the ownership and provenance of medals.

TATE GALLERY, Millbank SW1.
National collection of British painting up to 1900, and British and foreign art from impressionism to the present.

VICTORIA AND ALBERT MUSEUM, Cromwell Rd, SW7.
Greatest collection of fine and applied arts in Britain; strong on portrait miniatures, 19th-century furniture, jewellery, silver and many other specialities.

WALLACE COLLECTION, Manchester Sq, W1.
Miniatures, European paintings, sculpture, furniture, ceramics.

WELLCOME INSTITUTE, Euston Rd, NW1.
History of medicine.

Manchester

CITY ART GALLERY, Moseley St.
Famous 19th-century and pre-Raphaelite paintings (e.g. *Work* by Ford Madox Brown and *The Hireling Shepherd* by Holman Hunt), silver, English pottery.

SALFORD MUSEUM AND ART GALLERY, Salford.
Paintings and drawings of L. S. Lowry.

WHITWORTH ART GALLERY.
Nationally-important institution containing outstanding collection of English watercolours.

Newcastle-upon-Tyne

LAING ART GALLERY, Higham Pl.
Pottery, porcelain, glass, silver, and British art from the 17th century onwards.

Nottingham

CASTLE MUSEUM.
Fine collections of silver, ceramics and glass; watercolours by the Nottingham-born watercolour masters Richard Bonington and Paul Sandby.

Oxford

ASHMOLEAN MUSEUM, Beaumont St.
Fine collections of European oil-paintings, watercolours, prints, miniatures, old masters, modern drawings, European ceramics, English silver, coins, medals and Chinese and Japanese porcelain.

Sheffield

CITY MUSEUM, Weston Park.
Specialized collections of cutlery and old Sheffield plate.

Stoke-on-Trent

ARNOLD BENNETT'S HOUSE, 205 Waterloo Rd.
Personal relics of the novelist in his early home.

GLADSTONE POTTERY MUSEUM, Longton.
Galleries tracing the history of Staffordshire potteries; an early-Victorian 'potbank' with original ovens.

WEDGWOOD MUSEUM, Barlaston.
Extensive collection of early Wedgwood ware.

Wolverhampton

BANTOCK HOUSE, Bantock Park.
Fine collections of English painted enamels, Worcester porcelain and Staffordshire and Wedgwood pottery.

BILSTON MUSEUM AND ART GALLERY, Mount Pleasant.
Fine examples of English painted enamels.

Worcester

DYSON PERRINS MUSEUM, Severn St.
Finest and most comprehensive collection of old Worcester porcelain.

York

NATIONAL RAILWAY MUSEUM, Leeman Rd.
Development of British Railway engineering—good source
material for collectors of model trains.

Further reading

Allen, Bryan, *Print Collecting* (London: Muller, 1970)
Allix, Charles, *Carriage Clocks* (Woodbridge, Suffolk: Antique
Collectors' Club, 1974)
Battersby, Martin, *The Decorative Twenties* (London: Studio Vista,
1969)
Battersby, Martin, *The Decorative Thirties* (London: Studio Vista,
1971)
Baynton-Williams, R. H., *Investing in Maps* (London: Corgi, 1971)
Bedford, John, *Old English Lustre Ware* (London: Cassell, 1965)
Bedford, John, *Chelsea and Derby China* (London: Cassell, 1967)
Bedford, John, *Toby Jugs* (London: Cassell, 1968)
Bradbury, Frederick, *British and Irish Silver Assay Office Marks
(1544–1968)*, 12th edition (Sheffield: J. W. Northend, 1969)
Bristowe, W. S., *Victorian China Fairings* (London: A. & C. Black,
1971)
Britten, F. J., *Old Clocks and Watches and their Makers,* revised
edition (London: Eyre & Spottiswoode, 1969)
Castle, Peter, *Collecting and Valuing Old Photographs* (London:
Garnstone Press, 1973)
Chaffers, William, *Collector's Handbook of Marks and Monograms on
Pottery and Porcelain,* revised edition (London: W. Reeves,
1968)—standard work.
Coleridge, Anthony, *Chippendale Furniture* (London: Faber &
Faber, 1968)
Cooper, Jeremy, *Guide to Antique Street Markets* (London: Thames
& Hudson, 1974)
Cooper, Jeremy, *Nineteenth-century Romantic Bronzes* (Newton
Abbot: David & Charles, 1975)

Cotterell, H. H., *Old Pewter: Its Makers and Marks in England, Scotland and Ireland*, new edition (London: Batsford, 1968)

Cuss, T. P. Camerer, *The Country Life Book of Watches* (London: Country Life, 1967)

Davis, Derek C., *English and Irish Antique Glass* (London: Barker, 1965)

Davis, Derek C., *English Bottles and Decanters* (London: Letts, 1972)

Dowell, Anthony and Finn, Patrick, *Coins for Pleasure and Investment* (London: John Gifford)

Foskett, Daphne, *British Portrait Miniatures* (London: Spring Books, 1959)

Gaunt, William, *A Concise History of English Painting* (London: Thames & Hudson, 1964) (paperback)

Godden, Geoffrey, *Minton Pottery and Porcelain of the First Period 1793–1850* (London: Barrie & Jenkins, 1968)

Godden, Geoffrey, *Pottery and Porcelain Marks* (London: Barrie & Jenkins, 1969)

Godden, Geoffrey, *British Porcelain: An Illustrated Guide* (London: Barrie & Jenkins, 1974)

Godden, Geoffrey, *British Pottery: An Illustrated Guide* (London: Barrie & Jenkins, 1974)

Godden, Geoffrey, *Mason's Patent Ironstone China* (London: Barrie & Jenkins, 1971)

Godden, Geoffrey, *Illustrated Guide to Lowestoft Porcelain* (London: Barrie & Jenkins, 1969)

Goodison, N., *English Barometers 1680–1860* (London: Cassell, 1969)

Gordon, L. L., *British Battles and Medals* (London: Spink & Son, 1972)

Grimwade, Arthur, *Rococo Silver* (London: Faber & Faber 1974)

Harris, Ian, *The Price Guide to Antique Silver* (Woodbridge, Suffolk: Antique Collector's Club 1969)

Harris, Ian, *The Price Guide to Victorian Silver* (Woodbridge, Suffolk: Antique Collectors' Club, 1971)

Hayward, J. F., *English Watches* (London: Victoria and Albert Museum, HMSO, 1969)

How, G. E. P. and J. P., *English and Scottish Silver Spoons* (privately printed, 1952)—almost unobtainable, but the standard reference work on the subject.

Hughes, G. Bernard, *Antique Sheffield Plate* (London: Batsford, 1970)

Hughes, G. Bernard, *English Snuff Boxes* (London: MacGibbon & Kee, 1971)

Klamkin, Marian, *The Collector's Book of Wedgwood* (Newton Abbot: David & Charles, 1972)

Lewis, Roy Harley, *The Book Browser's Guide* (Newton Abbot: David & Charles, 1975)

Maas, Jeremy, *Victorian Painters* (London: Barrie & Jenkins, 1969)

Massé, H. J. L. J., *Chats on Old Pewter,* revised edition (London: Benn, 1969)

Oliver, Anthony, *The Victorian Staffordshire Figure: A Guide for Collectors* (London: Heinemann, 1971)

Oman, Charles, *English Domestic Silver* (London: Oxford University Press, 1957)

Peal, Christopher, *British Pewter and Britannia Metal* (London: John Gifford, 1971)

Pearsall, Ronald, *Collecting and Restoring Scientific Instruments* (Newton Abbot: David & Charles)

Peter, Mary, *Collecting Victorian Jewellery* (London: MacGibbon & Kee, 1970)

Pinto, Edward, *Treen and Other Wooden Bygones* (London: Bell, 1969)

Pinto, Edward and Eva, *Tunbridge and Scottish Souvenir Woodware* (London: Bell, 1970)

Purvey, P. F., *Standard Catalogue of British Coins,* part 4, *Coins and Tokens of Scotland* (London: Seaby, 1972)

Ray, A., *English Delftware Pottery* (London: Faber & Faber, 1968)

Reilly, Robin, *Wedgwood Jasper* (London: Letts, 1972)

Reynolds, Graham, *A Concise History of Watercolours* (London: Thames & Hudson, 1971) (paperback)

Sandon, Henry, *Illustrated Guide to Worcester Porcelain* (London: Barrie & Jenkins, 1968)

Seaby, P. J., *Standard Catalogue of British Coins:* parts 1 and 2, *Coins of England and the United Kingdom,* 13th edition (London: Seaby, 1974)

Shinn, C. and D., *Victorian Parian China* (London: Barrie & Jenkins, 1971)

Smith, Alan, *Illustrated Guide to Liverpool Herculaneum Pottery* (London: Barrie & Jenkins, 1970)

Snodin, Michael, *English Silver Spoons* (London: Letts, 1974)

Symonds, R. W., *Thomas Tompion: His Life and Works* (London: Spring Books, 1969)

Towner, Donald C., *English Cream-coloured Earthenware* (London: Faber, 1957)

Wardle, Patricia, *Victorian Silver and Silver Plate* (London: Herbert Jenkins, 1963)

Williams-Wood, Cyril, *Staffordshire Pot-lids and their Potters* (London: Faber, 1972)

Wintersgill, Donald, *The Guardian Book of Antiques* (London: Collins, 1975)

Wood, Christopher, *A Dictionary of Victorian Painters* (Woodbridge, Suffolk: Antique Collectors' Club, 1972)

In addition to the above, Faber publishes a large series of scholarly monographs on collecting, and the Antique Collectors' Club publishes a series of price guides to antique silver, ceramics, pewter and many other collecting fields—all updated with yearly lists.

Made in ancient Greece about 540 BC, this Attic black-figured amphora was formerly in England's Nostell Priory collection and was sold at auction in 1975 to a private buyer

6
Greece

Introduction

It may seem incongruous, surrounded by the awesome relics of classical Greece, to think of buying antiques in Athens, and indeed export regulations make it difficult to take out major antiquities, important icons or Byzantine silver. Everything of first-rank importance is officially registered and buyers should check with their dealer to see whether a piece has been cleared for export. Generally a written permit has to be obtained from the Greek Ministry of Education. It is possible to buy Greco-Roman antiquities of the kind dug up by farmers—coins, small pieces of pottery, votive offerings—but official permission to export should always be sought. Export regulations permitting, Athens is a good centre for ancient Greek coins, Byzantine silver and jewellery, and Greek and Byzantine icons, though it may be a very expensive place to buy them. Objects from the period of Turkish rule and the 1823 war of independence can be freely exported, including weapons, jewellery, costumes, silk embroideries, rugs and household artefacts. Buyers have less risk of being sold a fake from this period than from Byzantine and Hellenistic times.

It is customary to bargain with Greek dealers, though not so intensively as in Turkey. Most antique dealers in Athens are centred in the Monastiraki area, especially on Pandrossou Street. One interesting—possibly unique—specialist shop in Athens is Petrograd, which deals exclusively in antiques and works of art from pre-Revolutionary Russia. The flea market at the end of Ifestou St sells mostly junk, but it may be possible to pick up the odd piece of embroidery, Turkish antiquity or carved box. The best time to visit the market is on Sunday morning when farmers come in from the outlying villages to sell their family treasures.

Collectors should beware of modern pottery in old designs masquerading as antiques, also of cheap silverware and enamelwork.

Specialities

Coins

Ancient Greek coins form a fascinating collecting theme, tracing both the history and the art of the Hellenistic world. Each city state in ancient Greece had its own coinage; that of Athens was particularly handsome and there were also interesting issues from Sicily and the Aegean Islands. Greek coins were original works of art featuring the legendary heroes of the ancient world like Alexander the Great. They also featured natural subjects—a homely touch—like the bee on the silver tetradrachm of Ephesus and the ear of barley on the silver 'third stater' of Metapontum. Byzantine coins, even the gold issues, are still quite modestly priced in comparison with the Greek coinage, which is expensive except for certain bronze issues.

Icons

Greek icons were more primitive in style and in consequence are less sought after than Russian and Byzantine icons, and they are also more easily faked. On the other hand, they can have a charm all their own just because of this artless simple quality. Collectors should beware of street dealers offering icons, as these are most likely to be modern or outright fakes. Good icons, bought from a reputable dealer, are expensive in Athens and must be cleared for export; all icons of any age and value are registered centrally.

The trade

Athens

Dealers
George ALEXOPOULOS, Pandrossou 44.

AMIS du LIVRE, Valaoritis 9 (615562).
Large stock of books, including rare and out-of-print editions, especially Byzantine history; engravings, drawings, maps.

ANTIKA (John Yannoukos), Amalias 4 (3232220) and Athens Tower, Messocion 2 (705881).
Furniture, icons, ivories, hardstones, carpets, porcelain.

DEMETRAKOU, Haritos 27 (913511).

GAZAROSSIAN & VITALI, Pandrossou 58 and 75 (3213123/67).
Antiquities, terracotta, icons, carpets, coins, silverware.

George GOUTIS, Pandrossou 40 and 47 (3213212/044).
Antiques, coins, icons, objets d'art. Open Mon.–Fri. 0900–1400, 1700–2000.

C. HARITAKIS, Valaoritou 7 (621254).
Furniture, Georgian and Victorian silver, icons, porcelain, antiquities.

KAUFMAN, Bucarest 11 (624252).
Rare books.

LAMBRIDIS, Solonos 101 (620670).
Antiques, paintings.

John MARTINOS, Pandrossou 50 (222458).
Antiques, especially of Turkish period.

PANDONA, Kolokotroni 3 (224840).
Antiques, jewellery, objets d'art, Greek art.

Dionisios PANU, Ifestou 24 and Pandrossou 3 (3219685).

PETROGRAD.
Specialist in antiques and works of art from pre-Revolutionary Russia.

Homere ROUSSOS, Pandrossou 69 (234480) and 2 rue du Stade.
Antiques, old paintings, coins, medals.

Euripides SEPHERIADES, Praxitelous 9 (33574).
Coins.

Dimitris SERRAS, Voukourestiov 38 (625367).
Furniture, objets d'art.

Galerie TSANTILIS, Mitripoleos 31
Objets d'art.

ZOUMBOULAKIS, Kriezotou 1 (613433).

Markets
Flea Market, Monastiraki Square and Hermes St
Open Sat. and Sun. mornings.

Flea market, end of Ifestou
Open Sun. morning and other times.

Museums

Athens

BENAKI MUSEUM, Odos Koumbari 1.
Greek and Byzantine art including icons, Coptic and Islamic art (Arabic, Turkish, Persian), Greek costumes, embroideries, peasant art, Chinese porcelain, ancient Greek and Byzantine jewellery, Ottoman ceramics.

MUSEUM OF SACRED ICONS OF THE ARCHBISHOPS OF ATHENS, Archbishop's Palace, 21 Ayias Filotheis (237654).
Open only to specialists.

NATIONAL ARCHAEOLOGICAL MUSEUM, Tositsa 1 (817717).
NUMISMATIC MUSEUM, National Archaeological Museum, Totsitsa 1
250 000 examples of ancient Greek, Roman and Byzantine coins.

I. AND D. PASSAS MUSEUM OF EUROPEAN AND ORIENTAL ART, Evelpidou 2 (812372).
Chinese art, paintings.

PINACOTHEQUE NATIONALE, MUSEE ALEXANDRE SOUTZOS, Vass. Constantinou 50.
14th/20th-century European paintings; 17th/20th-century Greek paintings, sculpture and engravings.

Fine Irish silver coffee pot in rococo style, by John Moore of Dublin, 1760

7
Ireland

Introduction

The novelist V. S. Pritchett once described Dublin during Horse
Show Week as resembling 'a great country house by the sea, in the
old days, alive with hospitality . . . a good deal of Irish life is really
going on in a lost early Victorian paradise'. Much the same
metaphor springs to mind in thinking of the Irish antique scene;
the most typical Irish antiques all have an affinity with country-
house life—silver, Waterford glass, fine prints, portraits and
miniatures, Belleek porcelain, handsome guns and leather bookbindings, and classic well-made furniture, the mahogany
darkened by two centuries of peat smoke.

The craftsmanship of the 18th century (in 1786 there were 28
cabinet makers and a dozen carvers and gilders working in
Dublin) was such that even the heavy brass doorlocks of country
houses, encased in mahogany, are in demand in antique markets.
The houses themselves in all their pristine glory can be seen in
many old Irish prints, which are of architectural and historical
interest as well as decorative appeal. The Irish country houses
open to the public are also well worth visiting to sample the
flavour of Ireland's Ascendancy culture. Powerscourt, alas, was
destroyed by fire in 1974 just as the Slazenger family was
preparing to open its contents to the public, but Carton, Westport
House and Castletown among others are rich experiences. Bantry
House, on the shores of Bantry Bay, has some furniture and
tapestries supposedly once the property of Marie Antoinette
which were salvaged from the wreck of the Tuileries during the
French Revolution.

Silver and glass are of course the two chief fields in which
collectors look for Irish craftsmanship, but there are few bargains

to be had in either nowadays. It is probably cheaper to buy Irish Georgian silver in London than in Dublin, on the principle that wherever local interest is strong the price goes up, but there is certainly a great selection of it in Dublin. It is worth thinking also of the 19th-century Irish silver, which experts say is underrated— its florid exuberance may not be to everyone's taste. Dublin has many first-rate dealers specializing in Irish silver and glass, most of them clustered in the streets running off Grafton St, the fashionable shopping throughfare. Louis Wine in Dublin is *the* prestige dealer in Irish silver, though a thick wallet is needed to buy anything here and the assistants give the impression of knowing if it is not thick enough. J. W. Weldon, also in Dublin, has a good stock of reasonably-priced 19th-century silver. Irish silver prices have on the whole been slower than English silver prices to recover from the 1969/70 collapse in Georgian silver. Early Georgian Irish silver is in any case scarce; not much was made before 1714 because Ireland at that time could not support a luxury market to any great extent.

Around 1770 Ireland was becoming prosperous and Dublin a capital of style and craftsmanship, particularly in the decorative arts, to match any in Europe. This was reflected not only in the greater volume of silver production, but also in the flourishing publishing business—and in the preponderance of fine engravers, most of them anonymous, who served the silversmiths, book publishers and map and print makers.

Irish collectors are more interested now than they used to be in 18th-century work, once regarded (along with Dublin's Georgian architecture) as a legacy of the disliked English Ascendancy. They go for solid investments like silver, Irish furniture and oil-paintings; they are not keen on watercolours and prints (except for Malton's views of Dublin), which may indicate the possibility of bargains in those areas, and they have certainly shown no tendency to climb on to trendy collecting bandwagons like biscuit tins, bottles and similarly intrinsically worthless fads.

The Irish antique trade is very much centred on Dublin—good silver and glass can be bought in Cork but it is very expensive. Dubliners still love to comb the Liffey quays for bargains, though what is found there now is mostly rubbish or reproduction. Still, it is worth a Saturday-morning stroll just to enjoy the Joycean views of rosy brick facades and faded gilt lettering along the waterfront, with the opportunity of a rummage through the dusty secondhand furniture and tattered prints. There are several auction rooms on the north quays whose weekly sales are worth a visit. The north side of fashionable St Stephen's Green has one or two antique markets patronized by the locals on Saturdays, while on the south side near the Shelbourne Hotel the auctioneer James Adam holds good-class sales every few weeks of paintings, silver, furniture and works of art.

The Irish antique trade has prospered appreciably since the influx of British and American best-selling writers brought about by the Irish Republic's tax-free conditions for creative artists. Several have bought imposing country houses and are busily filling them with Irish antiques. There are now three major antique fairs each year when dealers get together to buy and sell. the Irish Antiques Fair in Dublin—a fashionable occasion during Horse Show Week, pinnacle of the Dublin social round—the Limerick fair, and the Cork Antique Fair inaugurated in 1975.

Specialities

Books

Dublin in the late 18th century was a flourishing centre of publishing (often of brazenly-pirated editions, there being no such thing as copyright in those days) and book-binding. Irish leather bindings were solid and durable, somewhat coarse perhaps compared to the best Continental or English work, but nevertheless are keenly collected in Ireland. So are the pirated editions of 18th-century London-published works. Irish country-house libraries (such as that of Westport House) are good places to see the work of local book binders. Dublin dealers Figgis Rare Books and Falkner Grierson can advise on buying.

Ceramics

The Belleek porcelain factory in Co. Fermanagh, established in 1857, made particularly delicate Parian ware distinguished by its glistening white glaze—it was once described as being like barley sugar—and its naturalistic decoration, often using marine motifs such as seashells. Early Belleek ware, combining both hard- and soft-paste techniques, is rare now. In fact its delicacy, especially the characteristic openwork Parian baskets, makes it hard to find undamaged pieces. The Belleek factory also produced some onstone ware and painted or transfer-printed earthenware; it is still making Parian-type ware to traditional designs.

Irish Delft ware was in the main stream of the blue-and-white tin-glazed earthenware produced in various parts of Europe in the 18th century. The largest factory was that of Henry Delamain in Dublin, noted for its beautiful landscape painting. Mason's Ironstone is also widely found in Irish antique shops: this hard-wearing handsome English ware was popular with middle-class Irish families in the 19th century.

Coins

Ireland offers a fascinating field to the coin collector, with pre-Ascendancy issues ranging from 1185 to 1649, but many of the coins are extremely scarce. They were all of silver or base metal except for the very rare Inchiquin gold issues. Commonly-found issues include the silver pennies of King John and Edward I and the harp issue groats of Henry VIII.

Firearms

Dublin was a thriving centre of gun-making in the 18th and 19th centuries and an impressive display of this work can be seen at the National Museum. The most famous of many family firms was that of William and John Rigby, which flourished in the mid 19th century. The Rigbys were the first in this part of Europe to make gun barrels of alternate iron and steel wires forged together and then twisted, rolled and coiled around a mandrel in imitation of Kurdish 'Damascus' barrels. These weapons were finished in acid to bring out the pattern and were among the most beautiful ever made. The Rigbys also made fine duelling pistols and small screw-barrel pocket-pistols in pairs, as did several other makers.

Dublin makers with approximate dates of working included: Matthew Collins (1750s), John Harrison, Daniel Muley (1800s), Farrell McDermott (1800), John Langson (1810), James Eames (late 18th century—famous for duelling pistols), Nicholas Clarke (1800), Thomas Fowler (1820), William Dempsey (1820), J.

Marsh (1775 — boxlock pocket pistols), Lewis Alley (1775), George Turner (1815), James and Thomas Calderwood (1850), William and James Kavanagh (mid 19th century), E. Trulock and Son (19th century) and Mark and John Pattison (19th century). Outside Dublin the best-known name was Westerman: there was John Westerman of Kilkenny and William Westerman of Cork.

Glass

Irish glass was heavier and more deeply cut than English; Ireland offered a golden opportunity to English glass makers when the Excise Act of 1777 doubled the tax on the weight of glass. In 1783 the Waterford Glass House was established by the Penrose brothers and the same year saw the start of the Cork Glass Co. which remained in production until 1818. The Waterford factory was closed in 1851 but reopened some years ago and is producing fine modern glass including copies of early designs. Old Waterford glass is now difficult to find and correspondingly expensive. It is generally thought that antique Waterford always had a blue or greyish tinge from the lead in the mixture, but this is not necessarily so. Characteristic of Waterford ware were elaborately cut vases, drinking glasses, jugs and other dinner-table appurtenances, as well as magnificent chandeliers, examples of which can be seen in Irish stately homes such as Westport House. Highly esteemed are the huge serving dishes on stems, sometimes with a curled rim, called turnover bowls. Waterford decanters usually had three neck rings and mushroom-shaped stoppers. Belfast was also a glass-producing centre in the late 18th and early 19th centuries; the Belfast Glass Co. was noted for its decanters.

One Dublin expert in both glass and ceramics is Mrs. Jackson of Rembrandt Antiques. Collections of Irish glass can be seen at the Ulster Museum in Belfast, National Museum in Dublin and Victoria and Albert Museum in London.

Paintings

Ireland is not generally thought of as having a great painting tradition, but 18th-century Irish painters such as George Barrett (senior and junior) and William Ashford were of international stature. As with Scottish artists, many Irish artists, particularly portrait painters (in which Ireland was strongly represented), found they had to migrate to England to find clients in spite of the fact that from 1700 onwards pictures were being imported into Ireland to grace the new town and country homes of the Ascendancy.

In the 19th century Irish sculptors were more admired than Irish painters; the *Art Journal* in 1861 said that Ireland had contributed more good sculptors to 'the British School of Art' than painters. Leading sculptors included Thomas Kirk, Christopher Moore, Sir Thomas Farrell, John Hogan and John Edward Carew. Some particularly fine portrait busts were done during this period.

The most underrated 19th-century painter, even now, is James Arthur O'Connor (1792-1841), 17 of whose sombrely romantic landscapes hang above the main staircase in Westport House. His work is well represented in the National Gallery in Dublin and he is generally regarded as the father of modern landscape-painting in Ireland. Other 19th-century painters to look for include: William Sadler II, who painted many scenes around Dublin; William Mulready, who designed the first cover for the Penny Post in 1840; Edwin Hayes, an eminent marine painter; Sir Frederick William Burton, an accomplished watercolour artist interested in Irish history and folklore; and Richard Bridges Beechey, a marine painter of dramatic flair. The major Irish artist of the period was undoubtedly Daniel Maclise of Cork, a monumental history painter (he did two large frescoes for the House of Lords) whose stature has been recognized after nearly a century of neglect. His early work ranged widely through genre scenes, allegorical pictures, fairy paintings and a famous series, executed for a magazine, of lithographic cartoons of literary celebrities. Among 19th-century portrait painters the most prolific was Stephen Catterson Smith the Elder, who specialized in female subjects. The work of Sir Martin Archer Shee, a portrait painter in the grand manner, was underrated until recently.

Among modern Irish artists, Jack B. Yeats's powerful and romantic evocations of Irish landscapes and Dublin scenes were the dominant influence. The paintings of Sir William Orpen, the biggest name in the Irish School before 1914, and of the poet 'AE' (George Russell) were cheap until fairly recently. W. J. Leech's Dublin scenes had a luminous nostalgia and Paul Henry was another distinguished name of the early 20th century—he also did poster work. The Municipal Gallery of Modern Art in Dublin has a splendid collection of Yeats.

Among contemporary artists the outstanding name is Camille Souter, whose treatment of light recalls Bonnard and whose early works in the *tachiste* manner are now eagerly sought.

The Wellesley-Ashe Gallery in Dublin has a good stock of paintings, both oil and watercolour, under £500.

Pewter

Most Irish pewter was made around Cork. The most generally-collected items are the sets of early 19th-century ale and spirit measures known as 'haystacks' from their distinctive shape. These, the equivalent of Scotland's 'tappit-hen' measures, are quite cheap individually but a set of eight in good condition could cost £800.

Portrait Miniatures

Ireland had a number of distinguished miniature painters. Rupert Barber (1736–72) was also noted as an enamellist. George Chinnery RHA (1774–1852) was born in London and is best known for his scenes of India and China; signed miniatures by him are rare. Of the Cork brothers Adam and Frederick Buck (1759–1833 and 1771–1840), Adam was the better artist. He worked in Dublin for a time, doing miniatures and small watercolours, while Frederick specialized in officers' portraits. Frederick Buck's work is the exception to the general rule that very few Irish miniatures can now be found for less than £100— the average is £300–£600. Some other leading Irish miniaturists, most of whom worked in the 18th century, were: Samuel Collins, John Comerford, Simon Digby, Thomas Frye, Gustavus Hamilton, Nathaniel Hone (who also did large landscapes, usually featuring cows), Denis Brownell Murphy, George Place, Charles Robertson and R. S. T. Roche. A 19th-century name to note is Samuel Lover, a man of versatile talents (composer, musician, novelist, illustrator) who was encouraged to take up miniature-painting by his friend John Comerford.

Prints and Maps

The prize for any print collector would be a set—extremely expensive now—of the famous series of 25 views of Dublin buildings done by James Malton during 1790/91. The etching and aquatinting was done by Malton himself. Small modern reproductions are quite commonly seen. Before this, in 1780, a series of architectural elevations of important Dublin buildings, now of great historic interest, was published by Pool and Cash. A particularly fine series of Irish country-house views was engraved by Thomas Milton from contemporary drawings and paintings between 1783 and 1793; 12 were reissued by the Irish Georgian Society in 1963. A later series of similar views by J. P. Neale has recently been widely reproduced. Mezzotints were done in Dublin by Thomas Beard (scarce), John Brooks and Andrew Miller. Thomas Frye's portrait mezzotints of the mid 18th-century are keenly sought after. Maps of towns and counties were often decorated with vignettes of more than mere artistic interest —Desmond Guinness, founder of the Irish Georgian Society, says that Noble and Keenan's map of Co. Kildare in 1752 was the only engraving to show Carton, seat of the Dukes of Leinster, with its original colonnades, which were removed in 1817. The well-known portrait painter and lithographer Daniel Maclise of Cork also did engravings, many of them for topographical books. Barrow's *Tour Round Ireland* (1836) contained four illustrations drawn and etched by Maclise. Etchings by him are also in an edition of Carleton's *Traits and Stories of the Irish Peasantry* and two woodcuts after his drawings are in Hall's *Ireland, Its Scenery and Characters* (1841).

Silver

Ireland has had a tradition of fine metal-working since 1800 BC, and Irish silver is different from any other. Domestic silver was first made in 1637, the year a royal charter was granted to Dublin's Goldsmith's Co., and Trinity College in Dublin has the earliest piece of hallmarked silver, a communion flagon of 1638. All Irish silver had to be assayed in Dublin and the mark of origin has always been a crowned harp.

Very little was made north of Dublin, though in the 17th and 18th centuries silver was made at Youghal, Galway, Cork,

Kilkenny (rare) and Limerick. Cork was the second silver-making centre of Ireland (Limerick the third). Cork silver is now rare but some can still be found near its place of origin. It was made from about 1660 when the identifying mark was either a tower or two towers flanking a three-masted sailing ship: the Cork civic arms. An interesting oddity for collectors (because technically illegal) is the Republican silver made by Messrs Egan of Cork (a firm still in existence) to prevent their men from being thrown out of work when they could no longer send their silver to be assayed in Dublin during the Civil War of 1922. An output of 26.9kg (950 oz) was produced between June and September that year, marked with two towers and a *two*-masted sailing ship; in all there were 60 or 70 pieces of well-designed hammered silver. Because they were not properly assayed in Dublin they were never offered for sale on the open market. Spoons are a particularly good way of collecting Irish provincial silver—they often have special characteristics, such as the bright cutting typical of Limerick.

Dublin 18th-century silver is sound and simple in form, but the rococo spirit flowered to fine advantage in the dish ring, the most distinctive of Irish silver articles—a pierced silver stand for keeping bowls of hot punch off the polished table top. The Victorians misnamed them 'potato rings' and sometimes served baked potatoes in them, wrapped in a napkin. Other particularly Irish items included 'freedom boxes', about the size of a circular snuff box and, indeed, designed to be used for snuff or tobacco once they had fulfilled their original function of holding charters of civic freedom given to worthy citizens. They usually had the city's arms on the lid and many came from Cork, which was notably generous in bestowing its honours. They are much collected and average about £700 each. The helmet shape often thought characteristic of Irish silver was in fact designed by Robert Adam and was not peculiar to Ireland, though many 18th-century Irish pieces were made in this classic design. The harp-shaped handle, however, was typical; so were two-handled cups and three-legged sugar bowls and cream jugs. The latter were often decorated in exuberant rococo style, and in the period 1740–70 Irish silversmiths went through a phase of nostalgia for country motifs, decorating dish rings and other pieces with milkmaids, cows, birds, farm animals and farmhouse patterns. These curiously rustic designs on sophisticated silver pieces are now avidly collected in Ireland but are not to everyone's taste.

Very typical of Irish silver, especially Limerick work, was bright cutting, a very attractive form of decoration designed to make the silver gleam with movement in flickering candlelight.

Everyone thinks of Georgian silver in connection with Ireland, but Irish 19th-century silver is, some think, unfairly neglected and thus still reasonable in price. Much of it was florid and ornate in the Victorian style, but the work of James Le Bas, the most prolific Dublin maker, is worth hunting out. At the end of the 19th century there was some very interesting and attractive silver in the Celtic manner inspired by the Celtic revival which influenced all the arts.

Some notable Dublin makers were: Robert Calderwood, William Townsend, William Woodhouse, James Taaffe, John Lloyd, Thomas Burton, George Wheatley, John Sherwin, John Nixon, John Moore, Joseph Jackson, John Hamilton, Richard Sawyer, Thomas Walker, Christopher Haines, Thomas Sutton, John Kelly, Thomas Williamson, William Thompson, William Hughes. Cork had Stephen Walsh, George Hodder, the firm of Terry and Williams, Thomas Lilly, William Clarke and Richard Goble. The most celebrated Limerick maker was Joseph Johns, famous for two-handled cups, and there were also two distinguished dynasties named Robinson in the 17th and 18th centuries.

The National Museum in Dublin and Victoria and Albert Museum in London have good collections of Irish silver.

The trade

Belfast

Dealers

BELL Gallery, 4 Alfred St (28021).
19th-century English paintings, 20th-century Irish paintings, maps, prints, rare books on Irish subjects.

CALDWELL Galleries, 40 and 56 Bradbury Pl (23311).
18th- and early 19th-century furniture, ceramics, paintings, silver.

KAVANAGH Antiques, 40-1 Smithfield Sq (23959).
Large stock of general antiques including coins, medals, pistols,
silver, glass and Victoriana. Closed Wed. after 1300.

John & Charlotte LAMBE, 41 Shore Rd (77761).
Antique furniture, silver, glass, china, pictures.

SINCLAIR'S Antique Gallery, 26 Arthur St.
Jewellery, china, glass.

A. THOMPSON, 11 Lisburn Rd (20063).
Paintings, drawings, prints.

Cork

Dealers
The ANTIQUE SHOP, 17a Academy St (22950).
18th- and early 19th-century Irish and English furniture, silver,
glass, china. Open Mon.–Sat.

FEEHAN, 2 Bridge St (26079).
18th/19th-century silver, furniture, clocks, bronze, porcelain,
rare books. Open Mon.–Sat.

LEE Bookstores, 10 Lavitts Quay (22307).
Secondhand books, especially Irish history.

MARLBORO Antiques, 33 Marlboro St (56652).
Specialist in clocks; brass, copper, glass, porcelain.

Markets and fairs
Flea market, Coal Quay.
Open every morning.

Antique market, St Francis Hall.
Open Sat.

CORK ANTIQUE FAIR.
Yearly in early April.

Dublin

Dealers

ANTHONY Antiques, 7 Molesworth St (777222).
Brass, copper, oil-paintings, silver, furniture.

Edward BUTLER, 14 Bachelor's Walk (743485).
17th/19th-century furniture, glass, porcelain, paintings, works of art.

John CALLERY, 40 South William St (770615).
Silver, paintings.

CITY Antiques Ltd, 3 Dawson St (777960).
18th/19th-century English and French furniture, paintings, porcelain, silver, glass.

DANKER, 10 South Anne St (774009).
Silver, plate, paintings, jewellery.

John DOOLY & Sons, 29-30 Dawson St (771250).
Fine antique furniture, Irish and English glass, chandeliers, silver, sporting prints, paintings, china. Open Mon.–Fri., also by appointment.

DUBLIN Art Shop and Cluna Studio, 110 St Stephen's Green (56632).
18th/19th-century silver, porcelain, glass, copper, jewellery, small furniture, samplers, Belleek ware.

FALKNER GRIERSON, 4 Molesworth Pl.
Rare books, especially 18th-century literature.

FIGGIS Rare Books (Neville Figgis), 15 St Frederick St.
Mr Figgis of the famous Hodges Figgis bookshop has set up his own establishment in a Georgian house, specializing in antiquarian books with an Irish section strong on history, topography and modern Anglo-Irish literature in fine editions (Shaw, Yeats, Gogarty, etc.). Open Mon.–Fri. 0900–1700 approx. Mr Figgis is there himself on Fri.

FINE ART Showrooms, 27 South Anne St (772142).

Antique Irish and English silver, jewellery, paintings, furniture, glass, porcelain.

Fred HANNA, 28/9 Nassau St (771255/6).
Secondhand book section; old prints and maps of Irish interest.

HIBERNIAN Antiques, 1 Molesworth Pl (763824).
Furniture, silver, paintings, glass.

Gerald KENYON, 36-7 South William St (773945).
Ceramics, paintings, 18th/19th-century furniture.

KILDARE Antiques, 19 Kildare St (63570).
18th-century porcelain and pottery, especially Belleek; miniatures, Georgian silver. Closed weekends.

R. McDONNELL Ltd, 8-9 Molesworth St (762614).
Antique furniture, paintings, silver, glass, curios.

NEPTUNE Gallery, 42 South William St (787349).
Modern and antique paintings, prints, maps, sculpture.

NUMBER FOUR Antiques (Mrs Marianne Newman), 4 Molesworth St (779534).
18th/19th-century furniture, glass, porcelain, pewter, copper, lamps, clocks, pictures.

Kevin O'KELLY & Co. Ltd, 21 Wellington Quay (771028).
Coins, medals, silver, jewellery.

John O'REILLY, 27 South Anne St (772142).
Antique silver, old Sheffield plate, jewellery, paintings, porcelain, furniture.

ORIEL Gallery, 17 Clare St (763410).
17th/20th-century paintings of English and Continental schools, especially Irish.

ORMOND Antiques, 32 Lower Ormond Quay (741569).
18th/19th-century furniture, glass, porcelain (including Belleek), pewter, copper, clocks, pictures.

REMBRANDT Antiques (Mrs Jackson), 24 South Anne St (779374).
18th/19th-century silver, porcelain, glass, jewellery, copper, pewter, works of art; expert in glass and ceramics.

J. W. WELDON, 55 Clarendon St (771628/2742).
Diamonds, jewellery, silver, coins, works of art.

WELLESLEY-ASHE Gallery, South Frederick St.
Good stock of oils and watercolours priced under £500.

Jane WILLIAM, 23 Molesworth St (767857).
18th- and early 19th-century English furniture, porcelain, glass, miniatures, objets d'art.

Louis WINE, 31-2 Grafton St (773865).
Leading dealer in early English and Irish silver; jewellery, glass, pictures, china, furniture, objets d'art.

Markets and fairs
IRISH ANTIQUES FAIR, Mansion House.
Yearly on 1st Tues. in Aug.

Auctions
James ADAM & Son, 26 St Stephen's Green (763881).
Sales monthly, announced in the *Irish Times* and *Irish Independent*.

BALFE'S Auction Rooms, 4 Lower Ormond Quay (741263).

IRISH FINE ART Auctions Ltd, Bachelor's Walk.
Clearance sales of antiques Tues., 1915; also specialist coin sales and country sales.

SHEERAN'S, 25 Bachelor's Walk (47097).
Sales Thurs.

Ennis

Dealers
HONAN, Barrack St (21137).
Long-case and wall clocks, glass, curios.

Galway

Dealers
ALEXANDER Antiques, Eyre Sq (2693).
17th/19th-century furniture, porcelain, clocks, paintings.

KENNY'S Bookshops and Art Galleries, High St (2739).
Antiquarian books, especially of Irish interest; old prints and paintings by Irish artists.

Limerick

Dealers
THOMOND Antiques, 37 Cecil St (45433).
18th/19th-century furniture, silver, porcelain, paintings, objets d'art.

Markets and fairs
Antique fair
Yearly in Oct. or Nov.

Tipperary

Dealers
COURTVILLE Antiques, The Corner House, St Michael's St (51249).
18th/19th-century small furniture, silver, porcelain, jewellery, paintings, miniatures, objets d'art.

Waterford

Dealers
The ANTIQUE SHOP, O'Connell St.
18th/19th-century furniture, silver, china, glass.

Museums

Belfast

ULSTER MUSEUM
Good collection of Irish glass.

Dublin

CHESTER BEATTY LIBRARY, 20 Shrewsbury Rd.
Fine collection of medieval and Oriental manuscripts, including the oldest known manuscript of the New Testament.

JOYCE MUSEUM, Sandycove, nr Dublin.
Material associated with the writer is housed in the old Martello Tower he once occupied. Open 1100–1600, summer only.

MARSH'S LIBRARY, nr St Patrick's Cathedral.
Important collection of old books on theology and medicine; Greek and Latin and Semitic rarities.

MUNICIPAL GALLERY OF MODERN ART, Parnell Sq.
Half of the famous collection of French impressionists formed by Sir Hugh Lane (the other half is in the National Gallery, London); also a fine collection of paintings by Jack B. Yeats.

NATIONAL LIBRARY AND MUSEUM, Kildare St.
The library has an important collection of Irish books, newspapers and manuscripts. The museum has an Irish Antiquities Division with such famous treasures as the 8th-century Tara Brooch; the Ardagh Chalice, also 8th-century; the Cross of Cong; and the 12th-century Lismore Crozier; also ancient Irish gold jewellery, fine collections of Irish silver and glass and impressive displays of portrait medallions and firearms.

NATIONAL GALLERY OF IRELAND, Merrion Sq.
One of the best collections of old masters in Britain or Ireland; also Irish artists of the 18th and 19th centuries.

ROYAL IRISH ACADEMY, Dawson St.
Extensive collection of old Irish manuscripts.

TRINITY COLLEGE LIBRARY.
Apart from the priceless 8th-century Book of Kells, it has Ireland's largest collection of books and manuscripts, the 9th-century Book of Armagh, a first edition of Dante's *Divine Comedy* and four Shakespeare folios.

Stradbally

MUSEUM OF STEAM ENGINES
Not to be missed by collectors of railwayana. Open daily 1400–1800, May–Sept.

Further reading

Bennett, Douglas, *Irish Georgian Silver* (London: Cassell, 1972)—the definitive work on Irish Georgian silver.
Bennett, Douglas, *Irish Silver* (paperback, forthcoming).
Bradbury, Frederick, *British and Irish Silver Assay Office Marks (1544–1968)*. 12th edition (Sheffield: J. W. Northend, 1968).
Cotterell, H. H., *Old Pewter: Its Makers and Marks in England, Scotland and Ireland*, new edition (London: Batsford, 1968)
Davis, D. C., *English and Irish Antique Glass* (London, Barker, 1965).
Jackson, Right Rev. Robert Wyse, *Irish Silver* (Dublin: Mercier Press, 1972)—a useful little book worth looking out for.
Seaby, B. A., *Standard Catalogue of British Coins:* part 3, *Coins of Ireland* (London: Seaby).
Strickland, W. G., *A Dictionary of Irish Artists* (1913)—essential reading for art collectors pending the publication of a new book on Irish painting by the Knight of Glin and Anne Cruickshank; an original set of the two volumes now costs about £60 but a reprint by Irish University Press (1969) is available at £26.25.
Warren, Phelps, *Irish Glass* (London: Faber & Faber, 1970).

*This rare and important Faenza dish painted with a mythological scene is
dated November 1503 on the back. It was sold at auction for £27,000*

8
Italy

Introduction

Italy is on the whole an expensive country for visiting collectors, and it is important to remember that for anything of major importance it is likely to be extremely difficult to obtain an export permit. Fakes are also a hazard for the unwary, particularly in Roman and Etruscan antiquities, which are nowadays a dangerous field for collectors since the digging up of these relics is illegal (though it goes on all the time) and possession could result in a very nasty situation at the Customs on departure.

Italian collectors, who have grown enormously in number as a result of Italy's prosperous years, tend only to be interested in Italian art and antiques. Consequently, anything non-Italian in the antique shops is likely to be underpriced—e.g. French pictures of the 18th and early 19th centuries and (in Rome) pictures of the European romantic schools, particularly those by German artists who gravitated there during the heyday of 19th-century cultural travel.

The thing to remember about Italian art is that it is intensely regional; every region had its own school of painting, for instance, and often excelled in other artistic fields. One example is Piedmontese silver, which owed much to French influence in that region. Florence is associated with the early renaissance and with superb craftsmanship in bronze, very little of which is available to collectors today; Rome with the high renaissance, Venice with glass and the crown of renaissance painting, Naples with Capodimonte porcelain. This regionalism persists in the form of local patriotism among collectors, so that dealers in, say, Turin buy for the local market. More than ever, Venice is the place for Venetian paintings, Genoa the place for the Genoese school, and so on.

Florence, however, is overall the most important centre for the antique trade. Its Biennial Antiques Fair claims to be the most important in Europe and it certainly offers something for the collector of every bank balance as well as items of extremely high quality—from £10 to £500 000 in the words of Giuseppe Bellini, founder of the fair and the doyen of Florentine antique dealers. In Florence can be found the finest Continental and English furniture, tapestries, porcelain and pottery—especially Capodimonte and Italian majolica—Sèvres china, ivories, Venetian glass, early paintings, sculpture and renaissance furniture. Bellini asserts crisply that Florence is also *the* centre for the best dealers—'They know what they are doing; some others could as well be selling potatoes.' Many collectors who know Italy bear this out and add that Florence, for all its imposing dealers and galleries, offers a wide selection at moderate prices.

Recently collectors in the Florence area have been displaying a keen new interest in art of the 14th and 15th centuries. Primitives, being highly fashionable, are expensive, though the 16th century is currently neglected and therefore relatively cheap. Paintings of the 17th and 18th centuries are also a promising field for foreign collectors, and a slow interest is beginning in the neoclassical period of the 19th century. It was not, however, until the early years of this century that Italian painting regained its true place in world art. The revival was led by a group of young Futurist artists that included Carlo Carrà, Unberto Boccioni, Luigi Russolo, Gina Severini and Giacomo Balla.

Generally the wealthy industrial cities of the north offer a richer hunting-ground for antiques than does the south; Turin and Milan are excellent centres for silver. Here, as elsewhere in Europe's big urban centres, collectors are increasingly developing a taste for rural artefacts of a simpler past, such as painted hard-carved pieces of wood from Sicilian donkey carts. These can sometimes be found at the flea market at Porta Portese in Rome, as well as in Sicily itself at shops in Taormina and the flea market at Palermo. Antique picture frames are another popular item with Italian collectors; so are gothic prayer stools and, in Venice, small carved stone Lions of St Mark, which make attractive bookends as well as ornaments.

Italy has very few specialized dealers; most are of the old-fashioned general type. Wherever one buys—at dealers or in markets—it always pays to bargain.

Specialities

Bronze

Baroque bronzes, produced by little-known artists and influenced by Bernini, were made in Rome, Florence and Foggini.

Drawings

Italy is a particularly prolific source and there are masses on the market.

Firearms

Milan was a centre of fine weapons, renowned for its sword blades. Other centres with high reputations were Genoa and Brescia, which had 200 sword workshops in the early 17th century. Some of the finest and most exquisitely decorated firearms ever made came from a village near Brescia called Gardone; they are known as Brescia pistols and carbines and were made by the Cominazzi family. The industry began here in the late 16th century and each craftsman signed the part of the weapon for which he was responsible. Brescia weapons were noted for the fine chiselling of their steel mounts and were exceptionally light and well-balanced in the hand. Among names which appear most frequently are Angelo Lanzarino (sometimes A. L.) and, in the second half of the 17th century, Pietro, Bartolomeo, Giovanni and Vincenzo Lanzarino. The Francinis were another Gardone family making fine weapons.

Glass

Italy provided two supreme centres of glass-making: Rome and Venice, the latter of which dominated European glass from the 13th to the 18th century. The best Venetian glass now seems to make its way to the Federal Republic of Germany and Switzerland—dealer Zeitz in Hanover has bought up several major collections in recent years. The earliest surviving example of Venetian glass dates from the 11th century, and by the 15th century Venetian glass was in its extravagantly coloured, enamelled, gilded and whorled heyday. Glass makers on Murano discovered a transparent, colourless, glass metal of pliable texture which enabled them to make airy and interlaced forms, such as the *latticinio* technique where clear and opaque canes were twisted together in lacy patterns. Much of the Venetian glass made today is of a type to appeal only to *nouveaux riches* taste.

Jewellery

Italian families dominated 19th-century jewellery design, particularly Castellani of Rome (whose mark was two crossed Cs) and Giuliano, who worked in London. Cameo carving was a Neopolitan art—in fact it is still practised for the tourist trade.

Maps and Prints

Italy became important in the field of map-making at an early stage because of its geographically prominent position in the medieval world. The earliest Italian sea charts were made in the 14th century, and many early manuscript maps of the Italian peninsula have survived. The two most important centres of map-making were Rome and Venice and the peak period was the 16th century. The Venetian cartographer Jacopo Gastaldi and the Roman map engraver Antonio Lafreri were two of the greatest names. Venice, an important centre of 15th-century engraving, is a good source of maps and prints.

Medals

Medals of the 18th century have been overshadowed by those of the renaissance but are interesting historically. Tuscan and Neapolitan medals were probably the finest in the 18th and early 19th centuries. Neapolitan craftsmen in the last quarter of the 18th century produced particularly fine classical designs.

Porcelain and Pottery

Lead-glazed earthenware was produced at Bologna in the 15th

and 16th centuries. Majolica—otherwise known as Italo-Moresque ware from its Moorish origins—was tin-glazed earthenware decorated in rich colours such as green, blue and purple. It reached its peak in the 16th century and was widely imitated elsewhere in Europe. The highest price paid for a piece of majolica in recent years was £55 000 for a Gubbio plate painted and decorated with lustre on a biblical theme by Giorgio *Andreoli*—the highest auction price on record in 1975 for *any* piece of Italian pottery.

The first-known European porcelain was made in Florence under Medici auspices. Porcelain was produced in Venice at an early stage when a Meissen goldworker called Hunger brought the secret in 1720, and production of Capodimonte ware, made of a soft-paste porcelain, was started near Naples soon after that. (King Charles III of Naples took as a bride a Polish princess who brought a quantity of Meissen porcelain with her dowry.) The factory was later transferred to Buen Retiro. True Capodimonte ware of 1743–59 is extremely rare and unlikely to be found by casual collectors. Translucent and generally pure white, it was used in figures modelled by Gricci (lovers, Italian Commedia dell' Arte figures, fishermen, religious subjects, etc.). Naples porcelain, founded in 1771, was a translucent glassy paste; the early ware had a yellowish tinge, later becoming creamy or pure white, and the mark was a crowned N. Figures were made, also plates decorated with a central medallion enclosing rustic scenes of peasants in traditional costume.

Silver

Northern Italy, particularly Milan and Turin, is the place to look for Italian silver; Piedmontese silver was especially fine because of the French influence. Genoa was a centre of silversmiths in the 17th century, but not so much survives there. A great deal of church plate in both silver and gold is still around; before Italy was unified in the 19th century each princedom possessed a centre of plate production. Much, however, was lost during wars, particularly Napoleon's campaign in the late 18th century. The work of famous renaissance goldsmiths such as Benvenuto Cellini would today be outside the scope of all but the wealthiest collectors.

The trade

Florence

Dealers

Dealers are found along Ponte Vecchio, Piazza Pitti, Via della Spada, Via dei Fossi, Via Tornabuoni, Borgo S. Jacopo and Via Borgognissanti.

ALINARI'S, Via Strozzi 19r.
Old prints.

N. BAROCCHI & Son, Lungarno Archibusieri 8 (1st floor) (287637).
Open Mon.–Sat.

BARTOLOZZI, Via Maggio 18 (282905, 215602).
15th/19th-century furniture, works of art. Open Mon.–Sat.; appointment advisable.

Giuseppe BELLINI, Lungarno Soderini 5 (24031).
The doyen of Florentine antique dealers, specializing in bronze and porcelain among many other items; fine paintings, tapestries.

Belli & Della BRUNA, Via Borgognissanti 20r.

CAMICOIOTTI, Via S. Spirito 9 (273137).
Bronze.

CAMPACCI, Via dei Fossi 32r (295181).

Carlo CARNEVALI, Borgo S. Jacopo 64r (295064).
Italian majolica, sculpture. Appointment advisable.

Leone CEI, Via dei Fossi.
Gold inlay work.

DAUPHINE CHESNE, Via Lorenzo il Magnifico 17r (471149).
Italian furniture, ceramics, old masters.

FRASCIONE, Via S. Spirito 19 (283784) and Corso Italia 26 (272283).
Old masters.

Luciano FUNGHINI, Via dei Fossi 32r (294216).
Faience, porcelain.

Maria FUNGHINA, Via dei Fossi 41r (221171).
Antiquarian books, drawings, engravings.

GIORGI, Via Vigna Nuova 51 (211631).
General antiques, paintings. Auctions.

Maria GIORNI, Via Martelli 35r (284967).
Old books, prints.

GUIDI, Via del Porcellana 3 (287010).
Antiques, works of art.

Gustavo MELLI, Ponte Vecchio 44, 46 and 48 (211413).
Silver, jewellery, small antiques.

Galleria OGNISSANTI, Via Borgognissanti 46 (239907).
Italian paintings, majolica, bronze.

PALLESI, Via dei Fossi 7/1 (296916).

ROMANELLI, Lungarno Acciaioli (296047).

Lo SDRUCCIOLO, Via Maggio 13 (296568).

Markets and fairs
Flea market, Piazza del Ciompi.
Open Mon.–Sat.

BIENNIAL ANTIQUES FAIR, Palazzo Strozzi.
Over 100 leading dealers from Italy and as far afield as Thailand and the Philippines. Yearly in mid Sept.

Auctions
GIORGI, Via Vigna Nuova 51 (211631).
See 'Dealers'.

PALAZZO INTERNAZIONALE DELLA VENDITE ALL'ASTA,
Palazzo Corsini, 11 Prato 56 (293000).

Old and modern paintings, prints, stamps, drawings, porcelain, tapestries, silver, carpets. Sales monthly, announced in principal newspapers and periodicals.

Genoa

Dealers
BOSSI, Via Assarotti 7.
Pictures.

Fiera del LIBRO, Via XX Settembre (540197).
Books.

JULIANI, Via Garibaldi 10 (291493).
Silver.

Bottega d'ARTE, Via Garibaldi 1 (297466).
Faience.

ODDONE, Via Rocco Lurago 10 (201439).
Drawings, carpets, paintings, bibelots.

Libreria Leo OLSCHKI, Lungarno della Zecca Vecchia 22 (662475).
Old and rare books, drawings and prints; specialist in books on art, the humanities, Italian literature and science. Open Mon.–Sat. 0900–1300; also afternoons by appointment.

RUBINACCI, Via Garibaldi 8 (298758).
Old masters.

Milan

Dealers
Antique dealers are found along Via S. Spirito, Via Manzoni, Corso Magenta, Via Montenapoleone, Via Durini, Via della Spiga, Via S. Andrea, Via Bigli and Via Borgogna.

ALLE ANTICHI ARMI, Via Bigli 24 (792318).
Arms.

ARS ANTIGUA, Via Mozart 9.

A. BENSI, Via S. Spirito 15 (793007).
Silver, porcelain, 18th-century pictures.

Marco BRUNELLI, Via Montenapoleone 18 (790924).
Italian and French antiques.

CAMPANA, Via Manzoni 43 (664617).
Antiquities.

Galleria CARINI, Via Durini 7 (700270).
19th-century and modern pictures.

CASA d'ARTE, Via Montenapoleone 22 (780348).
Antique silver, jewellery, Russian icons.

Dr Sandro COMOLLI, Via Rossari 5 (701837).
Majolica, weapons, scientific instruments, porcelain, miniatures,
art deco, paintings.

*CO-OPERATIVE ANTIQUARI d'ITALIA, Via Chiaravalle 7
(878940).*
Furniture, paintings, silver, jewellery, ceramics, Auctions.

*FINARTE (Istituto Finanziario per l'Arte), Piazzetta M. Bossi 4
(877041).*
Pictures, porcelain. Auctions.

Galleria d'Arte GERI, Corso Venezia 10 (702939).
Pictures, general antiques. Auctions.

Il MERCANTE DI STAMPE, Corso Venezia 29 (704402).
Antiquarian books, prints.

Galleria SIANESI, Via Durini 25 (700989).
Ancient and modern pictures, contemporary Italian masters.

A. SUBERT, Via della Spiga 22 (799594).
Silver, faience, clocks, watches, scientific items.

TACCANI, Via S. Spirito 24 (781248).
Porcelain, miniatures.

Galleria VITTORIO EMANUELE, Piazza del Duomo.

N. ZECCHINI, Via S. Andrea 14 (704049)
Clocks, watches, 17th/19th-century paintings, miniatures, silver.

Markets and fairs
Flea market (fiera), under the Arengario arcades, nr Cathedral.
Good for old books. Open Fri.–Sat.

FIERA DI SIMGALLIA, Piazza Calatafini.
Everything imaginable for sale. Open Sat.

Spring fair, nr church of S. Guiseppe.
Few antiques. Yearly on 19 March.

FIERA DI SAN AMBOSIO, Piazza S. Ambosio and adjoining streets.
Most important antique fair, selling antique furniture, good porcelain and silver, prints, paintings and, especially, rare books. Yearly on 7 Dec. for 15 days. San Ambosio is the patron saint of Milan.

FIERA DI SANT'ANGELO, Piazza S. Angelo.
Old books and religious items among the birds and flowers. Yearly on 1st Mon. after Easter.

Auctions
CO-OPERATIVE ANTIQUARI d'ITALIA, Via Chiaravalle 7 (878940).
See 'Dealers'.

Galleria d'Arte GERI, Corso Venezia 10(720939).
See 'Dealers'. Monthly catalogues.

FINARTE, Piazzetta M. Bossi 4(877041).
See 'Dealers'.

MANZONI, Via Manzoni 38(701117).

Naples

Dealers
Dealers can be found on Via Constantinopoli, Piazza Carolina, Via Norelli and Trinita Maggiore.

G. de FALCO, Corso Umberto 24 (320736).
Coins, medals.

Libreria DEPERRO, Via dei Mille 17-19 (393687).
Antique books, prints.

Galleria GIOSI, Via Chiatamone 6 (394555).

SEPE, Via S. Maria a Cappella Vecchia 14.
19th-century pictures.

Rome

Dealers
Good streets for antique-hunting are Via del Coronari, Via Bocca di Leone, Via del Babuino, Via Frattina, Via del Corso, Via Margutta, Via Condotti (very expensive and touristy), Via Sistina and Via Mario de Firo Fiori. There are a few shops for prints and maps on Piazza Navona and the streets near it.

APOLLONI, Via del Babuino 133-4 (672429).
Objets d'art, pictures, drawings, silver, contemporary paintings.

Studio Numismatico BARANOWSKY, Piazza Silvestro 13 (6791502).
Roman, Greek and Italian coins.

BULGARI, Via Condotti 9-10 (6793876).
Rare jewellery, antique silver.

I. del BORGO, Via Guilio 8 (659817).
Paintings, porcelain, icons, drawings.

Alberto di CASTRO, Via del Babuino 102 (672269).
Silver, paintings.

LUKACS-DONATH, Via Veneto 183(471252).
Porcelain, faience, silver, small 18th-century antiques.

MORANDOTTI, Corso Vittorio Emanuele 141(651867).

Stampe Artistische PACITTI, Via dei Banchi Vechi 59(650391).
Prints, maps.

PICCIATI Fratelli, Via di Priscilla 41(832696).
Arms. Appointment advisable.

QUERZOLA, Via del Babuino 153(6790568).
Rare books.

SANTAMARIA, Piazza di Spagna 35.
Coins and medals, especially Greek and Roman.

G. TANCA, Salita del Crescenzi 12(655272).
Old prints, drawings, paintings, porcelain, small silver, antique jewellery.

TRADARDI, Via Margutta 99(6792885).
Bronze, paintings.

V and L VENEZIANI, Via Frattini 15, Via Gregoriana 40(675824).
Fine Italian faience.

Markets
Flea market (fiera), Piazza di Porta Portese and Via Portuense, Trastevere district.
Open Sun. to 1200. Beat the asking price down at least four times.

Auctions
L'ANTONINA, Piazza di Spagna 93(6792064, 674009).
Important sales of pictures, furniture, porcelain and objets d'art.

FINARTE, Via Quattro Fontane 20(463564, 482968).

SALGA, Via Due Macelli 70(6791275, 6780750).

Turin

Dealers

Antique dealers abound on Via Giolitti, Piazza Costello, Via Maria Vittoria and Via Bognino.

BELDI, Via Giolitti 1 (546963).
Silver, jewellery.

Galleria COHEN, Via S. Federico 41 (518769).
Rugs.

GABINETTO DELLA STAMPE E ARTE ANTICA, Via Volta 9.
Original engravings, lithographs, drawings by old and modern masters.

Daniele GHIGO, Corso S. Maurizio 52 (831636).
Oriental art, carpets, tapestries.

Libreria Antiquaria PREGLIASCO, Via Accademia Albertina 3 bis (877114).
Rare books, especially in Latin.

Mari RAVIOLA, Corso Vittorio Emanuele 11 (546851).
Greek and Roman antiquities.

C. & G. ROSSI, Piazza S. Carlo 161 (553582).
Important stock of coins, Italian and French pictures, 18th-century silver, paintings, clocks, etc.

SILVESTRI, Via Maria Vittoria 27 (545432).
Paintings.

Libreria Antiquaria Soave, Via Po 48 (878957).
Antiquarian books.

ZURLETTI, Via Roma 358 (510579).
Watches, clocks.

Markets

Flea market (fiera), Porta Palazzo.
Open Sat. morning.

Venice

Dealers

Antique dealers are found in little streets around Piazza S. Marco and behind the Accademia gallery on Calle Larga S. Marco, Via S. Maria del Giglio and Via XXII Marzo.

Giocondo CASSINI, Via XXII Marzo and Piazza S. Marco 2424 (31815).
Antiquarian books.

G. DOMINICI, Calle Larga S. Marco 659 (23892).
Objets d'art, antique silver.

M. S. REDOLFI Maurizio 2663 (26840).
Bronze, porcelain, furniture.

Pietro SCARPA, Ponte S. Moise 2089 (27199).
Specialist in old-master drawings, paintings, Roman glass. Appointment advisable.

Museums

Florence

ARCHEOLOGICAL MUSEUM, Piazza S. Annunziata 9.
Etruscan antiquities.

BARGELLO MUSEUM.
Arms, armour.

BIBLIOTECA ESTENSE.
Antique maps.

CASA BUONAROTTI, Via Ghibellina 70.
Michelangelo's house. Closed Tuesday.

NATIONAL MUSEUM OF SCIENCE HISTORY, Piazza del Giudici 1 (276493).

Optical and astronomical instruments, maps, atlases. Closed Mon.

PALAZZO MEDICI-RICCARDI, Via Cavour 1.
Objects relating to the Medici family.

STIBBERT MUSEUM, Via Stibbert 26 (486049).
Arms, 16th-century armour.

Milan

CASTLE OF THE SFORZAS, Piazza Castello.
Paintings, arms.

MUSEO TEATRALE ALLA SCALA.
Capodimonte porcelain.

PINACOTECA AMBROSIANA, Piazza Pio XI (20123).
Famous collection of Leonardo paintings.

POLDI-PEZZOLI MUSEUM, Via Manzoni 12.
Botticellis, Tiepolos, 15th-18th century Murano glass, antique Persian carpets.

Naples

NATIONAL ARCHEOLOGICAL MUSEUM, Via Museo 18 (340418).
Roman and Greek glass, silver, jewellery, bronzes from Pompeii.

MUSEO NAZIONALE DI CAPODIMONTE (410801/81).
Arms, armour, superb paintings, Capodimonte and other porcelain.

Rome

MUSEO NAZIONALE DI VILLA GIULIA, Piazzale di Villa Giulia 9 (350719).
Etruscan ceramics, bronzes, terracotta.

MUSEO NUMISMATICO DELLA ZECCA, Via Principe Umberto 4.
Coins.

VATICAN MUSEUMS.
World's largest collection of antiquities, galleries of maps and tapestries, the Raphael Rooms, a 25-room art gallery, the Sistine Chapel ceiling and *Last Judgment* by Michelangelo.

CASTEL SANT'ANGELO.
Weapons, armour.

Turin

BISCARETTI AUTO MUSEUM, Corso Unita d'Italia 40 (677666).

ARMERIA REALE (Royal Armoury).
Arms, armour.

MUSEO EGIZIA, Via Accademia della Scienze 6 (44091).
The second most important museum of Egyptian art in the world.

Venice

PALAZZO DUCALE.
Arms, armour.

BIBLIOTECA MARCIANA.
Maps.

Further reading

Pollard, Graham, *Renaissance Medals* (London: Phaidon, 1967)
Rackham, Bernard, *Italian Majolica* (London: Faber, 1964)
Stazzi, Francesco, *Italian Porcelain* (London: Weidenfeld, 1967)

Cream pan of tin-enamelled earthenware, marked with the monogram AK in blue. Delft, late 17th century

9
The
Netherlands

Introduction

Generally speaking, the best countries for antiques are those which have nurtured a prosperous merchant class who could afford to buy silver, glass, porcelain, books and pictures for their homes, and where these accumulated treasures have not been dispersed by war or revolution. Although the Low Countries have been a battlefield many times in their history, the bourgeoisie has remained stable and wealthy enough to sustain the principle, and the Netherlands is a particularly good example, with its long period of maritime power and rich trading empire in the East supplying the comfortable existence of the burghers in their gabled mansions in Amsterdam, Utrecht and The Hague.

. Although no longer the bargain-hunting paradise for foreigners that it was a few years ago, the Netherlands remains immensely important in the international antique trade, as witnessed by the 1974 takeover by Sotheby-Parke Bernet of the Amsterdam auction house Mak van Waay. (Christie's of London also holds sales in Amsterdam). In 1975 the first International Fine Art Dealers' Fair took place at Maastricht, and the annual summer Delft Antique Fair has long been an event of major importance on the art world calendar.

Like neighbouring Belgium, the Netherlands experienced a great cultural explosion during the rule of the Dukes of Burgundy in the 15th century, when the Flemish school of painting was founded with the painter brothers Hubert and Jan van Eyck. The subsequent roll of Dutch painters lies at the very heart of North European civilization: Brueghel, Hieronymus Bosch, Frans Hals, Rembrandt, Rubens, Albert Cuyp, Jacob van Ruysdael, Jan Vermeer, Pieter de Hoogh, van Gogh and dozens of minor masters. In 1600, with a population of only a million, the Dutch were the most prosperous people in Europe and the money markets of Europe were centred on Amsterdam. Few countries have matched the concentration of artistic genius which flowered in the century that followed.

Besides producing some of the world's greatest painters, the Netherlands was also at various times foremost in the arts of engraving, map-making and producing finely-bound books and made silver and ceramics of outstanding quality. Cultural life was intensely regional; each province had its university of distinction (none prouder than Leiden, the scholarly town where Rembrandt was born), and such artefacts as silver, clocks and ceramics differed in style from area to area, as did the various fields of printing. The Netherlands produced especially fine landscape painters, the art being introduced in Amsterdam by the Flemish painter Vinckeboons (1576–1629). By 1609 the seven predominantly Protestant provinces in the north, known as the Dutch Republic or Holland, had finally gained their independence from the 12 Catholic provinces in the south. This resulted in the decline of religious and mythological pictures and the development of small paintings for the home, including landscapes, marine painting, domestic scenes and interiors.

The provincial antique shops, are not necessarily the very best hunting grounds for regional art today as most objects of importance have gravitated to the cities. In Amsterdam the main concentration of antique shops is to be found in the street called Rokin; other streets with dealers include Spiegelstraat, Singel, Damrak, Kalverstraat, Prinsengracht, Prins Hendriklaan, Hoofstraat, Leidistraat, Keizersgracht and Utrechtsestraat. The weekly flea market on Waterlooplein, though fun, does not usually yield anything of real collecting interest, but Amsterdam's galleries and museums provide an unrivalled appreciation course in Dutch art, and for book and print lovers there is no more agreeable city for browsing. In The Hague the better-quality antique shops are found in the Denneweg, the Noordeinde and nearby streets. In Leiden the Saturday market includes at least one antique dealer, and the flea market in the Havermarkt at Arnhem can be a source of real bargains on summer Saturdays.

The Netherlands' leading antiques periodical, *Antiek,* appears 10 times a year and contains summaries in English.

Specialities

Books

The Low Countries have always been a centre of great importance for the antiquarian book trade; the region was unrivalled for its magnificent book production in the 16th century and Antwerp was the first major centre for printing houses. Book-binding was also a famous Dutch art in the 17th century, characteristic bindings being highly embossed on silvered or gilded leather. Albertus Magnus of Amsterdam (1642–89) was a distinguished name, and the workshops of H. le Maire (Amsterdam) and J. D. de Swart (The Hague) were already well established in the 17th century. The early 20th century saw some excellent private-press books produced.

Some Amsterdam book dealers are: Scheltema & Holkema, Albert de Lange (with a big foreign-language department), Schroder & Dupont and de Slegte. There is also an antiquarian books centre at N. Z. Voorburgwal 264 with a fine collection of books, maps and engravings, and several shops near the University gates sell books, prints and maps.

Cast iron

Cast ironwork was a typical art form of the Low Countries, though posing obvious difficulties for travelling collectors. Leading dealers are Becker and Massee both in Amsterdam, and Dirven in Eindhoven.

Clocks

Bracket and long-case clocks were made, many with the unique 'double striking' system evolved in the Netherlands and decorated with much inlay work. Zaandam north of Amsterdam was a prolific area, and decorative clocks were made in Friesland.

Drawings

Drawings were an outstanding feature of the golden age of Dutch art. Fine collections can be seen in the print rooms of the Rijksmuseum (Amsterdam) Boymans Museum (Rotterdam),

Teyler Museum (Leiden) and Groningen Museum—particularly for Rembrandt drawings. Modern (19th- and 20th-century) drawings are well represented in the Gemeente Museum (The Hague) and Stedelijk Museum (Amsterdam).

Glass

Glass-making was introduced to the Netherlands by Italians who worked in Antwerp and other centres. The first glass kiln was in Middleburg around 1580, and by 1611 there were 10 in Amsterdam and the quality was said to rival that of Italy. Early 17th-century Dutch glass had obvious Venetian influences; later a distinctive Dutch style emerged.

The Dutch adapted the Italian art of glass-engraving to a high degree of artistry, on green-and-white glass *Roemers,* flute glasses and goblets; the poet Anna Roemer, an amateur glass artist, made notable engravings of flowers and insects. There are fine collections at the Rijksmuseum (Amsterdam) Boymans Museum (Rotterdam) and Gemeente Museum (The Hague). Well-known engravers included W. van Heemskerk, C. J. Meyer, W. Mooleyser, Marinus van Gelde, Stamproen and de l'Hormel. Later engravers included S. J. Sang (fl. 1750) and a Leiden craftsman known simply by his initials, W. O. R. At the start of the 18th century diamond-point stippling became a distinctive art form; artists using this technique included F. Greenwood, A. Schouman, G. van Hoolart, J. van der Blyck and D. Wolff of The Hague, to whom a lot of unsigned work has been ascribed.

In the 17th century, at the height of the Netherlands' silver craftsmanship, there was a vogue for ornamental silver-mounted glasses which could be taken apart for cleaning. These are often seen in still-life pictures of the time.

At the beginning of the 20th century decorative glass was designed for the Leerdam factory by D. Copier and C. Lebeau (after 1920, Lebeau settled in Czechoslovakia). De Bazel and Berlage are other modern names to note.

Paintings

Dutch old masters, of course, are good buys, also 19th-century landscapes which became so overpriced in the UK as a result of big investment buyers like Jim Slater. Van Gogh, first of the

Dutch modern masters, was followed by the Amsterdam impressionist school founded by Breitner and Israels. Art nouveau painters included Jan Toorop and Johan Thron Prikker; then came the Bergen school with Hendrik Chabot, Kees van Dongen, Jan Sluyters, Piet Mondriaan and Leo Gestel. This developed into a stark cubist school known as *De Stijl,* practised by Mondriaan and Theo van Doesburg.

Pewter

Pewter was a speciality of all the Low Countries, characterized in the Netherlands by sturdiness and simplicity of design along with brass and copperwork. It is important to be careful in distinguishing between old and new—some modern pewter is made from the original 17th-century moulds. Antique kitchen moulds are popular with local collectors and visitors alike.

Pottery and porcelain

Delft ware—the tin-glazed earthenware originally produced to imitate the first imported Chinese porcelain early in the 17th century—was first made only in blue and white, with much use of Chinese motifs, but later in other colours. Blue-dash chargers are commonly found—large dishes with blue splashes around the edges. Apothecary jars are also popular with collectors. The most successful of the Delft factories were those of the van Eenhoorn, Hoppesteyn, Kocks and Fictoors families. Potteries were set up by Delft-trained craftsmen at The Hague, Rotterdam, Schiedam and Arnhem, the latter being the only one with its own mark, a rooster. In the 17th century there were about thirty factories making Delft ware, but many were put out of business by the later success of English stoneware. Now only the Royal Factory at Delft survives, making Porcelain Fles in which many of the new designs are identical with the old.

Delft earthenware varies enormously in kind and in quality. To obtain an overall view, collectors should see the large collections at the Rijksmuseum (Amsterdam), Gemeente Museum (The Hague), Arnhem Museum (Arnhem) and Musée du Cinq-uantenaire (Brussels). Genuine old Delft ware can be picked out by its colour, fineness of glaze, intricacy of design and skill of execution. Leading dealers include van Schraften in Delft, Hart in

Amsterdam, and Aardewerk and van Kleef in The Hague. The old blue-and-white Maastricht pottery, no longer made, is worth looking for, with its genre pictures of Dutch life.

Around 1750 attempts were made to reproduce Saxon porcelain and some dinner, tea and coffee services were made at Loosdrecht, Weesp and The Hague. Then the industry moved to Amsterdam (Amstel porcelain). Biscuit porcelain imported from Germany and Tournai in Belgium was decorated at The Hague.

Wall tiles of earthenware painted in many colours and then tin-glazed—the majolica technique—were a great Dutch speciality, a favourite decorative theme being fruit such as grapes and oranges. The best were made in and around Rotterdam. Rijkers in Amsterdam has a stock of more than 5000 tiles in floral, ornithological and maritime themes. The Lambert van Meerten Museum in Delft has the most complete collection of painted tiles and early Delft ware.

In the 19th century, after a fallow period, Dutch ceramics revived with Porcelain Fles in Delft attempting reproductions of early designs and introducing new ones. In 1884 the Rosenburg factory was opened at The Hague where T. Colenbrander made vividly-coloured designs until 1890 when he moved to factories in Gouda and Arnhem. At the turn of the century the big name in tiles was Toorop, and good ceramics of other kinds were designed by C. Lanooy, Bert Nienhuis, G. de Blancke and M. A. Zaalberg. A revival of white Delft ware was introduced in 1936.

Prints and Maps

The Netherlands has a great tradition of woodcut-engraving, originating in Utrecht at the end of the 15th century, Gouda and Haarlem. Jacob Bellaert of Haarlem moved to Antwerp in the late 15th century, where his work had great influence; other outstanding artists were: Jacob Cornelisz van Oostzanen of Amsterdam, who improved on Bellaert's technique; Cornelis Anthonisz, his pupil, whose style was more mannered; Jan Swart; and Lucas van Leiden the painter, who engraved on copper as well. Rembrandt in his etchings done after 1639 became one of the greatest graphic masters.

Hendrik Goltzius was one of the greatest Dutch engravers. His pupils included Pieter Soutman (1580–1657), noted for his reproductions of Rubens paintings using a combination of etching and engraving, and among Soutman's followers was Jonas Suyderhoef (1613–89), best known for engravings of Frans Hals portraits. The brothers Boetius and Schelte à Bolsward, who worked in Antwerp in the mid 17th century, were particularly noted for their reproductions of Rubens's landscapes. The technique of mezzotint, which made possible better reproductions of oil-paintings with their full tonal values, was discovered by Ludwig van Siegen of Utrecht; other skilful exponents included Jacob and Wallerant Vaillant, Jacob Gole, Blooteling and Cornelis Troost.

In the second half of the 18th century a collector named Ploos van Amstel made fine aquatint copies of coloured drawings. Artists who worked in lithograph included A Allebe (1838–1927), Jan Veth (1864–1925), H. J. Haverman (1858–1928), S. Moulijn (d.1930) and T. van Hoytema (1836–1917). R. Roland Holst (1867–1939) worked in a stylized manner and was noted for his poster designs. Probably the outstanding graphic artist of his generation was Marius Bauer (1867–1932), who produced a series of political lithographs for the weekly *De Kroniek*. Later etchers included, most notably, A. P. Derkzen van Angeren, (b. 1878), who did river views of great beauty, and G. Haverkamp (1872–1926). The mid century revival of the Dutch engraving tradition was led by P. Dupont, with portraits, views of Paris and pictures of farm animals.

The woodcut tradition continued into the 20th century with names such as J. G. Veldheer, W. O. J. Nieuwenkamp (stylized, art nouveau, mainly tropical landscapes), Jan Mankes, Dirk Nyland, J. F. E. Klooster and M. C. Escher. There are several distinguished present-day artists working in woodcut (Bulder, Mauve, Rueter and van Gelder), as well as lithographers and etchers.

In its heyday of maritime power the Netherlands produced some of the earliest and finest masters of map-engraving. Probably the finest atlas of all time was that engraved by the Blaeu family of Amsterdam in 1662; called the *Atlas Major*, it comprised 596 maps in 12 volumes, and a set changed hands recently for £30 000. Abraham Ortelius, Dutch contemporary of Gerard Mercator, produced a map of North America in 1573 depicting California correctly as a peninsula—many later maps still incorrectly showed it as an island.

The antique book centre at O. Z. Voorburgwal 264, in

Amsterdam, has a fine collection of maps and engravings, and several bookshops near the University gates sell prints and maps. The Rijksmuseum in Amsterdam has probably the world's finest collection of prints, especially etchings.

Silver

Dutch silver tended to be heavy but was of impressive dignity and workmanship; 17th century work is similar to that of Augsburg. The silver content was guaranteed by the hallmarking system: the lion rampant meant 925 parts sterling silver, the lion passant 835 parts (with a greater alloy content—this was generally employed in Europe for articles in daily household use). Until 1812 every city had its heraldic-style hallmark: three crosses denoted Amsterdam, a stork The Hague. Then in 1814 a standardized system was introduced throughout the Netherlands, after which all Dutch pieces had to bear the head of Minerva, the year, the hallmark and the maker's mark.

First established at Utrecht in the late 14th century, Dutch silvercraft had flowered into a style of rich renaissance ornament by the 16th century. Some fine examples can be seen in the Rijksmuseum in Amsterdam. However, the great national period was the 17th century with its emphasis on embossed work, and many cups and dishes from this period have survived, made in Amsterdam, Alkmaar, Delft, Haarlem, The Hague, Utrecht, Leeuwarden and elsewhere. As the Dutch merchant classes grew more prosperous silver grew more baroque, and the van Vianen family of Utrecht made particularly fine work of this type. Some of the work of Christiaen van Vianen (the son) is in the Victoria and Albert Museum in London. Other makers associated with the baroque style were: Johannes Lutma of Amsterdam (1585–1669), some of whose best work is in the Rijksmuseum; H. C. Brechtel, Anton Grill and G. Vuysting of The Hague; and P. Groen of Delft. In the 18th century the spread of mercantile wealth caused table silver to come widely into use and Dutch silver craftsmen then began to follow fashionable French styles.

During the 16th and 17th centuries a famous school of silversmiths worked in Friesland, where pieces of typical Frisian silver can still be bought. A characteristic vessel called a 'brandy bowl', resembling the two-handled Scottish 'quaich', was usually richly engraved. The museum in Leeuwarden has a good collection of old Frisian silver, as does the Rijksmuseum. Frisian makers to note included Rintie Jansz and the van der Lilie family of Leeuwarden, and Claes Jansz Baardt of Bolsward who specialized in fine flower ornament. Old Frisian watch chains with massive seal fobs may be an interesting buy.

The trade

Amsterdam

Dealers

Jacob AALDERINK, Spiegelgracht 7 and 15 (230211).
Chinese, Japanese and other Oriental works of art.

David R. ARONSON, Nieuwe Spiegelstr 39 (233103).
Antique furniture, Delft ware, Chinese porcelain, silver, jewellery, clocks.

J. F. BEEKHUIZEN, Nieuwe Spiegelstr 49 (63912).
Pewter, bronze, furniture, 16th- and 18th-century sculpture.

Jan BECKER, Willemsparkweg 117 (729865).
Leading dealer in cast ironwork.

BODES & BODE, Nieuwe Spiegelstr 30 (231310).
Antique jewellery, pearls, silver, precious stones; classical, primitive and Oriental art.

Kunsthandel P. de BOER, Herengracht 512 (236849).
15th- and 17th-century old-master paintings. Open Mon.–Fri. 1000–1700; Sat. 1000–1300; also by appointment.

Paul CASSIRER & Co., Keizersgracht 109 (248337).
Paintings and drawings by old and modern masters.

J. DENIJS, Leidsegracht 48 (236431) and Nieuwe Spiegelstr 29 and 32.
Antique furniture, silver, porcelain, jewellery.

DOUWES Gebr, Rokin 46 (236208).
Important 16th- and 18th-century Dutch and Flemish old masters, both paintings and drawings; Barbizon school, impressionists.

ERASMUS Antiquariant en Boekhandel, Spui 2 (230535).
Antiquarian books.

van GENDT & Co., Keizersgracht 610 (234107).
15th/16th-century books, philosophy books, illustrated books, manuscripts. Auctions.

Jacob GIELING, Spiegelgracht 7 (232064).
Oriental porcelain, sculpture, bronze, prints, books.

Mathieu HART, Rokin 122 (231658).
Furniture, clocks, porcelain (especially Delft), pewter, copper, brass.

Bernard HOUTHAKKER, Rokin 98 (233939).
Old-master Dutch and Flemish paintings, prints, books.

Roel HOUWINK, Nieuwe Spiegelstr 31 (221774).
17th-century oak, bronze, pewter, prints, books. Open Mon.–Sat. 0900–1800; also by appointment.

M. ISRAEL, N. Z. Voorburgwal 264 (just behind the Royal Palace).
Fine collection of books, maps and engravings in a 16th-century house.

JUGENDSTIL WATERLOO, Berenstr 4 (238317).
Art nouveau.

D. W. KINEBANIAN, Heiligeweg 35 (67019).
Antique carpets and tapestries.

A. D. KRUYVER, Prinsengracht 578 (247691).
Dutch copper, brass, Bohemian glass, opaline bronzes. Open 0900–1700; also by appointment.

Albert de LANGE, Damrak 62.
Books, especially foreign-language.

Hans MARCUS, Keizersgracht 574 (234544).
Old maps and prints, drawings, etchings, lithographs, finely-illustrated books. Also in Düsseldorf.

J. J. MASSEE, Nieuwe Spiegelstr 34 (253371).
Leading dealer in cast ironwork.

Joseph MORPURGO, Rokin 108 (235883).
Chinese and Continental porcelain, glass, Delft ware, 17th/18th-century furniture, silver, sculpture, bronze, jewellery, clocks, Asiatic art, prints, books.

NIJSTAD Antiquairs Lochem, Rokin 86 (223830).
Silver, glass, 17th/18th-century paintings, sculpture, tapestries, Chinese and European porcelain. Open Mon. 1400–1630; Tues.–Fri. 1000–1630; appointment advisable.

T. F. NOLF, Herengracht 82 (64555).
Nautical instruments, mercurial barometers, chronometers, etc. Appointment necessary.

PREMSELA & HAMBURGER, Rokin 120 (249688).
Antique silver, renaissance jewellery, objets d'art.

H. M. J. RIJKERS, Nieuwe Spiegelstr 64 (230832).
Ceramics, including over 5000 tiles in floral, ornithological and maritime themes.

SCHELTEMA & HOLKEMA, Rokin 74.
Books.

H. SCHLICHTE BERGEN, P. C. Hooftstr 53 (793005).
Dutch and Flemish old-master paintings, prints, books, sculpture, bronze.

SCHRODER & DUPONT, Keizersgracht 516.
Books.

Jacques SCHULMAN, Keizersgracht 448 (233380).
Coins, medals, decorations; Egyptian, Greek and Roman antiquities. Open Mon.–Fri. 0900–1730; Sat. 0900–1400.

J. de SLEGTE, Kalverstr 11-13.
Books, mainly secondhand and remaindered stock, but sells collectors' items upstairs.

Bernhard STODEL, Rokin 70 (231692).
Mainly 18th-century antique furniture, Chinese and Continental porcelain, silver, clocks.

A. VECHT, Rokin 30 (234748).
Medieval, renaissance and Oriental sculptures and works of art: fine glass, Delft ware.

Geerd WITNEN, Spiegelpleintje 1 (225681).
Antique clocks.

Markets
Flea market, Waterlooplein.
Little of real collecting interest. Open weekly.

Auctions
CHRISTIE'S, Singer Museum, Larem (just outside Amsterdam).
General antiques and Dutch items. Sales 3–4 times yearly. Based in London.

van GENDT & Co., Keizersgracht 610 (234107).
See 'Dealers'.

SOTHEBY MAK VAN WAAY (Jan Pieter Glerum), Rokin 102 (246215).
Wide range of fine-art objects. Sales 3–4 times year, which last about a fortnight each.

Arnhem
Markets
Flea market, Havermarkt.
Can be a source of real bargains. Open Sat. in summer.

Breda
Galerie des ARTS, Raadhuisstr 28 (52291).

Pewter, bronze, iron, glass, porcelain, sculpture. Open 0900–1800; also by appointment.

La CHARRETTE, Baronielaan 29 (45672).
Pewter, copper, furniture, porcelain, paintings.

J. M. KAROLY, Torenstr 23 (42726).
Antiques, curiosities.

KUYPER & Zn, Haagdijk 64-6 (37281).
China, silver, furniture. Open Mon.–Sat. 0900–1800; also by appointment (always advisable).

Theo PELS, Ulvenhoutselaan 147 (51765).
Pewter, bronze, iron, oak furniture. Open 0900–1800; also by appointment.

M. H. SCHREURS, Catharinastr 36-42 (39024).
Antique clocks. Repairs and restorations.

Delft

ACADEMIA, Oude Delft 101-3 (23426)
Books on mathematics, physics, chemistry and art; old prints.

W. van BOKHOVEN, Oude Delft 226 (124427).
17th/18th-century oak furniture.

't BROUWERHUYS, Voldersgracht 29 (140716).
Objets d'art.

Galerie FELIUS, Markt 73 (30445).
Primitive art.

van SCHRAFTEN, Vrouwenregt 10 (126193).
Old Delft pottery.

Fairs
DELFT ANTIQUE FAIR
Fair of major importance at which every exhibitor must be a member of the Dutch Antique Dealers' Association and every

piece must be vetted by two independent juries. Yearly in summer.

Eindhoven

A. H. BIES, Boschdijk 221 (431377).
Dutch and Flemish 17th-century paintings, Dutch romantic paintings. Open Mon.–Sat. 0900–1800; also by appointment.

J. DIRVEN, Keizersgracht 15 (24889).
Early furniture, sculpture, ivories, enamel, pewter, glass. Open Mon. 1400–1800; Tues.–Fri. 0900–1800 Sat. 0900–1230.

Dick van LEEUWEN, Gestelsestr 81 (29410).
Metalware

Galerie TIEMAN, Kerkstr (437377).
17th-century paintings, 15th/16th-century sculptures, bronze, ivories, pewter, Limoges. Open Mon. 1300–1730; Tues.–Sat. 1100–1730; also by appointment.

The Hague

A. AARDEWERK, Jan van Nassaustr 76 (240987).
Fine antique silver, Delft ware, Chinese and Continental porcelain, clocks, glass, jewellery, furniture.

G. CRAMER, Oude Kunst, Javastr 38 (630758).
Dutch and Flemish old-master paintings, prints, books.

Meijer ELTE B.V., Korte Poten 13 (639781).
Rare early illustrated books, fine bindings, atlases, maps, drawings, prints.

Galerie HOOGSTEDER, Surinamestr 26 (601620).
Dutch and Flemish old masters, prints, books.

van KLEEF, Noordeinde 152a (605881).
General antiques (especially 18th-century), pictures, large stock of Delft ware.

S. van LEEUWEN, Noordeinde 164a (605741).
Furniture, china, glass, clocks.

W. STRUYK & Zn, Kazernestr 148 (605554).
Porcelain, furniture.

C. J. J. WEEGENAAR, Frederikstr 12 (462874).
Antique furniture, porcelain, sculpture, bronze, clocks, pewter.

Rotterdam

Jac BARENDSE, van Speijkstr 145-7 (361019, 148604).
General antiques, furniture, porcelain, pewter, bronze.

Kunsthandel C.P.A. & G. R. CASTENDIJK, Mecklenburglaan 51 (138937).
Porcelain, furniture, sculpture, bronze, prints, books, paintings.

E. van DAM, Henegouwerlaan 34 (125556).
Fine 17th/18th-century furniture, 17th-century Dutch seascapes, objets d'art.

Charles van der HEYDEN, Westersingel 21 (360342).
16th/18th-century furniture, objets d'art, mirrors, clocks, prints, books, tapestries, pewter. Open 1000–1730; also by appointment (always advisable)

F. KATS, Zwaerdecroonstr 26 (764475).
Antique clocks and watches.

A. KOEKKOEK, Mathenesserlaan 171 (363642).
Chinese and Japanese porcelain and faience.

Utrecht

Muzuikantiquariaat JOACHIMSTHAL, Wolter Heukelslaan 59, PO Box 2238 (510715).
Musical scores (1st editions), musicological literature, prints, manuscripts. Open Mon.–Sat.; appointment necessary.

F. KLEIJN, Oudkerkhof 38 (310856)
Pictures, sculpture.

G. A. LISMAN, *Vismarkt 10(22758)*.
General antiques.

A. D. M. SMULDERS, *Vismarkt 3(313533)*.
Sculpture, furniture, pewter, copper.

Museums

Amsterdam

RIJKSMUSEUM.
Major collection of fine arts, including Dutch silver, drawings, Dutch glass, a large collection of Delft ware and probably the world's finest collection of prints (especially etchings).

STEDELIJK MUSEUM
Good collection of 19th/20th-century drawings.

Arnhem

ARNHEM MUSEUM.
Large collection of Delft ware.

Delft

LAMBERT VAN MEERTEN MUSEUM
The most complete collection of early Delft ware and painted tiles, housed in a timbered mansion.

Doorn

MANOR CASTLE
Home of Kaiser Wilhelm II in exile, now preserved as a museum.

Gouda

DE MORIAAN PIPE MUSEUM
Clay pipes dating from 1617, tobacco jars and other smokers'

items. Gouda was the Netherlands' chief pipe-making city in the 17th century.

Groningen

GRONINGEN MUSEUM
Fine collection of drawings, particularly by Rembrandt.

The Hague

GEMEENTE MUSEUM, Stadhouderslaan 41.
A fine collection of antique musical instruments, ceramics (including a large collection of Delft ware), drawings (especially of 19th and 20th centuries) and paintings (including the definitive collection of works by Mondrian). Open Mon.–Fri. 1000-1700.

NETHERLANDS POSTAL MUSEUM, Zeestr 82.
A 'must' for stamp collectors. Open Mon.–Fri. 1000–1700; Sat. 1000–1300; Sun. 1300–1700.

ROYAL COIN CABINET, Zeestr 71b.
Complete collection of Dutch coins; also foreign coins, and medals. Open Mon.–Fri. 1000–1300, 1400–1700.

'sHertogenbosch

CENTRAL NOORDBRABANTS MUSEUM.
Large collection of coins, weapons, maps and manuscripts. Open afternoons.

Leeuwarden

LEEUWARDEN MUSEUM
Dutch silver, including a good collection of old Frisian silver.

Leiden

*RIJKSMUSEUM VOOR DE GESCHIEDENIS DER NA-
TUURWETENSCHAPPEN (History of Science Museum), Steenstr 1.*
Scientific instruments, including early globes, microscopes, themometers, etc.

TEYLER MUSEUM
Good collection of drawings and prints.

Rotterdam

BOYMANS MUSEUM.
Fine collections of drawings and Dutch glass.

MARITIME MUSEUM.
Ship models, maps, prints, globes.

Schiedam

P. MELCHERS SPIRITS COLLECTION, Langehaven 74.
A unique collection of over 5000 miniature bottles of spirits and liquors from more than 50 countries. Schiedam is a well-known gin-producing centre.

Further reading

Ash, Douglas, *Dutch Silver* (Cambridge: Golden Head Press, 1965)
Dooijes, D., *The Dutch Poster* (Amsterdam, 1968)
Gans, M. H. and Klinkhamer, T. M. Duyvene de Wit, *Dutch Silver* (London: Faber, 1961).
Imber, Diana, *Collecting Delft* (London: Arco, 1968)
Jonge, C. H. de, *Delft Ceramics* (London: Pall Mall, 1970)
Jonge, C. H. de, *Dutch Tiles* (London: Pall Mall, 1970).

This little carved and polychrome figure of a female saint holding a heavy book under her arm stares realistically out of glass eyes – a typical example of Portuguese church art

10
Portugal

Introduction

The political revolution in Portugal which started in 1974 has resulted in considerable changes in the art market in that country. From the visitor's point of view, customs attitudes towards the taking out of works of art and antiques have become much tougher since many wealthy Portuguese fled the country taking assets in the form of antiques such as coins and silver. It is always advisable now to get a receipt for everything one buys. On the other hand, for the same reason antiques are cheap now in Portugal, especially silver, the characteristic gilded and polychromed wood-carvings, Chinese export porcelain—a legacy of Portugal's imperial days —coins and pottery.

In the 16th century Lisbon was one of the richest and most beautiful cities in Europe, and as the capital of an Eastern empire it had a prosperous merchant class with the resources to patronize artists and to furnish their homes with fine things. The Portuguese were the first Europeans to trade in China, which accounts for the large quantity of Chinese export porcelain still to be found in Portugal's antique shops. The first blue-and-white ware was made especially for exporting to Portugal and the earliest examples in Portuguese ownership date back to 1541.

Portuguese painting never achieved the greatness of the schools in neighbouring Spain, but it was important on its own account by the 15th century. The discovery of gold and diamond mines in Brazil meant that by the middle of the 18th century Portuguese royalty was able to indulge in patronage of the arts on a grand scale. Portuguese kings imported Italian artists of the rococo school to design and decorate palaces and churches, and the rococo spirit was very influential in Portugal at this time, affecting the design of everything from silver to sculpture. Much of this fine work, however, was destroyed in the devastating earthquake of November 1755, which demolished two-thirds of Lisbon.

Lisbon, Braga and Oporto were lively artistic centres in the 18th century—Oporto in particular being a focus of painting and sculpture. Perhaps the best painter of the end of the 18th century was Francisco Vieira, who became known as Vieira Portuense; born in Oporto in 1755 he worked in Rome with another distinguished compatriot, Domingos Antonio de Segeuira. Portuense also worked for a time as a designer for the famous Bodoni printing-press in Verona, and in London, where he exhibited at the Royal Academy in 1789 and 1790.

Portugal's main contribution to the mainstream of European art has been in the decorative arts of the 18th century, particularly in carved woodwork and painted ceramic tiles, known as *azulejos*, a tradition shared with Spain. Silver was also a notable field of craftsmanship, especially in the early 16th and 18th centuries, and gun-making achieved considerable heights, though overshadowed by the Spanish tradition in arms and armour.

Specialities

Carvings

Gilded and polychromed wood-carvings were among Portugal's greatest contributions to the European artistic heritage. Church woodwork from the renaissance survives and collectors can find baroque wooden angels and polychrome statues.

Coins

Portuguese 18th-century gold coins slumped in value by 60 per cent in 1975 because Portuguese collectors were frantically selling what they could outside the country in the wake of the political upheavals. By the end of 1975 Portuguese gold was selling at barely 30 per cent above its melt worth and the field was grossly undervalued. In any case, coins without effigies such as the Portuguese gold issues are always less attractive to collectors and thus cheaper, than coins bearing the heads of kings and queens.

Firearms

Portugal has a little-known tradition in fine gun-making centred on the late 17th and early 18th centuries. The weapons were mostly flintlock or snaphaunce, rarely come on the market and are indistinguishable to most eyes from the better-known products of the Spanish workshops. Sotheby-Parke Bernet recently published a new translation of a rare 18th-century treatise called *Espingarda Perfeyta (The Perfect Gun)*, which with its diagrams and drawings from the original plus photographs of weapons in the translators' collections is expected to spark new interest in this little-explored field of the armourer's art.

Porcelain and Pottery

Chinese export porcelain is the big buy in Portugal, for reasons outlined in the 'Introduction', and many Lisbon dealers specialize in this ware. After the immense popularity of the first imports from China by Portuguese traders local faience factories attempted to cash in on the trend, but this was followed in the 17th century by an increasingly national flavour in motifs. The result was an attractive hybrid product unique in Europe at that time, a full century before the introduction of Delft ware.

Lisbon, Coimbra, Braga and Oporto were leading faience centres. The Royal Rato factory (1767–1835) was one of those which tried to copy the Chinese imports; it also copied or adapted patterns from French, English and Saxon porcelain. The mark was FR with the monogram TB or SA for Thomas Brunetto or Sebastian de Almeida, and tableware was made based on forms predominant in silver of the time, painted in the Turin or Savona style. Botanical motifs were popular, also coats of arms.

Majolica in the Ming style was produced at Lisbon and Braga in the form of dishes, vases, bottles, ewers and chemists' jars. Another notable faience manufacturer was the Bica do Sapato factory in Lisbon, founded at the end of the 18th century. An interesting collection of its ware can be seen at the Museu Nacional de Arte Antiga in Lisbon. Oporto ceramics from the late

18th to mid 19th centuries were of high quality and much was exported to Brazil. Oporto was also a great centre for the import and sale of the popular Staffordshire creamware and Queen's ware.

Portuguese faience is not generally regarded as an artistic achievement on a par with Portugal's ceramic tiles or wood-carvings, but it had an appealing freshness and down-to-earth quality. Pottery produced in the south of Portugal had a dense colouring; that of Lisbon was characterized by a more refined type of decoration, that of Oporto by delicate tints, and that of the Minho district by an infectious gaiety. At the time of its best flowering the British colony in Portugal—mainly connected with the port-wine trade—had the foresight to collect a good deal of the native pottery.

The Vista Alegre factory near Aveiro, founded in 1820, is still in production and has a showroom in Lisbon and its own museum.

Scientific Instruments

Portugal is a prolific source of compasses, sextants and navigational instruments of all kinds, no doubt as a result of its golden age of exploration and navigation in the 15th and 16th centuries.

Silver

Some magnificent silver was made around 1500, some of which survives in the form of ewers, dishes and chargers, but very little outside museums. Some of the best Portuguese silver was made in the 18th century, much of it following English neoclassical designs from 1750–1800, though before that the rococo designs typical of 18th-century Portugal were more apparent. In the 19th century there was a period of distinctively Portuguese work in the 1860s and 1870s. Silver dealers in Portugal are still well stocked with French and English silver of the 18th century and Oporto is a good centre. Wrought-gold work was a Portuguese speciality—see the Cathedral treasures in Coimbra and in museums in Lisbon and Oporto.

Tapestries

Arriolos carpets, originally woollen embroideries based on Oriental rug designs, are being produced today at the Portuguese tapestry studio from both old and contemporary designs. Tapestries are still widely used in interior decoration.

Tiles

Tin-glazed ceramic tiles of Arabic origin, called *azulejos*, were the most notable product of the Portuguese potter's art. They have been called 'the poor man's art' and originally came from Andalucia at the end of the 15th century. Examples of the 16th century had designs in relief, often geometrical in pattern, and these were followed by some splendid designs of garlands and flowers (the Fronteira Palace in Lisbon has some of the most beautiful). Tiles from the 18th century can be distinguished by their use of landscape decoration, biblical or sporting scenes. Lisbon was the main centre of production (polychrome tiles were used in thousands to rebuild the city after the earthquake of 1755) with lesser factories at Coimbra and Oporto. Originally made in as many as six colours, they became limited to blue and white in the late 17th century—hence the name *azulejos*—as part of the craze for Chinese ware.

The trade

Lisbon

Dealers

Elena ADORNO, Rua de S. Bernardo 16 (663376).
Furniture, paintings, old jewellery, Chinese export porcelain.

ALMEIDA Basto, Rua do Ouro 52 (30309).
Coins.

Pedro A. BAPTISTA (Galerias Star), Ave Sidónio Pais 4 (539021).
Antique silver and jewellery.
Also in Oporto and Praia da Rocha.

Salgueiro BAPTISTA, Rua do Alecrim 87 (362069).
Chinese porcelain, antique furniture.

BIBLARTE, Rua de S. Pedro de Alcântara 71 (33702).
Antiques, rare books, porcelain, works of art.

A. Taveres de CARVALHO, Ave de Republica 46 (770377).
Rare books, illustrated manuscripts, maps, prints.

António COSTA, Rua do Alecrim 76 (325889).
Chinese porcelain, pictures, furniture.

CRUZ-PEREIRA Antiguidades, Rua Dom Pedro V 65 (320645).
Chinese porcelain and ivories, pictures, furniture, decorative items.

DECORAL, Rua do S. Bernardo 70a (662578).
Country antiques.

DINASTIA Antiquarios Leiloeiros e Galeria d'Arte, Rua da Escola Politécnica 183 (668973).
Antique furniture, porcelain, pictures. Auctions.

Bazar DUQUE, Calçada do Duque 43a (367660).
17th/19th-century furniture, clocks, porcelain and religious objects.

GUERRA, Ave 5 de Outubro 12 (52604).
Prints, paintings, porcelain, furniture. Open 0900–1300, 1500–1900; also by appointment.

LIVRARIA HISTORICA e ULTRAMARINA, Travessa da Queimada 28 (368589).
Rare books, maps, prints.

Americo MARQUES, Rua da Misericórdia 91-2 (34977).
Rare antique books, manuscripts, maps, old prints.

Joaquim MARTINS, Rua José Esevão 2c (47072).
General antiques, wood-carvings, furniture, glass, porcelain.

José MAYER, Rua do Loreto 18 (322881).
Silver, porcelain, china.

MITNITZKY, Rua Victor Cordon 1a (326863).
Porcelain, engravings, paintings, glass, furniture. Open
0900–1900; appointment always advisable.

OURIVESARIA de SANTA ELOI, Augusta 181 (361787).
Antique silver, jewellery.

A. PEREIRA, Rua Dom Pedro V 145 (326121).
European 18th-century pottery and porcelain.

PERSIA Antiga, Rua da Imprensa Nacional 116b (674493).
Oriental carpets.

*PINTASSILGO & FERNANDES, Rua da Escola Politécnica 183
(668975)*
Ceramics, earthenware.

PRA ANTIGO, Rua de S. José 126-8 (366329).
Chinese porcelain, gold watches, ivory.

POPPER (Arte Antiga), Rua S. Sebastiao da Pedreira 29 (50589).
Antique and modern Persian carpets and tapestries.

SALAO DE ANTIGUIDADES, Rua Dom Pedro V 31-7 (325280).
Portuguese furniture, porcelain, (especially Chinese), faience,
wood-carvings, objets d'art. Closed Sat. afternoon in
summer.

Bazar SAN JOSE, Rua de S. José 162 (33416).
Furniture, paintings, prints, faience, porcelain, ivory,
bronze.

Galeria da SE, Rua Augusto Rosa 46 (864241).
18th/19th-century furniture, sacred antiques, Chinese porcelain,
Portuguese faience, glass, drawings.

António da SILVA, Praça Luis de Camões 40-1 (322728).
Jewellery, silver, snuff boxes, miniatures, enamels.

SIMOES & IRMAOS, Rua de S. Marinha 3(862527).
Religious paintings, drawings, glass, 17th/18th-century furniture, Portuguese faience.

*SOLAR-ALBUQUERQUE & SOUSA, Rua Dom Pedro V 68-70
(365522).*
Antique furniture, prints, statues, pewter, antique tiles of all
periods.

VULTOS & DUARTE, Rua de S. Marta 41a (43167).
Furniture, wood-carvings, arms.

Markets
*FERIA DA LADRA (flea market), Calçada de S. Vincente and 'Campo
Santaná' behind S. Vincente.*
Open Tues. and Sat.

Auctions
LEIRA & NASCIMENTO, Rua da Emenda 30(1st floor) (369498).
Furniture, porcelain, pewter, brass, large selection of antiques.
Sales 9–12 times yearly, mostly in winter.

SOARES & MENDONCA, Rua Luz Soriano 53(1st floor) (321312).
All types of antiques and works of art.

*DINASTIA Antiquarios Leiloeiros e Galeria d'Arte, Rua da Escola
Politécnica 183(668344).*
See 'Dealers'. Sales monthly.

Restorations
Alberto Mendes BARATA, Regueirão Anjos 7a (556812).
Antiques.

Pedro BOURGARD, Cidade Luanda 482(316157).
Paintings.

CORVELLO ATELIER Angelina Vidal 84 (843075).
Porcelain, faience.

ESPLENDOR, Calçada da Estrela 135a (677670).
Antiques.

Manuel Fernando RAMALHO, Cabo 49b (679202).
Antiques.

Oporto
Dealers
Pedro A. BAPTISTA Rua das Flores 235 (025142).
Antiques, jewellery. Also in Lisbon and Praia da Rocha.

BAPTISTA-JOALHEIROS, Rua Passos Manuel 2 (22831)
and Rua Sa da Bandeira 148 (27888).
Jewellery, silver, general antiques.

CASA AZUL, Praça Carlos Alberto 84 (23450).
General antiques.

COSTA, Rua Miguel Bombarda 200 (24594).
General antiques.

FERREIRA, Rua da Flores 283 (22606).

PORTO CARRERO (Baghana) Rua Dom Hugo 13 (34883).
Antiques, pictures, religious objects. Restorations.

Restorations
BAGHANA, Rua Dom Hugo 13 (34883).
See 'Dealers'. Antiques.

Manuel SEQUIRA, Praça República 9 (35852).
Pictures, drawings.

Praia da Rocha

Dealers

Pedro A. BAPTISTA, Hotel Algarve (Portimão 1101)
Antiques, silver, jewellery. Also in Lisbon and Oporto.

Museums

Lisbon

GULBENKIAN FOUNDATION MUSEUM.
The collection formed by the legendary multimillionaire Calouste
Gulbenkian, including Islamic art, 18th-century French wrought
gold, paintings, renaissance tapestries and art nouveau jewellery,
notably a magnificent display of lalique.

MILITARY MUSEUM.
Arms and armour from the 15th century onwards. Open Tues.–
Sun. 1000–1700; closed hols.

*MUSEU NACIONAL DE ARTE ANTIGA (National Museum of
Ancient Art).*
The world's finest collection of French silverware by the Germain
brothers; Portuguese ceramics.

NAVAL MUSEUM.
Old painted maps, antique navigational instruments, models of
ships from the time of King Henry the Navigator onwards.

Further reading

The Perfect Gun (Espingarda Perfeyta) (Sotheby–Parke Bernet)

A superb 17th-century Danish silver peg tankard made in about 1610 by Matthis Clausson

11
Scandinavia

Introduction

The cultures of Norway, Sweden and Denmark are very largely literary, so it is not surprising that books provide the best quarry for visiting collectors in Scandinavia. This is particularly true in Sweden, which has few book collectors, and where many early works in French and Latin as well as English can be found at prices well below their international market value.

Of the four Scandinavian capitals, Copenhagen is the most expensive for antiques and Oslo probably the least expensive. In Copenhagen many good antique shops can be found in the old quarter of the city off the pedestrian-only thoroughfare known as Stroget. In Stockholm the Old Town is again the place to look for antiques, but for almost everything except books buyers must expect to pay higher prices than elsewhere in Europe. One exception may be English silver, which is regarded by Swedish collectors as intrinsically inferior to their native product, but silver in Copenhagen is astronomically expensive.

Sweden experienced a flood of antiques, paintings and rare books on to the market a decade or so ago after the government abolished centuries-old entailment laws on land, houses and contents, thus enabling old families to dispose of their hereditary assets. Some say the move was simply to enable the richer Swedes to pay their taxes. Whatever the motive, one result is that though Swedish antiques are expensive they are usually of genuine provenance.

Scandinavia has a strong tradition in the graphic as well as the literary arts. Norwegian painting and sculpture date back to Viking times, while the country has produced a leading modern master in Edvard Munch. Swedish art reached its peak in the 18th century when, along with Swedish furniture of the period, it was greatly influenced by the French rococo style. Danish and Finnish painting both flowered in the 19th century, in a naturalistic mode, but on the whole the Scandinavian artistic impulse has tended to express itself in practical rather than purely aesthetic ways. Much Danish and Swedish artistic talent in this century has gone into industrial design and architecture. Russian influences abound in Finnish art.

Glass, ceramics and folk tapestries are areas in which collectors in Scandinavia can expect to find interesting work. Glass is a particularly good field, with wide variety and reasonable prices. A noticeable recent trend among collectors in both Sweden and Norway—as in other North European countries—has been the avid pursuit of rustic antiques such as old farming implements and household items such as spinning-wheels and old butter churns. Several shops in Stockholm and Oslo specialize in domestic antiques, and they can be seen to supreme advantage in those characteristic open-air folk-village museums of Scandinavia, notably the Frilandsmuseet, just outside Copenhagen, and Skansen near Stockholm, the oldest of its kind in the world.

Specialities

Books

All the Scandinavian countries are happy hunting-grounds for rare-book collectors. In Copenhagen one street, Fiolstraede, is a nest of antiquarian booksellers.

Brass and Copper

Old brass and copper articles are extremely popular now with Danish and Swedish collectors, after decades of neglect.

Coins

Swedish issues after 1873 are the most attainable; earlier issues in *fleur du coin* condition are scarce. The most sought after are the gold issues, particularly the de Ducat and Carolin series. A unique Swedish curiosity is 'plate money'—the largest form of currency ever made. Coins weighing as much as 18.2kg (40lb) of copper have been known, the equivalent of their value in silver.

Glass

Glass is a particularly good buy in Scandinavia. There is a wide range and it is quite reasonably priced. Sweden's supreme contribution was the Swedish chandelier, light and delicate in design and made of extremely fine crystal, mainly in the style known in Britain as the waterfall type. Gothenburg is a good centre for these. Glass was made in large quantities for the Swedish royal household and royal ciphers can be found on goblets modelled on English patterns of the 17th and 18th centuries. Superb art deco items were made in the period after the First World War by Orrefors and Kosta of Sweden, both of which are still in production today.

Norwegian glass was often characterized by applied beading decoration and many decanters had a distinctly nautical style. Norwegian glass of the 18th century, when Norway and Denmark were combined under a single crown, showed distinct English and Italian influences; glass makers from Newcastle were employed at the Nostetangen factory, which was in production from 1741 to 1777. Opaque blue-and-white glasses from the Empire and Biedermeier periods are among the most attractive of Norwegian glassware.

Household Antiques

Domestic antiques are a booming local interest in most Scandinavian countries, hence an expensive and difficult field for foreigners. A good selection, however, can be found at the shop of Oslo dealer Berntsen. Norway is a good source for household treen—items made from wood for drinking and keeping beer, making cheese and butter and serving food. These were often charmingly painted with roses, after the fashion of Norwegian painted furniture. Denmark is also quite a good place to find treen, along with country utensils made of brass and ceramics.

Painting and Sculpture

Some names to note in Scandinavian painting and sculpture include:

Denmark: Christopher Wilhelm Eckersberg, 19th-century painter; J. F. Willumsen, naturalistic modern painter, sculptor, ceramics designer and architect (two museums in Denmark are devoted to him); and sculptor Bertel Thorvaldsen.

Sweden: The 18th- and 19th-century painters are worth collecting. Look for Alexander Roslin (1718–93), A. Wertmuller (1751–1811), Marcus Larson (1825–64), F. Fagerlin (1825–1907), B. Nordenberg (1822–1902), B. Liljefors (1860–1939), Carl Larsson (1853–1919), the leading 19th-century landscape painter Carl Frederik Hill, and his contemporary Ernst Josephson.

Norway: Edvard Munch, of course, whose works would be beyond most purses; Isaac Grunewald, who studied under Matisse; Siri Dekert and Vera Nilsson, major expressionists; and sculptors Gustav Vigeland (Frogner Park in Oslo contains many of his works), Carl Eldh, Carl Milles and Arne Jones.

Finland: Albert Edelfeldt, 19th-century painter who was the first Finnish painter to become widely known outside his own country; Akseli Gallen-Kallela, who led the romantic movement but later turned to abstract themes (his home in Helsinki is now a museum); and Waino Aaltonen, the leading sculptor of the modern school. Younger sculptors to note include Kalervo Lallio, Aimo Tukiainen and Eila Hiltunen (who did the Sibelius monument in Helsinki).

Pewter

There has been a great revival of interest in pewter among local collectors, especially in Sweden where modern pewter is a flourishing trade; one of Stockholm's smartest shops is called Svenska-Ten (Swedish Pewter). Tall straight-sided pewter tankards were made in Denmark in the 17th century—in Britain the style was known as Danske pots. Norwegian pewter resembled Belgian and German pewter rather than British, due to the colour of the alloy. Collectors go for offbeat items outside the usual run of tankards and platters.

Porcelain and Pottery

Royal Copenhagen and Bing and Grondahl of Denmark are world-famous names in porcelain; collectors should look out for the translucent white antique figurines of the former and the blue anniversary plates of the latter. Copenhagen was the centre of both porcelain and faience production, though there was a characteristic black pottery from Jutland. Finland has the world's largest ceramics factory, the Wartsila-Arabia, established in the late 19th century. Faience was made in large rococo-style items in Herreboe in Norway from the mid 18th century, usually painted in underglaze blue or purple. Swedish faience was made in Rorstrand near Stockholm. Both Sweden and Denmark produced a creamy-white earthenware in the late 18th century. Sweden's prize porcelain is Marieberg, started in the second half of the 18th century—rare, similar to Mennecy. Look out for the beautifully-modelled cream pots with covers, delicately painted with flowers; also figurines and rococo candelabra. The mark is MB.

Prints

Martin engravings in Sweden are the most collectable of Scandinavian prints.

Silver

Silver is of especially fine quality in Sweden, where it has a higher intrinsic value than English silver and where there was little faking of hallmarks. Hallmarking was used in Denmark and Sweden from the 15th century and Norway from the 18th century. An antique Swedish silver bowl is a prize worth the capture, as one can usually be sure of its genuineness, and Swedish silver is more expensive than English silver in Stockholm antique shops. Horn drinking-vessels mounted in silver survive in some quantity from the 15th century and earlier in Denmark, Sweden and Norway. Silver tankards and beakers are available from the 16th to the 18th centuries. Scandinavian silver was modelled on English and French styles. Swedish silversmiths were greatly influenced by cubism in the 1920s and these articles are interesting collector's items. In Denmark, collectors should look for silver made by Georg Jensen in the early years of this century.

Snuff boxes, in both silver and gold and fashioned after Paris 18th-century styles, were a Swedish speciality.

Tapestries

Tapestry-weaving was primarily a folk art in Norway and Sweden, emanating from Flemish influences in the 16th century; it revived throughout Scandinavia in the 19th century. Norwegian examples were highly stylized in their figures. In Finland the founding of the Finnish Handicraft Association in 1879 revived old peasant weaving-techniques, and *ryijy*—originally horsecloths or sledge rugs—became popular as wall decorations in the 1920s. In Sweden they are known as *rya*.

The trade

Bergen (Norway)

Dealers and auctions
ANDERSEN, Kong Oscarsgaten 41 (211386).
Coins, medals, silver, rare books. Auctions.

Copenhagen (Denmark)

Dealers
Countess Irene AHLEFELDT LAURVIG, Laederstr 5a.
China, jewellery, snuff boxes, Chinese porcelain.

ANTIK (Mogens & Angelo), Kompagnistr 29 (126058).
Chandeliers, Christmas plates, glass, bronze, furniture, etc.

ANTIQUE-TRADING HOUSE (Ingvar M. Svensson), Studiestr 30 (148300).
Clocks, Continental porcelain, English and French furniture, drawings, paintings.

ART & PRINT (Frode Andersen), Kompagnistr 25 (BY 9762).
Old prints, maps, views. Open 1000–1730.

I. Fensmark BECKER, Kompagnistr 8 (PA 7237).
Important stock of Fabergé objects, 18th-century gold enamelled boxes, watches, clocks, jewellery, Copenhagen and other Continental porcelain, coins, medals.

C. BERNDORFF Fiolstr 25 (BY 7476).
Important stock of antiques including furniture, china, silver, glass, pewter and clocks. Closed early on Sat.

BOGHALLEN Antikvariat, Radhuspl 37 (117040).
Large stock of antiquarian and secondhand books; specialist in English literature, the arts and finely-bound sets; old maps, prints. Catalogues issued. Exhibitor at annual Antiquarian Book Fair in London.

BRANNERS Bibliofile Antikvariat, Bredgade 10 (159187).
Old and rare books, maps, views and decorative engravings.

Arnold BUSCK, Fiolstr 24 (PA 4990).
Books on Greenland; general antiquarian books especially on bibliography, typography, history, art, archaeology and architecture.

G. CASTELLA, Kompagnistr 16 (BY 4769).
Arms, model ships.

H. DANIELSENS, Laederstr 11 (BY 274).
Antique silver, general antiques.

FREDERIKSBERG Antikvariat, Gl Kongevej 120 (EVA 9708).
Books on Scandinavia, Danish literature, the arts, Greenland and heraldry. Catalogues issued.

Erik GOTTSCHALCH, Laederstr 13 (BY 7911).
Danish antique furniture, pewter, glass, mirrors and other items.

Freddy HANSEN, Gothersgade 34 (123618).
Glass, bric-à-brac, small items of collector interest.

Ludvig HANSEN, St Strandstr 16 (PA 1085).
Clocks, barometers.

HAMMERS Antique Silver, (The Silver Cellar), Kompagnistr 1 (BY 3634, PA 5567).
Large stock of antique and modern silver, precious stones.

Ole HASLUNDS Hus, Amagertorv 14 (158888).
Specialist in Oriental porcelain, English and French 18th-century furniture, clocks, barometers, early Scandinavian furniture, pewter and glass.

IVE Antiques, Hestemøllestr 3 (148171).
Fine stock of Danish and European pewter and brass, Oriental porcelain, rugs.

KAABERS Antikvariat, Skindergade 34 (BY 4177).
Old and rare books, maps, topographical prints.

KLEIS Kunsthandel, Ostergade 4 (MI 5360).
Danish artists of 1850–1940. Valuations and restorations.

Ella KRAEMER & CO., Pile Alle 55 (next to Carlsberg Breweries) (216083).
Old French bronzes, furniture, paintings, china (especially Sèvres), ivory figures, jewellery, candelabra. Open Mon.–Sat. 0900–1800; also by appointment.

KUNST og ANTIK, Kompagnistr 3 (PA 8309).
Paintings, prints, furniture, European and Chinese pottery, lamps, bronze, pewter, glass, curios.

LUNDBERG, Rådhusstr 8 (PA 4017).
Small items, bronze, bric-à-brac.

Ole MATHIESEN, Ostergade 8 (141208).
Large stock of antique clocks (bracket and long-case), specializing in pre-1800 period. Open Mon.–Fri. 0900–1730; Sat. 0900–1400.

A. MORTENSEN, Lille Kongensgade 6 (MI 3048).
Fine Continental and Scandinavian silver.

Anna MUNCH-MOLLER, Naboløs 3 (PA 1056).
Glass, antique jewellery.

ROSENKILDE & BAGGER, Kron-Prinsens-Gade 3(157044).
Large stock of old and rare books, maps, views.

Erling SCHROEDER, Lille Kongensgade 6(114048).
Specialist in 17th/18th-century European faience. Open
Mon.–Fri. 1300–1730; Sat. 1100–1400; also by appointment.

Erik VEJERSLEV, Hyskenstr 7(141583).
Glass, copper, brass, lamps, furniture, small items. Open
Mon.–Fri. 0900–1730; Sat. 0900–1300.

Fairs
ANTIKVITETSUDSTILLING.
Antique fair held yearly at end April/beginning of May in a
number of well-signposted venues in the city centre. Entrance
charge of 10 kroner. Prices tend to be high.

Auctions
Kunstauktioner ARNE BRUUN RASMUSSEN, Bredgade 33(136911).
10 sales yearly of Danish and foreign pictures (including some
modern sales), furniture, carpets, silver, porcelain and Oriental
objects. Special sales 2–3 times yearly of old masters, silver,
porcelain and Oriental works of art. Special sales of books, wine
and coins. See announcements in Copenhagen papers such as
Politiken.

Gothenburg (Sweden)

Dealers
ANTIQUE Konsthandeln, Södra Hamngatan 45(131067).
Antique furniture, china, silver, paintings.

B. W. BERRY, Geijersgaten 16(167748).
Antiques, Swedish 18th-century paintings, ceramics, silver.

BORJESSONS, Vastra Hamngatan 15(133177).
Important pictures, especially 19th-century Swedish paintings.

MELLGRENS Antikvariat, Ostra Larmgatan 17(105874).
Illustrated manuscripts, books with woodcuts and engravings,
maps, lithographs, Scandinavian books and graphic art.

TOBISONS Antikhandel, Kungsgatan 41 (115066).
Porcelain, silver, pewter, furniture.

Auctions
BOCKER & KONST, Hamngatan 29(113758).

GOTEBORGS STADS AUKTIONS WERK, Trede Langgatan 7 (245805).

Helsingor (Denmark)

Dealers
QUISTGAARD Antique, Bramstr 7 (214304).
18th-century furniture, Chinese porcelain, Danish silver and glass.

Helsinki (Finland)

Dealers in paintings, arms, glass, icons, furniture, general antiques.
Iso AITI, Pääskylänrinne 10, Helsinki 50 (763775).

Cose BELLE, Neitsytpolku 12a, Helsinki 14 (631613).

Antique BULEVARD, Bulevardi 5, Helsinki 12 (647286).

CHURCH HILL Antiques, Mantytie 3, Helsinki 27 (484025).

Galerie DONNER, Töölönkatu 8a, Helsinki 10 (444174).

KAGAN, Bulevardi 22, Helsinki 12 (638736).

LUX, Uudenmaankatu 7, Helsinki 12 (642345).

Brigit NYHOLM, Fabianinkatu 4, Helsinki 13 (626942).
Also carpets and silver.

OCCASION, Annankatu 15, Helsinki 12 (607923).

Dealers in books
ANTIKVAARINEN KIRJAKAUPPA, Pietarinkatu 18, Helsinki 15 (666913).

KESKUSTAN Antikvaarinen Kirjakauppa, Yrjönkatu 1, Helsinki 12 (605675).

KIRJAKUJA, Uudenmaankatu 4-6, Helsinki 12(633396).

LIBRARIA, Kasarminkatu 23, Helsinki 15(626321).

POHJOISMAINEN Antikvaarinen Kirjakauppa, P. Makasiininkatu 6, Helsinki 13(626332).

Other dealers
HORHAMMER, Yrjönkatu 11, Helsinki 12(628071).
Paintings, engravings.

KIN-JA Pohjoinen Esplanadikatu 27, Helsinki 10(663701).
Jewellery, silver.

MATROSOFF, Annegatan 15, Helsinki(631923).
Coins, medals.

WAHAJARVI, P. Makasiininkatu 7, Helsinki 13(663274).
Pictures.

Malmö (Sweden)

Dealers
Elisabeth ANDERSSON, Regementsgatan 20(11044, 971844).
Antique furniture, clocks, jewellery, chandeliers, paintings.

ARTINA, Stora Nygatan 7(19093).
China, weapons, general antiques.

ARTIUM, Kalendegatan 7(22580).
Clocks, glass, Chinese porcelain, ormolu, furniture. Open 1200–1700; appointment always advisable.

LENGERTZ Antikvariat-Bokhandel, Adelgatan 19 (122265).
Old books, maps, prints.

LILLA Antikvariatet, Södra Fordstadsgatan 20 (128778).
Illustrated books, natural-history books, Swedish first editions, books on the fine arts, prints, woodcuts.

Oslo (Norway)

Dealers
Kaare BERNTSEN, Universitetsgaten 12 (203429).
Antique furniture, fine silver, porcelain, glass, Norwegian furniture, jewellery, etc.

BORSUMS, Fr. Nansenspl 2 (410433).
Engravings, books.

CAPPELEN, Kirkegaten 15 (413660).
Incunabula, works on the arts, illustrated books, fine bindings, old maps; books on Greenland, Iceland and the Arctic.

DAMMS, Tallbodgaten 25 (410402).
Engravings, rare books, manuscripts, atlases, ship models.

HAMMERLUNDS, Tordenskioldsgaten 3 (412744).
Scandinavian antiques including glass, pewter, bygones and painted furniture.

HOLST-HALVORSEN, Universitetsgaten 14 (332904).
Paintings by old and modern masters, engravings, modern graphics (especially Edvard Munch).

NORLIS, Universitetsgaten 24 (336190).
Books.

SVEEN, Tordenskioldsgaten 5.
Antiques, curios.

Auctions
CITY AUKSJON, Nygaten 6.

WANGS, Kristian IV 12.

Stockholm (Sweden)

Dealers

AHLSTROM, Master Samuelsgatan 11 (101010).
Coins, medals.

N. M. AMELL, Regeringsgatan 52 (114191).
Fine Swedish and Continental antiques, porcelain, glass, furniture, paintings.

ANTIKAFFAREN SNACKAN, Trängsund 8 (205126)
Large stock of English and Swedish furniture, china, glass and silver. Open Mon.–Fri. 1000–1730; Sat. 1000–1500

ANTIK-KRONAN, Storkyrkobrinken 3 (219696).
China, glass, brass, pewter.

ASPINGTONS, Drottninggatan 73c (112160).
Antiquarian books and engravings.

BJORCK & BORJESSON, Kungsgatan 5 (200836).
Antiquarian books, especially early Swedish and on Linnaeus, botany and science; periodicals.

BUKOWSKIS, Arsenalsgatan 2 (104328).
All kinds of antiques and paintings. Auctions.

CAMP & Co. Riddaragatan 11a (616160).
Mechanical items, cameras, photographs.

CARAVAN OF ART, Storkyrkobrinken 5 (103055).
Antique Oriental tapestries, rugs, jewellery, especially Turkestan.

DAHLGREN Konsthandel, Jakobsbergsgatan 5 (204644).
China, silver, pictures, furniture.

Ake FALK, Nybrogatan 5 (113765).
Clocks, jewellery. Clock restorations.

FRANSKA Antikhandeln, Svartmangatan 11 (214163).
Prints, silver, weapons, medical instruments, furniture. Open Mon.–Fri. 1500–1800; Sat. 1100–1500; also by appointment.

K. G. L. FRITZES Hovbokhandel, Fredsgatan 2 (238900).
Rare books, especially on history, topography and the arts.

HANSSON, Storkyrkobrinken 6 (208691).
Copper, glass, china, paintings.

HEINBRANDTS Konsthandel, Norrlandsgatan 21 (207572).
Swedish 19th/20th-century pictures, copper, silver.

Lennart HEYMANN, Birger Jarlsgatan 1 (212721).
Oriental carpets and rugs, antique and modern. Open 1000–1730; appointment necessary.

Walter JOHANNSON, Kyska Brinken 24 (208474).
Swedish furniture, porcelain, small antiques.

KREUTER, Trängsund 2.
Antique silver.

LIBRIS Antikvariatet, Kommendörsgatan 14 (622131).
Books on history, science and Scandinavia; fine bindings, maps, prints.

C. H. LUNDGREN, Almlöfsgatan 3 (622582).
Japanese works of art, swords, mirrors, porcelain, glass.

MAGALIFF, Birger Jarlsgatan 13 (103603).
Antique porcelain, glass, jewellery, silver, paintings, furniture.

MOLLERS Antikvariat, Regeringsgatan 71 (214994).
Books, stamps, graphic art.

M. MOLVIDSON, Nybrogatan 21 (618684).
Important stock of Swedish and Continental fine antique porcelain, fine silver, glass, furniture.

NYBRO Galleriet, Nybrogatan 6 (604200).

Copper, gold and silver items; Swedish 20th-century water-colours and paintings.

REINIUS, Norrlandsgatan 2 (210401).
High-quality European pistols and guns, nautical items, European glass. Open Mon.–Fri. 1100–1600; Sat. 1100–1500, but closed Sat. in summer.

ROCKE & KRONBERG, Nybrogatan 42 (606007).
Swedish, English and Continental furniture, silver, china, paintings, glass.

SVENSK-FRANSKA, Standvagen 13 (639310).
20th-century drawings, lithographs, paintings, sculpture, engravings.

TERRINEN GRONA, Kopmangatan 13 (217761).
Antique glass, blue-and-white china. Open Mon.–Fri. 1100–1800; Sat. 1100–1500.

THULINS Antikvariat, Tysta Gatan 6 (603131).
Early scientific works, fine bindings, books on Scandinavia, old prints and maps, cookery books.

TIARA, Norrlandsgatan 8 (205955).
Antique jewellery.

Auctions
BUKOWSKIS, Arsenalsgatan 2 (104328).
See 'Dealers'. Important sales twice yearly in April and Nov.

STOCKHOLM STADS AUKTIONS WERK, Norrtullsgatan 6 (340720).

Museums

Copenhagen (Denmark)

FRILANDSMUSEET, just outside Copenhagen.

One of several regional museums of folk art, mostly in the open air with reconstructed village buildings.

MINERALOGICAL MUSEUM, Ostervolgade 7

MUSEUM OF MEDICAL HISTORY.

MUSEUM OF MUSICAL HISTORY, Abenra 34, Copenhagen K

ROYAL ARSENAL, Tojhusgade, Copenhagen K
A 'must' for arms collectors. The lower floor, described as 'the longest continuous room in Northern Europe', contains every kind of heavy *matériel* from late-medieval cannon to modern tanks.

ROYAL NAVAL MUSEUM, St Nicolai Kirke, Copenhagen K
Plenty to interest collectors of ship models.

Fredericia (Denmark)
FREDERICIA MUSEUM, Jernbanegade
Contains a unique collection of candlesticks in various materials.

Frederikshavn (Denmark)
MARITIME MUSEUM.

Helsingör (Denmark)
TECHNICAL MUSEUM, Ndr Trandvej 23
Traces Denmark's technological development through working machinery.

Helsinki (Finland)
BANK MUSEUM OF KANSALLIS-OSAKE-PANKKI, Aleksanterinkatu 42.
Special exhibitions which coin and banknote collectors should see.

Oslo (Norway)

HAERSMUSEET, Akershus.
Arms, uniforms, armour.

MUNCH MUSEUM, Toyengate 53.
Not to be missed for a crash course in the famous Scandinavian painter Edvard Munch.

NATIONAL GALLERY, Universitetsgaten 13.
Has 58 Munch paintings and covers the rest of Norway's painting and sculpture besides the art of the other Scandinavian countries; also Russian icons and a fine collection of French art since Delacroix.

NORSK SJOFARTSMUSEUM, Bydoynesveien 37.
Department specializing in steam shipping, often a neglected subject.

UNIVERSITETS MYNTKABINETT, Fredriksgaten 2.
Coins.

Skagen (Denmark)

FISHERIES MUSEUM.
For collectors of ship models.

Stockholm (Sweden)

DANCE MUSEUM, Filmhuset, Borgvägen.
History and aesthetics of the dance throughout the world.

MUSEUM OF MEDICAL HISTORY; Asögatan 146.

NATIONAL MARITIME MUSEUM, Djurgarden (reached by bus 47 and 67 from Stockholm).
Includes the famous Viking warship *Wasa*.

SKANSEN, Djurgarden.
Oldest open-air museum in the world, with 150 old buildings brought together from all parts of Sweden and set in a fine park.

This small Spanish shrine made of wood and silver in about 1520 portrays a kneeling monk with uplifted face praying to the Virgin and Child. The little oval frames above and below contain relics, neatly labelled with the names of saints

12
Spain

Introduction

No serious collector would choose to go to Spain in order to buy antiques or works of art, mainly because all major works are prevented from leaving the country (this has hampered the operations of Christie's in setting up as fine-art auctioneers in Madrid), but also because, as with many other European countries, there is very little to be found in Spanish antique shops which cannot be bought more advantageously in London. Exceptions are perhaps Spanish 19th-century paintings, which are rapidly gaining fashionable status, beautiful wood-carvings, and painted fans of 17th-, 18th- and 19th-century provenance. The latter are not signed but judged by the quality of the painting, they are extremely worthwhile buys and undoubtedly cheaper than outside Spain.

On the whole the art market in Spain is not organized and is of fairly recent origin. Auctioneers such as Duran in Madrid, the leading Spanish saleroom, have been going only a few years and still sell mainly second-rank goods which are overpriced by London standards, simply because first-rank work is hard to get out of the country. Duran, a jeweller by training, charges a hefty 30 per cent commission to vendors but nothing to buyers, and his catalogues give prices at which the auctioneer will accept starting bids. Sales are held in the evening, which makes it convenient for visiting businessmen to fit them into a busy schedule, and are well worth attending for entertainment value and education if nothing else.

Spanish collectors themselves have a strong bias towards English items—particularly English furniture and silver. At the present stage of their taste they tend to go for second- or third-rate examples of furniture such as George III chests of drawers, and there is a flourishing and very highly-skilled Spanish industry in the making of reproduction English furniture.

In Madrid those with only a few hours to spare to go antique-hunting should concentrate on El Rastro, the daily market which covers an entire network of streets such as Calle Ribera de Curtidores and Calle Carlos Arniches filled with antique and bric-à-brac dealers; many have high quality and higher price tags, though the market also harbours dealers in secondhand goods. One street almost entirely devoted to antiques is Calle del Prado, and there are a number of curio shops in the neighbouring Plaza de las Cortes and Carrera de San Jeronimo. Some specialize in wood-carvings, others in paintings, books, china, glass, ivory, furniture or religious sculptures. On Calle Ribera de Curtidores are several *galerias* with a number of stalls after the style of London's antique supermarkets—some dealers specializing in a particular field, others carrying a general stock. Bargains are not to be expected in El Rastro and collectors should be prepared to haggle as Spaniards do, waiting until at least two lower prices are named by the dealer before reaching a compromise. Philatelists will enjoy the Sunday-morning stamp market in the Plaza Mayor, where schoolboys rub shoulders with international experts in search of a bargain.

In Barcelona the antique shops are clustered around the Cathedral and especially in Calle de la Paja. Barcelona dealers have the reputation of being even sharper than those in Madrid and there are few bargains to be picked up there, though at 33 Calle de la Paja it's said that medieval parchments can be bought remarkably cheaply. In the 19th century Barcelona was an important centre for painters. Sketches by the gifted Catalan artist Mariano Fortuny (1838-1874) are still collectors' items, as are works by Santiago Rusiñol, who worked in an impressionist style. The great Spanish architect Antoni Gaudi designed furniture and ceramic tiles to go with his art nouveau buildings.

In Seville, to the south, there is a good chance of finding some of the rare Hispano-Moresque tin-glazed earthenware made in the 15th or 16th centuries, precursor of majolica and very sought-after. Toledo is historically important for the manufacture of fine weaponry—though more and better examples can be found in London salerooms than in Toledo itself—and its characteristic gold-inlay work on steel is still a flourishing craft.

Specialities

Books

Spain is a good source for book collectors, not only for Spanish books but also Italian and French. Madrid has some excellent antiquarian booksellers in the Cuesto de Moyano, the side streets near the Plaza de las Cortes and the Gran Via.

Carvings

Lovely carved wooden statues can be found, often of Madonnas or other religious subjects, but they are expensive. Collectors should beware fakes which have been 'antiqued' with a saltwater bath—the same treatment can be applied to copper or wrought iron.

Ceramics

Buen Retiro porcelain is the aristocrat of Spanish ceramics—an historical offshoot of Italy's Capodimonte factory which also took over Capodimonte's Gricci as chief modeller until 1770 and now commands equivalent prices in the saleroom (a Gricci figure can now exceed £20 000). Buen Retiro, rarely seen outside Spain, is found in Capodimonte-type figures (though the paste has a yellower tinge) and some tableware. There are splendid collections of Buen Retiro in the Madrid museums.

In pottery, Hispano-Moresque tin-glazed earthenware was made from 1200 to 1800, mainly at Malaga and Valencia. It had a strong Islamic influence and was known as the 'golden pottery'. No regular marks appeared on genuine Hispano-Moresque and reproductions were made from the mid 19th century. Talavera pottery, made in Castile from the 15th century onwards, today ranges in availability from the very old to pieces produced yesterday; it is attractive with a thick milky glaze sprigged with colourful decoration in blue, yellow, green and orange, and modern jugs come as cheaply as 50 pesetas. The designs of antique and modern pieces are often identical, so the ware should be bought from a reputable dealer. In the 18th century Talavera pottery lost its essential simplicity of decoration and became ornate, but this period saw some exceptional ware, especially in blue and white, produced in Catalonia and Aragon. In the early 18th century, Alcona in the province of Valencia was established as a centre of fine ceramics; the designs were more delicate than those of Talavera ware. Spanish pottery is still underrated as a whole compared to Italian majolica, Dutch Delftware or French and German faiences.

Also important in Spanish ceramic products were the tiles made in Seville and Toledo for the Spanish and Portuguese markets.

Firearms

Spanish firearms were among the most decorative of European weapons, and their makers pioneered some technical advances, such as the miquelet lock of the early 17th century which was to remain the basic mechanism in Spanish gun-making for 200 years. The best Madrid pistols had splendid silver fittings, often featuring gold inlay on the barrels. Provincial pistols were all fitted with belt-hooks and many were elaborately decorated with brass or silver. Pistols produced in Ripoll were characterized by their short grips with ball butts; the wood of the stock could be inlaid or overlaid with pierced ironwork, brass or silver, decorated with geometric patterns, birds or animals. In the 18th and 19th centuries Spanish gun barrels were highly regarded for their strength and safety of construction and quite widely faked in other countries. Some were reputed to be made of horseshoes—*de herraduras*—for extra strength, and perhaps good fortune. The breech on Spanish firearms was usually stamped with the maker's mark in gold. Pistols were rarely cased and there was no equivalent to the duelling or target pistol. Accessories were also rare.

Today, 17th-century Spanish pistols are scarce and costly except for the Ripoll ball-butt pistol, which was manufactured for more than a century. There is more chance to pick up an 18th-century example, probably made in Madrid or Barcelona; the value will depend on the maker and the richness of the decoration.

Glass

Glass-making in Spain is a long-established tradition dating from pre-Roman times. La Granja de San Ildefonso is the great name.

The factory, founded in 1728, dominated Spanish glass-making until the early 19th century. It employed Bohemian craftsmen who stamped their influence on its products. The pieces were very handsome and are much collected within Spain and consequently expensive. La Granja was famous for its chandeliers.

In Spanish glass, characteristic shapes are those of the *cántara* (a double-spouted pitcher), the *almorrata* (a rosewater sprinkler with four spouts) and the *porrón* (a long-spouted drinking-vessel with no handles). The most impressive pieces are said to come from Granada.

Ivory

Carvings of a religious nature, such as Christ on the Cross, exquisitely carved, can be found quite cheaply as there is little demand for them.

Paintings

The golden age of Spanish painting obviously being inaccessible to most collectors—certainly to even the richest foreign buyers—the 19th century has become highly fashionable. The period produced 300 or 400 Spanish painters worth attention in a small way, but the big names like Ignacio Zuloaga and Joaquin Sorolla (the leading Spanish impressionist) are now almost as pricy as French impressionists. The contemporary painter Benjamin Palencia is extremely popular; he used to paint pleasantly conventional landscapes but latterly has favoured what one Spanish collector describes as the green goat in a blue field type of subject. Spanish contemporary artists are well catered for in Madrid, which has more than 20 galleries specializing in such exhibitions. Spaniards themselves—the English taste again—go for sporting pictures, J. F. Herring prints, paintings of game and the like. These are regarded as highly chic.

Prints

Collectors should look out for attractive mezzotint engravings of paintings by Goya and other Spanish masters.

Silver

Spanish silver is of indifferent value intrinsically, but rare and for that reason expensive. Aragon, Castile and Salamanca were important centres, especially prosperous Castile. So much Spanish plate was melted down for coinage in the various 19th-century wars that most of what survives is church plate—that of the renaissance period is quite common and fine pieces still appear on the market. Barcelona, Madrid, Seville and Valencia were also centres of production.

Tapestries

Tapestry-weaving in Spain was originally started by Flemish weavers who migrated to Spain in the 14th century to maintain the imported tapestries of the nobility. The royal factory Santa Barbara, established by Philip V in 1720, produced a famous series of 45 tapestries in 1776–91 based on the cartoons of Goya. In the 19th and early 20th centuries the Royal Carpet Manufactory (Fabrica Real da Madrid) produced copies of gothic tapestries, Persian carpets and Aubussons (the latter in stronger colours than the French originals).

Tiles

Tiles were an Iberian speciality, but it is much harder to find them in Spanish antique shops than in Portuguese.

The trade

Barcelona

Dealers

ABRAHMS Art Gallery, S. Severo 11 (2322119).
Paintings. Open 1100–1330, 1700–2100; also by appointment (always advisable).

Juan BALDRICH, Baños Nuevos 19 (2225858).
Antiquities, furniture, paintings, silver, sculpture.

Enrique DOMENECH, Baños Nuevos 22 (2312886).
Spanish furniture, antiques, decorative items.

FALGUERAS, Plaza San José Oriol 4 (2187191).
Spanish furniture, armour, paintings, curios.

FONT, Nicaragua 69 (2399682).
Furniture, ceramics, sculpture, historical pictures, weapons.

Alberto GRASAS, Baños Nuevos 14 (3178838, 3180853).
Spanish furniture, paintings, ceramics, sculpture, armour.

Galerias LINARES, Plaza de Cristo Rey 2 bis (3101541).
Tapestries, historical ceramics, swords, silver, brocade, lace.
Open Mon.–Sat. 0900–1330, 1500–2000; Sun. morning.

Establecimientos MARAGALL SA, Petrixol 5 and 8 (2215816).
Specializes in modern Catalan paintings; also in 17th- and 18th-
century Flemish, Dutch and English paintings. Open 1000–1330,
1600–2000; appointment advisable. Also in Madrid.

*MENINAS as (Antonio Climent), Paris 205, Petrixol 18 and Minerva 7
(23112135, 2185775)*
Pictures, furniture, porcelain, carpets, jade, tapestries, silver.
Open 0900–1330, 1600–2000; appointment advisable.

*J. QUINTANA Antigüedades, S. Severo 7 (2217301), Paseo de Gracia 53
(2151980) and Paja 10 (2217940).*
Armour, bronzes, ceramics.

RELICARIO Antigüedades, Valencia 263 (2154322).
Porcelain, furniture, curiosities, glass.

SANES, Ave Generalissimo Franco 580 (2274471).
Carpets, Oriental art, furniture, paintings, sculpture, tapestries.
Open 0900–1300, 1600–1930.

TORRES, Balmes 470 (cnr of Paseo S. Gervasio) (2470649).
Oriental specialist; paintings, furniture, bronzes, engravings,
general antiques.

VALENTI (Fernando Valenti Clua), Provenza 308 (2154525).
Silver, furniture, decorative and interesting objects, general
antiques. Also in Gerona, Madrid and San Sebastian.

Markets
Los ENCANTES (flea market), Plaza de las Glorias.
Open Mon., Wed, Fri., and Sat. mornings.

Auctions
Ramón MIRO, Floridablanca 110-12 (2234140).

Sala VAYREDA, Rambla de Cataluna 116 (2273701).

Gerona

Dealers
VALENTI (Fernando Valenti Clua).
Silver, furniture, decorative and interesting objects, general
antiques. Also in Barcelona, Madrid and San Sebastian.

Madrid

Dealers
ALCOCER, Pelayo 68 (2320682) and S. Catalina 5 (2210538).
Fine antique furniture, paintings, ceramics.

ALENCON, Narcisos 60 and Prado 29 (2321494, 2313029).
Tapestries, ivory, porcelain, clocks, paintings, general antiques.

AUBASORO, Galerías Piquer (stalls 2 and 3) (2398460).
Porcelain, furniture, curiosities, silver, pictures, tapestries.

BARRIOPEDRO, Galerías Piquer (stall 21) (2398890).
Furniture, sculpture, armour.

*BENI, Galerías Piquer (stalls 20 and 46) (4672892) and Prado 7
(2315217).*
Arms, nautical antiques, motoring curios, decorative objects.

BERALIA, Barquillo 20 (2210873).
Old fans, lace, period furniture, old and modern pictures.

CASA y JARDIN, Estudio Padilla 21 and 32 (2767604).
Furniture, glass, ceramics, objets d'art. Open 0930–1330, 1630–2000; also by appointment (always necessary).

CASTRO MUNOZ (Maria de Castro Lage), Ribera de Curtidores 12 (2273419).
Furniture, pictures, clocks, ceramics, sculpture, carpets.

Juan CAYON, Fuencarral 41 (221083).
Coins, medals. Auctions.

Galeria Del CISNE, Paseo de Eduardo Dato 17 (4100722).
Modern Catalan paintings; 17th/18th-century Flemish, Dutch and English pictures. Also in Barcelona; see Establecimientos Maragall.

ESEX, Marqués de Cubas 19 (2223034).
Antiques, historical relics, Spanish furniture. Auctions.

FRESNO, Galerías Piquer (stall 26) (2280029).
Ceramics, sculpture, pictures.

Rodriguez GARCIA, Plaza de S. Ana 12 (2311785) and Galerías Piquer (stall 13).
Silver, numismatics, Spanish furniture, ceramics, sculpture.

Manuel GONZALEZ, Velázquez 40 (2762620).
Important stock of antiques, including porcelain, paintings, silver, tapestries and objets d'art. Open 0930–1330, 1630–2000.

Galeria LEGAR, Plaza de S. Ana 10 (2312614).
Spanish, Italian and Flemish paintings; French and Spanish furniture, sculpture, porcelain, books.

Abelardo LINARES, Plaza de las Cortes 11 (2214627).
Old masters, furniture, sculpture, porcelain, jewellery, pistols, crystal, etc.; antique and modern Spanish handicrafts. Open Mon.–Sat. 0930–1330, 1630–1930. Also in Palma de Mallorca.

Felix LLORENTE, Galerías Piquer (stall 54) (2270668).
12th- and 15th-century sculpture, 15th/16th-century paintings, French furniture.

Montero LÓPEZ, Pez 15 and Prado 3 (2224257).
Specialist in antique silver.

Ruiz LÓPEZ, Galerías Piquer (stall 59) (3395080).
Fine Spanish and provincial furniture, Spanish sculpture, primitive ceramics.

Antonio MOMPLET, Velázquez 27 (2752455).
Specialist in marine antiques; fine stock of Spanish general antiques.

Alvaro PATERNINA CRUZ, Velázquez 38 (five floors) (2753820).
English and French 18th-century antiques.

Antigüedades Rodríguez PENA, Prado 5 (2225682).
Gothic sculpture.

Laureano PINTO, Galerías Piquer (stall 63) (4673543).
Arms, furniture, bronzes, etc. Open Mon.–Sat. 1100–1400, 1700–2000; Sun. 1100–1400.

QUIXOTE, Plaza de España 11 (2475544).
Paintings, sculpture, engravings, ceramics, books, contemporary Spanish art.

RAMON, Galerías Piquer (stall 25) (2271492).
Arms, armour.

REY, Nuevas Galerías (2276146).
Spanish furniture, religious sculptures in wood.

Carlos RIOS, Nuevas Galerías (stall 25) (2307883).
Sculpture, pictures, 17th- to 19th-century Spanish furniture.

ROMERO FERNANDEZ, Prado 23 (2311416).
Important stock of antiques. President of Spanish Antique Dealers' Association.

ROSALES, Nuevas Galerías (2399871).
Furniture, glass, porcelain, brass.

J.J. ROTTENBURG, Almagro 27 (4190409).
Contemporary Spanish artists.

TENHE, Plaza S. Domingo 18 (2475451).
Lamps, glass, bronze.

USALLAN, Galerías Piquer (stall 27) (2276184).
Furniture, ceramics, sculpture, armour.

VALENTI SA (Fernando Valenti Clua), Velázquez 81 (2708958).
Furniture, silver, decorative and interesting objects, general antiques. Also in Barcelona, Gerona and San Sebastian.

Galeria el VIADUCO, Baile 12 (248 6452).
Paintings of all periods from 14th century onwards.

Markets
NUEVAS GALERIAS, Ribera de Curtidores 12.
Wide range of antiques, works of art, etc. Over 25 dealers.

GALERIAS PIQUER, Ribera de Curtidores 29.
Wide range of antiques, pictures, curios etc. Over 63 dealers.

EL RASTRO, Plaza Cascorro, Plaza del General Vara del Rey, Carnero, Rodas, Ribera de Curtidores, Carlos Arniches, Mira el Rio Alta and Ronda de Toledo.
Flea and bric-à-brac market. Open Mon.–Sat. 1000–1400; Sun. morning.

Stamp market, Plaza Mayor.
Open Sun. morning.

Auctions
Juan CAYON, Fuencarral 41 (221083).
See 'Dealers'. Sales of coins.

CHRISTIE'S Montalban 9.
Madrid office of the London auctioneers.

DURAN, Serrano 12(4013400).
Spanish and foreign art objects; paintings, silver, clocks, watches, bronze, coins, woodcuts, wood-carvings, furniture, ceramics, Oriental art, etc. Sales at end of every month. Catalogues on subscription.

ESEX, Marqués de Cuba 19(2223034).
See 'Dealers'.

JULFE, Nuevas Galerías, Ribera de Curtidores 29(2390011).

SASKIA (in conjunction with Sotheby's of London), Paseo Texeira 8 (4586106).

Palma de Mallorca

Dealers
Abelardo LINARES.
Old masters, furniture, sculpture, porcelain, jewellery, pistols, crystal, etc.; antiques and modern Spanish handicrafts. Also in Madrid.

San Sebastian

Dealers
VALENTI (Fernando Valenti Clua). Plaza Zaragoza 2(411825).
Silver, furniture, decorative and interesting objects, general antiques. Also in Barcelona, Gerona and Madrid.

Museums

Barcelona

GABINETE NUMISMATICO DE CATALUNA (Numismatic Museum), Parque de la Ciudadela.
Open 1000–1400.

MARITIME MUSEUM, Reales Atarazanas, Puerta de la Paz.
Open Mon.–Sat. 1000–1300, 1600–1800.

MUSEUM OF DECORATIVE ARTS, Palacio de la Vierreina, Rambla de las Flores.
Furniture, carpets, ceramics, glass, silver, etc. Open 1000–1400, 1800–2100.

Madrid

ARCHAEOLOGICAL MUSEUM, Serrano 13.
Notable for coins and a complete collection of ceramics from every period.

NATIONAL MUSEUM OF DECORATIVE ART, Montalban 12.
62 rooms of ceramics, furniture and other decorative arts from all regions of Spain. Open Tues.–Sun. 1000–1330; closed Aug.

NAVAL MUSEUM, Montalban 2.
Model ships, charts, nautical instruments. Open Tues.–Sun. 1000–1330.

ROYAL ARMOURY.
Visit in conjunction with the Royal Palace. A magnificent collection of old weapons and armour.

VALENCIA DE DON JUAN INSTITUTE, Fortuny 43.
Ceramics.

Further reading

Caiger-Smith, Alan, *Tin-Glaze Pottery in Europe* (London: Faber)
Frothingham, Alice Wilson, *Spanish Glass* (London: Faber)
Lavin, J. D., *A History of Spanish Firearms* (London, 1965)
Neal, W. K., *Spanish Guns and Pistols* (London, 1955)
Oman, Charles, *The Golden Age of Hispanic Silver 1400–1665* (London: HMSO, 1968)

This gold, enamel and diamond-set miniature repeating clock-watch measures only 6 cm in diameter. It was sold in 1972 for more than £5000

13
Switzerland

Introduction

Switzerland, a melting-pot of the three great European cultures which surround it—French, German and Italian—has skilfully managed since the late 19th century to keep out of all the great European wars. In consequence its art treasures have been kept together and safely preserved in museums and some of the wealthiest private collections in Europe.

The Swiss are tremendous collectors—it has been said they own more art per capita than any other people—and, as befits a country famous for the exquisite precision of its watch-making, they demand only the best. Geneva, which, largely due to the tax advantages enjoyed by its big international community, can lay claim to being the richest city in Europe, has in recent years become a leading centre for international sales, particularly of jewellery. Saleroom experts coming in from London find that the Swiss buy only top-quality goods; pieces with a slight blemish or imperfection which might easily get by in London, Paris or Munich are liable to be briskly rejected after close examination by a Swiss dealer.

Swiss collectors are very keen on English antiques, especially silver and furniture of the late Georgian period, and St James's Gallery in Lucerne is one of several dealers specializing in this field. But all over Europe there has developed a great interest in rustic antiques, reflecting perhaps a subconscious desire to get back to the reassuringly permanent roots of society in a period of urban unrest, disillusion and change, and the Swiss are also turning to such things as carved wooden chests and painted cupboards from their rural past.

Switzerland's whole artistic heritage in fact, through 600 years of bourgeois democratic culture, has been popular, almost folkloric, in character and as a result has tended to be underrated in the grand rollcall of European art. Now, with the movement towards the rustic and naive, it may well be due for a reappraisal. Wood-carving has been a characteristic expression of this popular culture, whose objects, under the generic name of Helvetica, can be found in many smart antique shops in Geneva, Lausanne, Zurich and Lucerne and at cheaper prices in the Alpine areas. Good places to study the old popular arts, including pottery, are the National Museum in Zurich, the Ethnological Museum in Basel, the Historical Museum in Berne, and the Engadine Museum in St Moritz. But Switzerland has also had a long and distinguished history in the graphic arts, particularly in landscape-painting and cartography. Zurich has been a centre of map-making since the 16th century, and Konrad Witz of Basel painted Europe's first exact representation of a landscape in 1444: the view of Mont Salève and Mont Blanc seen from Geneva which forms the background to his altarpiece *The Miraculous Draught of Fishes* (in Geneva's Musée d'Art et d'Histoire).

Geneva is the world's leading watch centre and a natural magnet for collectors in this field; it is expensive for antiques but the narrow alleys surrounding the Cathedral offer fascinating opportunities for browsing. Cheaper buys can be made in Geneva's flea market, the only one in Switzerland.

Zurich, one of Europe's top numismatic centres, is a city of *hauts antiquaires*, most of whom cluster about the Gross Munster in the old quarter. Streets of antique dealers include Dufourstrasse, Neustadgasse, Kirchgasse, Lowenstrasse, Taisstrasse, Neumarkt, Bahnhofstrasse, Ramistrasse and Rindermarkt. Galerie Koller in Zurich is an auction house of growing international importance, selling a wide range of fine-art objects from netsuke to musical boxes, Persian rugs to Swiss watches. Swiss auctions are usually held in late spring and autumn and attract keen international interest.

Annual antique fairs are held in Berne and Lausanne, and the latter city offers one of the most unusual museums in Europe which is a 'must' for Sherlock Holmes fans: the Museum of the Conan Doyle Foundation in the 1000-year-old Château de Lecens.

Many of the great Swiss private collections are not open to the public, but an exception is that of the late Baron Heinrich von Thyssen in Lugano, which is probably the finest private collection in Europe.

Specialities

Books

Switzerland is quite an important centre for rare books, but they are mostly of local topographical or historical interest. Some magnificent illuminated manuscripts were done in the Dark Ages and can be seen in the library of the Abbey of St Gallen. Book collectors should check the auction sales at Haus der Bücher in Basel. Leading dealers include: Mohler (Basel); Hegnauer (Berne); Gilhofer & Rauschburg (Lucerne); Cramer, Engelberts (Geneva); Bridel (Lausanne); Art Ancien, Galerie am Neumarkt, Laube and Schumann (Zurich). Bloch in Lausanne has an important stock of books on the history of medicine and science.

Clocks and Watches

Switzerland is obviously one of the best places possible for watch collectors. Geneva is the world's leading watch centre and has two very good watch auctions each year, at which the Swiss enamelled watches fetch particularly good prices. Specialist dealers include Chatelain in Lausanne and, in Zurich, Galerie am Neumarkt, Koller and Mannheimer. Schneider in Neuchâtel, Scherer in Berne and Colombo in Zurich deal especially in antique clocks. Geneva has a Museum of Watches and Enamels, including a fine collection of Geneva enamelled watches, as part of its Musée d'Art et d'Histoire. In Zurich, collectors should visit the Beyer Museum of Time Measurement.

Coins

Switzerland is a leading centre for coins, with the Swiss banks themselves investing heavily in fine gold and silver specimens, and Zurich vies with London as coin capital of the world. In Geneva, the Union Bank of Switzerland has opened a 'coin exchange' for gold and silver currency of all periods. There is a national coin collection in Berne. and leading numismatic dealers include: Munzen & Medaillen (Basel); Zbinden-Hess (Berne); de Mayo (Geneva); Dietrich and Sternberg (Zurich).

Firearms

Wherever German influence is strong one tends to find an interest in fine antique weapons. Leading Swiss dealers include: Markes (Basel); Galerie du Coq Muet (Lausanne); and Fischer (Lucerne). Antique weapons feature in the Galerie am Neumarkt sales in Zurich, and collectors may want to visit the Swiss Rifle Museum in Berne.

Helvetica

Wood-carving was a characteristic expression of the popular culture. Decoration, most often geometric chip-carving, is usually found on large objects such as chests, boxes, chairs and cradles, and there are magnificently exuberant painted cupboards in a primitive rococo style from the period 1740–1850 originating in the Appenzell and Toggenburg districts. Unique to Switzerland are ancient demonic-looking masks which might be African or Polynesian at first glance; they are still used for folk rituals in Grisons (where, incidentally, Switzerland's famous sculptor and painter Alberto Giacometti originated) and part of Valais. Rural and domestic objects from the past can be found at smart antique shops in Geneva, Lausanne, Zurich and Lucerne, and more cheaply in the Alpine areas.

Jewellery

Geneva has become a world centre for antique and fine 20th century jewellery, as witnessed by the fact that Christie's of London holds the cream of its jewellery sales there. Leading dealers include Dick (Lausanne) Baszanger and Lombard Joaillier (Geneva); in Zurich, jewellery is included in the Galerie am Neumarkt sales; in Berne, Howald's Erben holds an important stock of 17th/20th-century items, and jewellery is featured in dealer Dobiaschofsky's sales twice a year; in Basel, Markes is a dealer to visit.

Maps and Engravings

Cartography is one field where the Swiss early established an international reputation and Zurich, one of the oldest of the German Imperial cities, has been a centre of map-making since the 16th century. In the Zurich National Museum there is a city plan of Zurich by Hans Leu, c. 1497, which is extraordinarily accurate, and the 16th-century maps of Johannes Stumpf were landmarks of cartography. Also remarkable for their accuracy were the bird's-eye views of Zurich by Josias Murer and of Fribourg by Sickinger. In Basel, the publisher Matthius Merian issued a collection of copper-engravings of every city in Switzerland and eventually, the whole of Europe. From the 17th century onwards no other cities except Rome, Paris and Venice were so accurately portrayed in all their stages of development as Basel, Berne and Zurich. *Vedute*—pocket views produced for the tourist—were avidly collected in the 19th century and still are today. The landscapes were first etched on to copper plates (an artist called Aberli was the top man in the field) and the prints later tinted by hand.

Some leading dealers are: Mohler (Basel); Dobiaschofsky, Minder (Berne); Fischer (Lucerne); Cramer, Engelberts, Muriset (Geneva); Art Ancien and Koller (Zurich).

Painting

The great gothic master Konrad Witz, who worked in Basel in the first half of the 15th century and painted Europe's first exact representation of a landscape in 1444, and another German immigrant Hans Holbein, who also lived in Basel, dominated Swiss art in the 15th and 16th centuries; French and Italian renaissance influences were slow to percolate through because of the strong Swiss Protestant tradition of the late 16th century.

Later Swiss painting showed a strong romantic streak, however. The philosopher Jean-Jacques Rousseau, who came to live in Geneva before the French Revolution, spread the fame of Switzerland as an untouched natural paradise, and the 'discovery' of the Alps in the next century by jaded city dwellers produced shoals of Arcadian mountain landscapes. Two artists who specialized in mountain views were François Diday (1802–77) and Alexandre Calame (1810–64). By far the most famous name in Swiss painting before this century was the 18th-century mystical painter J. H. Fuseli (1741–1825), who was enthusiastically taken up by the English taste of the time. Other artists of note included: writer Salomon Gessner (1730–88)who also etched and painted; caricaturist Rodolphe Topffer of Geneva; portrait and horse painter J. L. Agasse (1767–1849); portraitist F. Massot (1766–1849), whose work can be seen in Geneva's municipal art gallery; Barthelemy Menn (1815–95), famous for his Geneva landscapes in a style resembling Corot's; Arnold Bocklin (1827–1901), whose romantic paintings can be seen in the Basel and Zurich city art galleries and were reproduced in thousands of cheap editions for 19th-century homes; Albert Anker (1831–1910), who brilliantly expressed the rustic nature of the Swiss national character; Rudolf Koller of Zurich (1828–1905), animal and genre painter; Frank Buchser (1828–90), landscape and genre painter; and Ferdinand Hodler of Berne (1853–1918), who was one of Europe's outstanding modernists of the period and strongly Swiss in character and whose remarkable frescoes are in the Zurich National Museum. In this century Switzerland's artistic fame rests principally on the painter Paul Klee, the painter and sculptor Alberto Giacometti and the architect Le Corbusier.

Porcelain and Pottery

Swiss popular art produced some interesting ceramics, including the unique polychrome pottery from Heimburg and Langnau in Berne, whose factories are still in production. There is a museum of Swiss 18th-century ceramics in Zurich called the Zunfthaus zur Meisen and a ceramics collection in Geneva (Musée Ariana). Most antique dealers in Swiss cities seem to carry some porcelain and faience, but there are a few specialists: Mehlhose in Basel (faience), Bloch-Diener in Berne (faience). Desarzens in Geneva (Continental and Chinese porcelain) and Ars Domi in Zurich.

The trade

Basel

Dealers

BASLER-KAENSCHTERLI (E. Schmutz), Dufourstr 32(232686).
Antique furniture, porcelain, faience and small items.

Ernst BEYELER, Bäumleingasse 9(235412).
Fine modern paintings.

René BIEDER, Barfüsserpl 21(250869).
Antiques, furniture, pictures, faience, glass.

HAFTER, Elisabethen Str 42(231358).
English antiques, especially furniture, silver, plate and scientific instruments. Open 0900–1200, 1400–1830. Also in Zurich.

Max KNOLL, Herbergsgasse 4-6(235174; private 236962).
16/17th-century silver, glass, bronzes, porcelain, etc. Open 0900–1200, 1400–1830; appointment advisable.

Max KNOLL Jr. (Seems)

Otto MARKES, Klosterberg 17(237008).
Jewellery, antique weapons, silver.

Heinz MEHLHOSE, Augustinergasse 7(251848).
Specialist in faience.

Karl MOHLER, Rheinsprung 7(259882).
Early maps, engravings, antiquarian books.

MUNZEN & MEDAILLEN (Dr Herbert A. Cahn), Malzgasse 25 (237544).
Specialist in early coins, medals and classical antiquities. Auctions.

Au PETIT TRESOR (Ruth Goetz) Klosterberg 21 (391213).

Marcel SEGAL, Aeschengraben 14-16 (233908; private 429942).
Porcelain, silver, pictures, general antiques.

Auctions
HAUS DER BUCHER, Bäumleingasse 18 (233088).
Antiquarian books, autographs, music.

MUNZEN & MEDAILLEN (Dr Herbert A. Cahn), Malzgasse 25 (237544).
See 'Dealers'.

Fairs
Foire d'Antiquités, yearly in Spring.

Berne

Dealers
Elsa BLOCH-DIENER, Kramgasse 60 and Obstbergweg 7 (220406).
Faience, Coptic textiles, Egyptian antiques, 17th/18th-century Swiss furniture, glass, sculptures, pictures. Open 0900–1830.

Hans DOBIASCHOFSKY, Laupenstr 3 (252372; private 423164).
Jewellery, old masters, drawings, engravings. Open Mon., Wed. and Fri. 0800–1200, 1400–1830; Tues. and Thur. 0800–1200, 1400–2100; Sat. 0900–1200, 1400–1700; Sun. 1030–2100. Auctions.

Eduard HEGNAUER, Kramgasse 16 (226415).
Antiquarian books; important stock of general literature, philosophy, fine arts and natural science.

E. HERMANN. Gerechtigkeitsgasse 79 (224810, 447484).
Swiss furniture and objects.

HOWALD'S Erben (Gertrud Howald), Gerechtigkeitsgasse 54 (221410).
Important 17th/20th-century jewellery, silver, objets de vertu. Open 0900–1200, 1400–1830; closed Mon.

KORNFELD & KLIPSTEIN, Laupenstr 49 (254673).
Specializes in fine prints and drawings. Auctions. Also in Zurich.

Paul MINDER, Gerechtigkeitsgasse 59 (220826; private 232847).
Antique furniture, glass, engravings, porcelain, objets d'art.

J. Otto SCHERER & Sohn, Kramgasse 26 (227369).
Antique clocks.

G. & L. ZBINDEN – HESS, Kramgasse 55 (28203).
Antiques, pictures, Helvetica, furniture, coins, porcelain, silver,
sculpture.

Fairs
Antique fair.
Yearly, end Feb.

Auctions
Hans DOBIASCHOFSKY, Laupenstr 3 (252372; private 423164).
See 'Dealers'. Sales twice yearly.

KORNFELD AND KLIPSTEIN, Laupenstr 49 (254673).
See 'Dealers'.

Galerie Jurg STUKER, Alter Aargauerstalden 30 (440044).
Porcelain, silver, paintings, jewellery, furniture, Swiss prints. Sale
yearly in Nov.

Geneva

Dealers
ART ANCIEN (Ernest A. Zumkeller), 23 rue Lefort (211211, 461411).
17th/19th-century paintings, engravings and watercolours;
bronze sculpture. Appointment necessary. See also 'Galerie
Zumkeller'.

*ARTS ANCIENS de Chine et Extrême-Orient (Mr Nguyen Tan-Phuoc),
16 rue de l'Hôtel-de-Ville (297190).*
Far Eastern and Indo-Chinese works of art; archaic bronzes,
Khmeres sculptures, jade, porcelain, lacquer, furniture, snuff
bottles, hardstone-carvings. Open Mon.–Fri. 0900–1200,
1400–1900; Sat. 0900–1200, 1400–1700.

BASZANGER & Cie (Lucien Baszanger), 6 rue de la Corraterie (244354).
Antique jewellery.

CHARBONNIER Antiquité, 19 rue de la Cité (282810).
18th/19th-century bibelots, Russian objects, curiosities, icons. Open 1000–1200, 1500–1900; closed Mon. morning.

Galerie Gérald CRAMER, 13 rue de Chantepoulet (325432).
Drawings, prints, sculpture, modern illustrated books. Open Mon.–Fri. 1000–1200, 1430–1830; Sat. 1000–1200; appointment advisable.

Galerie Edwin ENGELBERTS, 11 Grand'Rue (247965).
Illustrated books, original modern prints, paintings, etchings, lithographs, drawings.

J. FILIPPINI, 13 and 38 Grand'Rue (242520/246437).
Swiss, French and German furniture and objets d'art.

JADE Co., 3 rue Cornavin (320220).
Chinese works of art, jade, hardstones, coral, turquoises, etc. Also in Paris and New York.

Roland LAZZARELLI, 16 rue de l'Hôtel-de-Ville (255970; private 81154).
16th/19th-century paintings.

LOMBARD Joaillier, 19 rue de la Cité (213244/213399).
Antique jewellery, silver, Russian items. Open 1000–1700; also by appointment.

Marcel de MAYO, 7 pl de la Fusterie (257334/252107).
Coins.

Mme Marguerite MOTTE, 10 quai Général-Guisan (252151).
Antiques, paintings, furniture, porcelain. Auctions.

Galerie MURISET (Annie Muriset), 4 pl Molard (216001; private 366103).
17th- and 19th-century engravings of Switzerland etc. Open

Mon.—Fri. 1400–1900; Sat. 1000–1200, 1400–1900; also by appointment.

Paul ROSSIRE, 18 rue de la Corraterie (212699).
18th-century French furniture, silver, porcelain, faience, bibelots. Open Mon.–Fri. 1000–1200, 1400–1800; Sat. 1000–1200.

Galerie ZUMKELLER (Ernest A. Zumkeller), 30 Grand 'Rue (211211).
17th/19th-century paintings, engravings and watercolours; bronze, sculpture. Open Mon.—Sat. 1000–1900. See also 'Art Ancien'.

Markets
Flea Market, pl Isaac-Mercier.
About 50 dealers. Open Wed. and Sat. 0630–1800 (summer), 0700–1800 (winter).

Auctions
Watch auctions.
Sales twice yearly.

Christie's, 8 Pl de la Taconnerie (282544).
Jewellery sales.

Mme Marguerite MOTTE, 10 quai Général-Guisan (252151).
See 'Dealers'.

ROSSET, 29 rue du Rhône (289633).
Old and modern pictures, antique furniture, bibelots. Sales Mon.–Fri.

Lausanne

Dealers
Henri BLANC, 3 pl du Tunnel (233238; private 268620).
Furniture, silver, porcelain, 18th-century faience, bibelots, other objects. Appointment necessary. Auctions.

Librarie Felix BLOCH, 5 pl de la Palud (221328).
Important stock of books on history of medicine and science.
Open Mon.–Fri. 0900–1200, 1400–1800; appointment advisable.

Maurice BRIDEL, 1 ave du Théâtre (237735).
First and rare editions, fine bindings, incunabula, drawings,
prints, works of the French gothic period, books on the arts and
horses.

Daniel CHATELAIN, 10 rue de Pont (235854; private 325482).
Antique watches, clocks, jewels and musical boxes. Open Mon.
1330–1830; Tues.–Fri. 0800–1830; Sat. 0800–1700; appointment
advisable.

Galerie du COQ MUET (Jacques Schmied), 7 rue de l'Academie (234323; private 233253).
Specialist in arms and armour. Open Mon.–Fri. 0900–1300,
1330–1900; Sat. 0900–1200, 1330–1700; appointment always
advisable.

M. DESARZENS, 29 rue Centrale (238651).
Continental and Chinese porcelain.

Jacques DICK, 1 rue de la Paix (227819).
Important stock of antique silver and jewellery; general antiques.

Simone NEUFFER, 11 ave Cesar-Roux (232390; private 243409).
Small antique items. Open Mon.–Fri. 1400–1900; Sat. 1000–
1200, 1400–1900.

Galerie PEQUIGNOT (J.-P. Péquignot), 8 rue du Grand-Chêne (236249).
Old and modern paintings. Auctions.

Galerie POTTERAT, 8 ave du Théâtre (224453).
Oriental carpets, paintings, furniture, objets d'art. Auctions.

Michel RIGALDO, 7 and 9 escaliers du Marché.
Pewter, furniture, general antiques, copper, bronze, silver.

Au TEMPS RETROUVE (Carmen Porchet), 13 rue Caroline (225736)
Clocks, furniture, mirrors, etc.

Galerie Paul VALLOTTON (Claude and Maxime Vallotton), 6 rue du Grand-Chêne (2nd floor) (229166).
Antique furniture, works of art, glass, porcelain, pictures, bibelots. Open Mon.–Fri. 0900–1200, 1400–1830; also by appointment.

Fairs
Antique fair.
Yearly in Nov.

Auctions
Henri BLANC, 3 pl du Tunnel (233238; private 268620).
See 'Dealers'.

Galerie PEQUIGNOT (J.-P. Pequignot), 8 rue du Grand-Chêne (236249).
See 'Dealers'.

Galerie POTTERAT, 8 ave du Théâtre (224453).
See 'Dealers'.

Lucerne

Dealers
Fr. Mathilde BUEL, Hertensteinstr 12 (225523).
Antiques, works of art, Helvetica, furniture, porcelain, silver, sculpture, jewellery.

Galerie FISCHER, (Dr Paul and Arthur Fischer), Haldenstr 19 (225772/3).
Large stock of paintings, antiques, works of art, furniture, porcelain, silver, drawings, engravings, books, arms, armour, sculpture, Oriental items. Auctions.

GILHOFER & RAUSCHBURG GmbH (Axel Erdmann), Haldenstr 9/1 (236466).
Rare books, especially incunabula, humanism, old sciences and Americana; old and modern drawings and prints. Open 0800–1200, 1400–1800; appointment advisable.

Frl. M. KOPP, Weinmarkt 17 (228997).
Antiques, paintings, furniture, porcelain, silver, sculpture, carpets, small antiques.

Freddie KUNG, Haldenstr 7 (231415).
15th/18th-century; clocks, Greek, Roman and Etruscan antiques.

KUNSTHANDEL AG (Mrs May Steinmeyer), Haldenstr 12 (21387).
Old paintings, antiques.

Frl. Olga MAHLER, Haldenstr 5 (31383).
Porcelain, silver, sculpture, furniture, small antiques.

ST JAMES'S gallery, Unter der Egg 10 (222014).
English antiques, clocks, watches, prints, oil-paintings, silver.

WEY GALERIE, Haldenstr. 11 (225507).
Furniture, sculpture, 18th-century European porcelain, silver, icons, glass, paintings.

Joseph WILLIMAN, Theaterstr 3 (22444).
General antiques, furniture, pictures, porcelain, sculpture, carpets, small antiques.

Auctions
Galerie FISCHER (Dr Paul and Arthur Fischer), Haldenstr 19 (225772/3).
See 'Dealers'. Big international sales twice yearly in June and Nov.

Neuchâtel

Dealers
Jacques E. MEYLAN, 2 pl des Halles (52806).
General antiques.

Claude SCHNEIDER, Evole 9 (252289).
18th/19th-century French and Swiss furniture, porcelain, pewter,

silver; specialist in antique clocks. Open Mon.–Fri. 0800–1200, 1400–1830, Sat. 0800–1200, 1400–1700.

Zürich

Dealers

ARS DOMI (Frau DR A. Torre), Talstr 14 (273474).
Specialist in antique porcelain; silver, glass, etc.

ART ANCIEN, Signaustr 6 (479229).
15th/20th-century books, prints

Angelo COLOMBO, Münstergasse 8 (327785).
Specialist in Continental and English clocks, Gallé glass and art nouveau. Open Mon.–Fri. 1330–1830; Sat 1330–1600; also by appointment.

Erwin DIETRICH, Werdmühlepl 4 (270167).
Numismatic items.

Dr Walter FEILCHENFELDT, Freiestr 116 (447960).
Important impressionist paintings, drawings, old masters.

Galerie GROSSMUNSTER, Kirchgasse 28 (326026).
Swiss furniture and paintings.

Milon GUGGENHEIM, Alfred-Escher-Str 17 (252045).
Fine stock of silver, general small antiques.

HAFTER, Zeltweg 67 (476962).
English antiques, especially silver, plate and scientific instruments. Also in Basel.

Galerie Semiha HUBER, Talstr 18 (233303).
Modern pictures, sculpture, lithographs.

IMEO Ltd – GOLDEN CIRCLE, 7 Schoffelgasse (340706).
Chinese and Japanese arts, coloured stones, hardstone-carvings, jewels, ivories, prints, antique watches. Open 0800–1200, 1400–1730; also by appointment.

Galerie KOLLER, Ramistr 8 (475040; private 347543).
Fine 18th-century furniture (especially French), silver, clocks, porcelain, paintings, prints, engravings. Open Mon.–Fri. 0830–1200, 1330–1830; Sat. 0830–1200, 1330–1600; also by appointment. Auctions.

KORNFELD & KLIPSTEIN. Titlistr 48
19th/20th century art. Also in Berne.

LAUBE & Sohn (August Laube) Trittligasse 19 (328550; private 521633, 885374).
Old-master prints, 15th- and 18th-century illustrated books on Switzerland. Open Mon.–Fri., appointment advisable. Auctions.

Edgar MANNHEIMER, Sonneggstr 80.
Important stock of antique clocks and watches; scientific instruments.

Galerie MEISSNER, Florastr 1 (325110).
Fine stock of 15th/19th-century paintings and drawings.

Dr Fritz & Dr Peter NATHAN, Arosastr. 7(554550).
Important stock of 19th-century French and modern paintings; drawings, old masters. Appointment necessary.

Galerie am NEUMARKT (Walter Germann), Neumarkt 13(328358).
Jewellery, watches, clocks, books, graphic arts, paintings, drawings, Helvetica. Open 0900–1230, 1330–1830. Auctions.

SCHUMANN(Hans W. Neubauer), Ramistr 25(320272).
Books, modern engravings. Open 0900–1830.

Frank STERNBERG, Bahnhofstr 84(277980).
Coins, medals, ancient art. Open 1000–1200, 1500–1800; appointment advisable.

Antiquités TOUTES EPOQUES (Mme Berthe Tripet), Dufourstr 82 (320113; private 333923).
Antique furniture, works of art, glass, porcelain, pictures, bibelots. Open 0900–1200, 1400–1830; also by appointment.

André VOGT, Predigergasse 4 (474155).
Good stock of antique Swiss country furniture, mostly painted.
Open 1400–1830, Sat. 1000–1600; appointment advisable.

Auctions
Galerie KOLLER, Ramistr 8 (475040; private 347543).
See 'Dealers'. Internationally important sales of a wide range of
fine-art objects from netsuke to musical boxes, Persian rugs to
Swiss watches.

*LAUBE & Sohn (August Laube), Trittligasse 19 (328550; private
521633, 885374).*
See 'Dealers'.

Galerie am NEUMARKT (Walter Germann), Neumarkt 13 (328358).
See 'Dealers'. Specialist sales of watches, clocks, paintings, coins,
books, prints, weapons, model railways, etc.

Fairs
Foirie des Antiquaires,
Early autumn.

Museums
Basel

MUSEUM FUR VOLKERKUNDE, Augustinergasse.
A good place to study the old popular arts.

CITY ART GALLERY.
Including work by the romantic painter Arnold Bocklin.

Berne
HISTORICAL MUSEUM, Barfüsserkirche.
Including arts of the popular culture.

NATIONAL COIN COLLECTION.

SWISS RIFLE MUSEUM, Bernastr 5.
Of interest to antique-weapon collectors.

Geneva

BAUR COLLECTION, 8 rue Munier-Romilly.
A 'must' for collectors of Chinese and Japanese ceramics, jades
and prints.

HISTORY AND SCIENCE MUSEUM, Perle-du-Lac Park.
Antique scientific instruments.

MUNICIPAL ART GALLERY.
Including work of the portraitist F. Massot.

MUSEE ARIANA, 10 ave de la Paix.
Ceramics.

MUSEE D'ART ET D'HISTOIRE, rue Charles-Galland.
Including work by gothic painter Konrad Witz.

*MUSEUM OF ANTIQUE MUSICAL INSTRUMENTS, 23 rue
Lefort.*

*MUSEUM OF WATCHES AND ENAMELS, part of the Musée
d'Art et d'Histoire.*

Lausanne

*MUSEUM OF THE CONAN DOYLE FOUNDATION, Château de
Lecens.*
A 'must' for Sherlock Holmes fans—includes a replica of 221b
Baker St.

Lugano

*BARON HEINRICH VON THYSSEN COLLECTION, Villa
Favorita.*
Probably the finest private collection in Europe. Open Sat.–Sun.
in April–Oct.

St Gallen

LIBRARY OF THE ABBEY OF ST GALLEN.
Antiquarian books and illuminated manuscripts.

St Moritz

ENGADINE MUSEUM, Badstr.
Popular arts.

Zürich

BEYER MUSEUM OF TIME MEASUREMENT, Bahnhofstr 31
Clocks, watches, Open Tues., Thur. and Fri. 1500–1700.

CITY ART GALLERY.
Including work of the romantic painter Arnold Bocklin.

FRANZ CARL WEBER MUSEUM, Bahnhofstr 62.
Late 18th- to early 20th-century toys. Open Thur., 1500–1700.

KUNSTHAUS, Heimpl 1.
Including sculpture of Alberto Giacometti.

NATIONAL MUSEUM, Museumstr 2.
Popular arts.

THOMAS MANN ARCHIVES, Schönberggasse 15.
The author's manuscripts, library and study. Open Wed. and
Sat. 1400–1600.

ZUNFTHAUS ZUR MEISEN, Munsterhof 20.
Swiss 18th-century ceramics.

*UNIVERSITY MEDICO-HISTORICAL COLLECTION, Ramistr
73.*
Medical instruments and documents from primitive medicine to
the 20th century. Open Mon. and Wed. 1400–1700.

This Isnik pottery dish decorated in blue and turquoise dates from the late 16th century

14
Turkey

Introduction

A meeting place for East and West for 4000 years, Turkey is a rich layer-cake of art history. First came the Hittite culture (3000–1000 BC), then the Greek and Roman civilizations in Anatolia, the splendid marble bones of which can be marvelled at in some of the world's great classical sites—Ephesus, Pergamum, Troy, Didyma, Miletus. The magnificence of the Byzantine era then intervened before the rise of the Ottoman Empire, which stretched at one time from Vienna to the Persian Gulf and was for some 200 years politically and culturally a dominant force in Europe.

There are incalculable art treasures in Turkey—in 1909 it was said that masses of Ming, T'ang and Sung pottery were discovered, still in their original packing-cases, in the Topkapi Museum in Istanbul, and many archaeological sites have yet to be fully explored. Strict control is imposed on all archaeological remains and antiques leaving the country: visitors should always make sure when buying that export can be cleared with the authorities. One good method is to ask the dealer in Turkey to take the object to a museum; if the officials there approve its export they will issue a certificate.

Art objects available to buy come mainly from the Turkish Seljuk and Ottoman periods, post-Byzantine: basically silver, ceramics, jewellery, brocades, carpets and some icons. Izmir is a good source for the latter, but collectors should beware of fakes. Iznik ceramic tiles are famous for their brilliant colour and bold designs. It is sometimes possible to find Roman seals of semi-precious stones and Greek and Roman coins. Most of the available silver is 19th-century, but some very pretty pieces were made then, such as bowls for holding rosewater and typically filigreed holders for coffee-cups known as zarfs. Painting and sculpture were regarded as idolatrous—a legacy of Islam—but miniature-painting flourished at the court of the Sultans, being approved of so long as it was not displayed in public.

A visit to Istanbul's Great Covered Market (Kapalcarsi) is a must for any visitor to this fascinating city. Dealers in antiques are grouped together, as are dealers in gold, jewellery, leatherwork and other specialities. Here can be bought attractive Ottoman silverwork of the late 19th and early 20th centuries, such as plaited silver belts and cigarette cases of Armenian and Russian origin decorated with niello work—engraving filled with a glossy black alloy. Carpet hunters will probably find better bargains outside Istanbul, where many of the items offered will either be modern or so worn as to be worthless. One should always, always bargain. A bid of half the asking price is considered a fair basis for haggling. For objects over a value of 2000 Turkish lire, certificates must be obtained by foreign buyers to prove that the article was paid for in foreign currency cashed by an official bureau in Turkey.

But even if the rarer Turkish antiques are hard to come by, collectors in Turkey cannot help learning a great deal about Ottoman and Byzantine culture from the great museums in Istanbul, among them the famous Topkapi Museum, with all the treasures of the Sultans, and the Santa Sophia Basilica, built in the reign of the Roman Emperor Justinian and converted first into a mosque in 1453 and then into a museum in the 1930s.

Specialities

Bookbindings

Persian craftsmen brought to Istanbul by Sultan Selim I in 1514 gave the Ottomans the art of book-binding, which remained very Persian in style. Turkish binders excelled in decoration, elegance and delicacy of execution: a particularly Turkish speciality was the combination of polished leather with gold-painting and presswork. Metal was not normally used in Islamic bindings, though the Topkapi Museum in Istanbul has a collection of gold bindings studded with jewels. Sultan Suleyman's brother-in-law and vizier was reputed to own 130 Korans decorated with precious stones. Most 16th-century bindings were of leather, decorated with blind and gold tooling, filigreework over a coloured ground or stamped designs. Usually the cover decoration was dominated by a central medallion, as on carpets, and many of the designs were similar. Lacquer bindings with decoration in liquid gold, silver and pearl dust were also a Turkish speciality—a Chinese invention which the Ottomans picked up from the Persians.

Brass and Copper

Pieces dating back 200–300 years with attractive floral or geometric designs, some plated with tin for household durability, are among the best buys in Turkish antiques. Copperware is also a flourishing modern industry in Turkey.

Carpets and Rugs

Most Turkish and Anatolian rugs with their bold designs and vivid colours, predominantly blue and red, come from the two central provinces of Ankara and Konya. In the 19th century Izmir (or Smyrna as it then was) was the collection point for despatch to Europe, and today the chance of buying a good Turkish rug is much better in Izmir, Kusadasi or Konya than in Istanbul, where stocks tend to be heavily overpriced, hopelessly worn or modern. One London dealer in Oriental carpets who visits Turkey regularly on a buying circuit was recently asked £15 000 in Turkey for a Shirvan rug which would have cost £3000 at the most in London. Turkey has very strict regulations governing the export of antiques, old rugs and works of art, but provincial centres like Izmir and Kusadasi (a popular cruise-ship stop) are easier to get purchases out of than Istanbul. Once a collector has chosen a rug he should ask the dealer to take it to a museum; if officials there consider it reasonably common or already have an example they will probably release it for export.

There are good rugs to be had in the 50-year-old bracket, but little of any great age. The 1920s rugs can be picked up cheaply on the Izmir–Kusadasi–Konya–Ankara circuit without danger of running into fakes, though there is a quantity of worn-out merchandise which dealers will present as being 300 years old and which is not worth buying at any price.

The best advice to prospective buyers is to study the different types of Turkish rug carefully in London before visiting Turkey (London has been the centre of the Oriental-rug trade since 1900) until a firm idea crystallizes as to what to look for. In Turkey, foreign buyers should attempt to knock as much as 50 per cent off the asking price for rugs and carpets, ending up with at least a one-third discount after bargaining is finished.

Ceramics

Pottery was brought to Central Asia and Turkey by the Seljuks, and they and the Ottoman Turks later made decorative tiles for the interior and exterior of houses, mosques, palaces, fountains and baths. In the 15th and 16th centuries, particularly in the Iznik region 75 miles southwest of Istanbul, Ottoman ceramics achieved a richness of colour and design which won them a worldwide reputation. Early Iznik pottery copied Chinese blue-and-white designs, but late Iznik plates tended to be rather crude and their vivid tones somewhat discoloured. By 1900 Turkish pottery was being seriously collected in other countries and now, after a period of depression, its prices are again going up.

Modern Turkish pottery often uses Seljuk motifs, notably flowers such as tulips, carnations, roses and hyacinths, and geometrical patterns. The Yildiz factory, founded by Sultan Abdulhamit II and closed after his deposition in 1909, is in production again making high-quality porcelain, including copies of porcelain vases in the Topkapi Museum.

Jewellery

Antique filigree silver jewellery is typically Turkish, and there are many fine old pieces in gold and precious stones. In the main street of Antalya are shops where Roman seals made from semiprecious stones may be found.

Miniatures

Turkish art in this field, previously overshadowed by that of Persia, has come to be highly regarded by connoisseurs. Early

Ottoman miniatures were close in style and subject to those of Persia, but the later Turkish miniatures were characterized by movement and energy in contrast to the contemplative manner of the Persian artists. Turkish painters came to favour 'action' subjects such as historical events, though they also illustrated the Persian poets and did portraits of Ottoman notables such as Sultans like Suleyman the Magnificent—themselves patrons and active exponents of the arts. One splendid manuscript on the life of Suleyman, illustrated with miniature paintings, is now in the Chester Beatty collection in Dublin.

Silver

The history of Turkish silver goes back more than three centuries and involved the fusing of many Asia Minor cultures. Definite Turkish characteristics appeared for the first time in the 14th century. Later, important centres of silver were Erzurum and Van. The only method of hallmarking was by the Stamp Office, and if the three officials responsible dared to stamp silver of a lower alloy than that laid down by the Sultan's court they were beheaded. In consequence Turkish silver had a guaranteed quality of 900 parts of silver, and the reign of the Sultan—though not the maker—is identified in the mark.

Silver from the 16th century is practically nonexistent and that from the 17th century is rare. The earliest examples found today are on weapons forged from 'watered steel' and decorated with silver, gold and jewels. There are also 15th-century helmets covered in damascene work, and 17th- and 18th-century scimitars, daggers and guns decorated with silver arabesques.

Domestic silver dates from the 17th century, but collectors would be lucky to find such typical articles of that period as penboxes or portable inkpots. In the mid 18th century Turkish silver became strongly influenced by European design, especially French. Louis XV, Louis XVI and Empire motifs were popular—flowers, bouquets, garlands, ribbons, egg and dart and wave patterns—as was repoussé work. Articles from this period included mirrors, birdcages, lanterns and braziers, the hospitable waterpipe and the coffee-cup holder or zarf, usually made in pierced silver or filigree. The latter is an important element in Turkish silver, seen to fine advantage in such items as sweetmeat dishes, vases for a single rose or basins for holding rosewater.

In the 19th century collectors have more choice with many types of spoon, including some with bowls made of Turkish coins. Dealer Abdul in Istanbul has a fine selection of 19th-century silver. In general, it can be said that very little silver survives on the market from the pre-18th century era, and there are very few pieces with traditional Ottoman designs, probably due to the custom of melting down silver utensils whenever money was needed by the court. For silver of pre-18th-century vintage one has to turn, probably in museums, to weapons of the period, Koran covers or perhaps a rare pencase to see the fine arabesque decoration and Kufic lettering which was characteristic before European influences took over.

The trade

Ankara

Dealers
ANTIKITE, Anafartalas Caddesi.
The most important dealer in antiquities in the Turkish capital.

HODJA, Mesrutiyet Caddesi 19.
Antique jewellery.

MODA MODEL, Ulus is Hani.
General antiques, especially brass.

Istanbul

Dealers
ABDUL, Hotel Hilton (486360).
Fine Turkish silver.

ASEO, Carsil Kebir Sahaflar Sok 97 (227340).

CANSEVER EDIP, Sandalbedesteni 32, Kapalcarsi (227657).

KARAKUS, Sandalbedesteni 19, Kapalcarsi (270936).

Ali KAZGAN, ic Bedesten 26 and 35, Kapalcarsi (275256).
Antiques, ceramics, carpets, jewellery, silver, arms, armour.

Abdullah KENT, Zincirli Han 7-9, Kapalcarsi (273397).

ORIENT, Bankalar Caddesi, Bankalar Han Kat 5, no. 37.
Antiques, coins, Oriental art, carpets, antiquities, weapons.

SEVSEVIL LUTFI, Zincirli Han 106, Kapalcarsi (220977).

Ibrahim TOREDI, Cevahir Bedesteni Sokak 105, Kapalcarsi (227478).
General antiques.

Markets
KAPALCARSI.
Great covered market in which dealers in antiques are grouped together, as are dealers in gold, jewellery, leatherwork and other specialities. Wide variety of handicrafts and artwork.

Museums
Ankara

MUSEE D'ETHNOGRAPHIE, nr Bouloire de Talat Pacha (113007).
Folk costume and Turkish ceramics from the 15th to the 18th centuries.

NATIONAL LIBRARY (123132).
Ancient manuscripts and rare books.

Istanbul

ARCHAEOLOGICAL MUSEUMS OF ISTANBUL, Sultanmet (279070, 224093).
Famous collections of old coins and antiquities.

MUSEUM OF TURKISH AND ISLAMIC ART, Suleymaniye 6
Sifahane St (221888).
A rich feast of Turkish religious art, rare manuscripts, miniatures,
antique copies of the Koran in ivory-encrusted caskets,
metalwork, wood-carvings, ceramics including wonderful
examples of Iznik tiles, and the greatest collection in the world of
Islamic rugs, though only a small proportion are on display.

SANTA SOPHIA BASILICA.
Splendid Byzantine church containing many art treasures.

TOPKAPI MUSEUM (278110).
Probably the world's finest collection of Chinese porcelain, the
fabulous jewelled treasures of the Sultans, and fine collections of
antique arms and armour, enamels, Turkish miniatures and
glazed earthenware.

Further reading

Erdmann, Kurt, *Seven Hundred Years of Oriental Rugs and Carpets*
(London: Faber, 1970).
Lane, Arthur, *Guide to Tiles* (London, 1960)
Levey, Michael, *The World of Ottoman Art* (London: Thames &
Hudson, 1976)
Rice, D. Talbot, *Islamic Art* (London: Thames & Hudson, 1968).

Part Two
Eastern Europe

Introduction

Eastern Europe—the German Democratic Republic, Hungary, Poland, Czechoslovakia, Yugoslavia, Romania and Bulgaria, plus the USSR—is very largely a closed book to Western collectors, as it is in so many other aspects of life. (Albania is so entirely closed as not to be worthwhile including in a book of this type.) It remains both fascinating and frustrating to art lovers, because of the richness of a heritage which takes in Slavic folk art of many kinds, as well as Habsburg, Venetian and Ottoman influences, and which is built on a foundation of Greek and Roman antiquities whose surface is only now beginning to be uncovered. In Eastern European museums masterpieces of classical, gothic and baroque art may be enjoyed, but in the antique shops of its countries, run inexorably by the state, there is little of real age or value which is allowed to filter through to foreign visitors.

Most dealers who have anything to do with the 'Iron Curtain' countries know that there is very little that Western visitors can buy. In the USSR certainly the state buys up all the best items of pre-Revolutionary art—especially icons—and then lets them out to Western markets, where their value is well known, in a judicious trickle. In Czechoslovakia today the price of antique Bohemian glass is probably more than would be paid in London. In most East European countries, says one London dealer in icons who travels the Balkan area regularly, all that is left for Western buyers is 'rubbish'. Even the Czech state antique dealers say that antiques are of 'inferior quality' and that they would not advise a visit to Czechoslovakia for this purpose.

This is not to say that there are no antiques worth buying in these countries; it is just the extreme difficulty, if not impossibility, of getting export permits for anything of special interest. Local residents and diplomats can buy without difficulty and often find beautiful things—one French family in Moscow built up a fine collection of pre-revolutionary porcelain—but diplomats have the edge on other people of being able to use 'diplomatic bag' facilities, immune to customs inspection. And when a diplomatic family moves house the 'diplomatic bag' can literally assume the size of a container load. Some countries have stricter export regulations than others. In most, prohibitions against export of art objects relate to pre-revolutionary paintings or antiques, but in Romania nothing is allowed out—even of post-1945 vintage—if it is regarded as of national interest.

Yugoslavia and Czechoslovakia have the largest and finest collections of art treasures; according to one expert on Eastern European art the Serbian wall paintings of Yugoslavia and the baroque architecture of Prague are the greatest treasures in Eastern Europe. On the whole, painting is less outstanding than architecture, perhaps because social conditions prevented the emergence of a distinct school of painting and because aristocratic patronage tended to go to foreign artists. But Serbia was rich in Byzantine iconography and new treasures are being discovered every year.

For collectors the best advice is: enjoy the museums and art galleries but do not expect to pick up any treasures for a song in a dusty back street shop in Prague, Gdańsk, Sofia or Bucharest. In Yugoslavia the market is freer than in the other countries, but prices will probably be no less than in Vienna or Paris.

In all the Eastern European countries the best chance of a bargain—and of an export permit—lies in books or prints, particularly those of Western provenance which do not attract the 'national interest' label. A Western news agency correspondent in Moscow managed to buy a set of original Hogarth engravings for well below their market value and to export them without difficulty. Nearly all the Eastern European capitals are rich in secondhand booksellers; in the USSR, Poland and Czechoslovakia there are still relics of old libraries being broken up, and local dealers do not know or are not interested in the values of many of the 18th- and 19th-century Western books.

The other possibility is to invest in modern work. Folk art is of a high standard throughout most of Eastern Europe and in most countries the authorities are anxious to promote its sale. In Poland the work of contemporary coin and medal designers matches the best of the past, and it is certainly worth considering forming a collection of modern Polish numismatic items.

Whoever travels in Bulgaria today will see the countless Thracian grass-covered burial mounds which dot the countryside. From one of them came this marble relief of a bearded horseman, now in the Archaeological Museum, Sofia

15
Bulgaria

Introduction

The stunning exhibition of golden treasures from Thrace mounted by the British Museum in conjunction with the Bulgarian government in 1976 opened many eyes to the marvellous tradition of workmanship in this former Roman province. Bulgaria reached its artistic peak in the Middle Ages, when finely-painted ceramic icons and the glass made at Preslav in the 10th century ranked among Europe's finest artefacts. In the 19th century, at the end of 500 years of Turkish rule, during which time Bulgarian culture had been kept alive in the remote Orthodox monasteries, the country had a cultural renaissance, and icons of refreshingly primitive style were produced at that time.

Today, nine specialist museums have been set up for the display of icons alone, and no fewer than 25 towns have been declared 'museum towns' for the importance of their architecture and art history. Bulgarians take their art seriously. Painting in particular is a public art, with painters working on what in the West would be advertisement hoardings. In small towns artists from the local painters' union decorate the gable ends of houses or the walls of the public library. Fine paintings from the national renaissance period of the 19th century can be seen at the Monastery Museum in Rila, 30 miles south of Sofia.

Altogether there are 201 state-supported museums and about 25 000 cultural monuments of various kinds in this country with a population of only 9 million, and archaeological excavations take place at an average 120 sites a year. Sofia is a city resting literally on 7000 years of history and it has had the layer-cake of its heritage cut open in a most dramatic way. Above ground is a modern urban landscape; below the surface, in subways and underground rooms, the antique streets, towers, gates, baths and churches are preserved as if through a window on another age.

Bulgaria has always been famous for its folk arts: textiles, woodcarvings, icons, pottery (faience was made in the 9th and 10th centuries and revived in the 19th-century renaissance), goldsmithing, ironwork, leatherwork and hand-weaving. Modern versions of Persian rugs are still made. Copper, silver and pottery ware is also made in the old traditional designs.

There is, however, no antique trade as such. In Bulgaria's pre-revolutionary society there was virtually no cultured middle class with a knowledge of antiques, and before 1944 only a few Bulgarians could afford or were interested in collecting. These few kept—and still keep—their treasures within their own families, and if antiques or works of art do change hands it is done privately. Individuals may legally sell only to the Hemus Foreign Trade Organization in Sofia, which is concerned with books, works of art, musical instruments (antique and modern) and sheet music; Hemus then sells these to the public, reaping a fat profit, and can issue a certificate, known as a *belezhka*, to permit export.

There is really no prospect of finding good antiques, paintings or icons in Bulgaria, but there are secondhand shops in Sofia where conceivably finds could be made among the bric-à-brac and outright junk. Anything bought in a secondhand shop can be freely exported. Two of the secondhand shops, in Graf Ignatiev Street and Rakovski Street, sell mainly junk such as broken cameras and worn-out plated cutlery, but the one in Georgi Dimitrov Street and in Kirov Street by the main market are recommended as better prospects. Coin collectors should visit the numismatic shop on Vitosha Street which sells old and valuable coins and which can issue an export certificate. There are two secondhand bookshops; the larger, Antikvarni Knigi in Graf Ignatiev Street sells mainly 'nearly new' textbooks, but there is a more interesting, small bookshop housed in a near-shack at the bottom of Vitosha Street. Some reproduction (but not very old) maps have been seen there also.

Finally, there are two markets in Sofia worth investigating: the Gipsy Market where, apparently, interesting items can occasionally be found, and the Peasant Market where junk items are sometimes on display.

The trade

Sofia

Dealers

ANTIKVARNI KNIGI, 19 ul Graf Ignatiev.
Secondhand books, mainly 'nearly new' textbooks.

HEMUS, 6 blvd Rouski.
Books, works of art, antique and modern musical instruments, sheet music. Export certificates.

RAZNOIZNOS, 1 ruse Assen.
State organisation for export and import.

Bookshop, bottom of ul Vitosha.
Books, maps.

Numismatic shop, ul Vitosha.
Old and valuable coins. Export certificates.

Secondhand shops, ul Georgi Dimitrov and ul Kirov.
Recommended.

Secondhand shops, ul Graf Ignatiev and ul Rakovski.

Markets

GIPSY MARKET, nr the cemetery.
Open Tues. and Fri.

PEASANT MARKET, behind Georgi Dimitrov Arch nr the canal.

Museums

Sofia

NATIONAL ARCHAEOLOGICAL MUSEUM.
Housed in a 15th-century mosque, it possesses important gold

treasures from the 4th century BC, Alexander's tombstone and marble remains from Roman sites, an important collection of icons and other mural paintings, and one of the world's richest numismatic collections but is rarely open.

NATIONAL ART GALLERY.
Works mainly from the period of Bulgarian renaissance in the 19th century. An annexe in the crypt of the Alexander Nevski Cathedral holds the main collection of medieval Bulgarian art, with many beautiful icons and illuminated gospels.

Rila

MONASTERY MUSEUM.
A priceless treasury of ancient icons, medieval wood-carvings, gold and silver ornaments, richly-embroidered ecclesiastical vestments and more than 16 000 rare books, mostly in manuscript.

Czechoslovakia is renowned for its traditional engraved glass. This Bohemian beaker, decorated with a portrait of the Emperor Leopold I, dates from about 1690

16
Czechoslovakia

Introduction

Czechoslovakia came into existence as an independent state
following the first world war. It was created from three lands:
Bohemia, Moravia and Slovakia. The Kingdom of Bohemia had,
with Moravia, been part of the Habsburg dominions since the
period of the Thirty Years War (1618-48), while Slovakia formed
part of Hungary. Prague, the capital of modern Czechoslovakia,
had been the capital city of Bohemia and one of the principal cities
first of the Holy Roman Empire and then of the Austro-
Hungarian Empire, with a history going back to the early middle
ages.

Czechoslovakia has in some ways suffered less from war and
occupation than other countries of the area now designated as
Eastern Europe. All of them were occupied or partitioned by
foreign powers for generations, but the Austrian hegemony over
Bohemia from 1528 to 1918 was in many ways more beneficial
than the Turkish rule of the Balkan countries to the south. In the
14th century Charles I of Bohemia (1347-78) became Holy
Roman Emperor, as Charles IV, and Prague became the centre of
Europe, both politically and culturally. In the sixteenth century
Rudolf II, a Habsburg ruler (1576-1611), moved his capital from
Vienna to Prague. Prague is still said to be the most beautiful city
north of the Alps, with a greater variety of art and architecture
packed into a small space than anywhere else. Lying in the
geographical heart of Europe, it is in fact west of Vienna, and
Czech culture still has an indefinably Western European feel
about it.

The history of fine arts in Czechoslovakia goes back to neolithic
times, and there are German, Jewish and Hungarian influences as
well as Czech and Slovak. A continuous artistic heritage can be

traced back to the early middle ages, while during the gothic period, the golden age of Bohemian art, Prague was known throughout Europe as the 'city of a hundred spires'. Following the Thirty Years War the art and architecture of the country became predominately baroque, imparting a memorable legacy in painting, sculpture and engraving. In the 19th century there was a national artistic upsurge and a school of Czech art became firmly established. In the 20th century Czech artists played leading roles in the development of art nouveau, surrealism and cubism.

Czechoslovakia has always been strong in the decorative arts. Bohemian glass of course is famous throughout the world, and Bohemian baroque silver, virtually unknown outside the country, was the next most important decorative medium; each piece was literally unique. Furniture, bookbindings, embroidery, lace, pewter and wrought ironwork were also important, and there was a fine native tradition of wood-carving, icon-influenced painting on glass and handsome folk ceramics, all from various regions of Slovakia.

Antique shops in Czechoslovakia, as everywhere else in Eastern Europe, are mainly run by the state. In the old part of Prague may be seen the odd antique shop which looks like a relic of pre-Communist days but which in fact is probably part of a state chain. These are mostly devoted to bric-à-brac, Austro-Hungarian kitsch of the type beloved by the lower middle class in the reign of Franz Josef—pen stands ornamented with ironwork and cheap green stone, surmounted by the Imperial eagle, and lamps made out of figurines of girls and youths in flowing William Morris-type draperies. Nám Prikope is one of Prague's chief shopping streets for antiques, among other things; Krizovnicka has fascinating bookshops on either side, where the visitor may find many interesting items.

The usual procedure for foreigners is to obtain coupons for foreign currency at the Tuzex shops and then to exchange these coupons at the antique shops, but in the end the cost may be more than the price at home. Some Tuzex shops in the big tourist hotels sell modern Bohemian glass, porcelain from Karlový Vary (Carlsbad) and wood-carvings. The import and export of Czech currency is prohibited and all currency transactions must be noted on the visa form. The export of antiques is permitted if the buyer obtains a certificate from a state concern such as Artia in Prague.

Specialities

Glass

Around 1700 the mechanization of water power enabled glass cutters in Bohemia and Silesia (now Polish territory) to make their craft faster and more accurate. The early 18th century was the greatest period of Czech glass-engraving, when it became superior even to that of Venice. The technique was introduced by Kaspar Lehman and Bohemian glass was characterized by the baluster-form goblet with deep engraving. Portrait busts in high relief were a popular form of glass decoration, and in the rococo period gilding was added to the cutting and engraving. Bohemia did a roaring trade in glass trimmings for chandeliers (introduced in 1724), in mirrors and in artificial jewellery made from coloured glass. Some antique Bohemian and Silesian glass can still be found in Czech antique shops, but even in 1968, before the Soviet invasion, prices were more expensive than in London.

Painting and sculpture

Czech gothic art was outstanding in painting and sculpture (see the National Gallery, Prague); foremost among native painters were the Master of Vyssi Brod (c. 1350), Master Theodorik (c. 1360) and the Master of Trebon (c. 1380). The statues on the Charles Bridge in Prague speak eloquently of the great age of baroque, and two artists who gained a wider fame were the Slovak painter Jan Kupecký and the engraver Vaclav Hollar.

In the national artistic upsurge of the 19th century the foundations of a Czech school of painting were laid by Josef Manes (1820–71) and Josef Navrátil (1798–1865). By the second half of the century Czech art was firmly established, with fine landscape, historical, portrait and genre painters. The leading sculptor of the period was Josef Mylsbek, who was born in the tumultuous revolutionary year of 1848 and lived until 1922; he sculpted the figure of St. Wenceslas (Sv. Vaclav) which commands Wenceslas Square (Vaclavske náměsti) in Prague and is regarded as the founder of modern Czech sculpture.

In this century many important Czech artists settled in Paris after the First World War, though Alphonse Mucha, perhaps the most famous, returned home in the end. Expatriate Czech artists played a leading role in the fermenting art movements of the early 20th century, especially surrealism and cubism.

The trade

Bratislava

Dealers
ANTIQUITES, branches at Jiraskova 16, Nalepku 17 and Leningradska 7.

TUZEX, Gorkeho 12.
Coupons for foreign currency.

SLOVENSKA KNIHA, branches at Mickiewiczova 10 (50164) and Sedliarska 9(30117).
Rare books.

Prague (Praha)
Dealers
ANTIQUITES, branches at Narodni trída 43, Melantrichova 9, Mikulanska 7, Nosteka 7, nám Mutsku 9, Narodni trída 24, Presslova 5, Ponic 35, Simackova 17, Uhelny trh. 6, ul Smaltovny 25, Vaclavske nám 60 and Vinohradska 45(254781).
Auctions at Mikulanska 7.

ART CENTRUM, V. Jame 10 and Starostrasnicka 25(220652/3).

ARTIA, Ve Smeckach 30(2460410)
.State commercial import/export and publishing organization.

Galerie DILO, Narodni trída 37(220962).

GALERIE, Narodni trída 30.

KNIHA, Diazdena 5 (221861).
Rare books.

KNIHA, branches at Karlova ul 2 (234282) and (240275) and ul Radice 1.
Rare books, paintings, graphic art.

TUZEX, Rytirska 13.
Coupons for foreign currency.

Antiquarian book export centre, Stepanska 65.

Markets
Collectors' exchange market, Vaclavske nám
Chiefly banknotes, coins and stamps. Open Sun. morning.

Auctions
ANTIQUITES, Mikulanska 7.
See 'Dealers'.

Museums

Brno

MORAVIAN MUSEUM.
Moravian folk art, especially ceramics.

Prague

DVORAK MUSEUM, Villa Amerika, corner of Bozena Nemcova ul. and Diezenhoferova ul.
Memorabilia of the composer.

FAUST HOUSE, Karlovo nám.
Commemorates the ill-fated Prague student who originated the legend through his supposed pact with the devil.

MUSEUM OF NATIONAL LITERATURE.
Medieval literature and incunabula, including a 9th-century Bible manuscript.

NATIONAL GALLERY.
The collection of gothic art is one of Europe's great treasures.

NATIONAL LIBRARY.
World's largest collection of the writings of John Wycliffe, the 14th-century scholar who translated the Bible into English.

NATIONAL MUSEUM, Vaclavske nám.
Numismatic section with 250 000 Czech, Moravian, Silesian, Slovak and foreign coins; one of Europe's best collections of musical instruments.

SMETANA MUSEUM.
Memorabilia of the composer.

Further reading

Hettes, Karel, *Glass in Czechoslovakia* (Prague, 1958).
Poche, E., *Bohemian Porcelain* (Prague: Artia).
Rhodes, Anthony, *Art Treasures of Eastern Europe* (London: Weidenfeld, 1972).

A Potsdam goblet decorated with a portrait of Queen Sophia Dorothea, surmounted by a crown and eagle

17
German Democratic Republic

Introduction

About the time that East–West trade was opening up in the 1950s, the German Democratic Republic was a fruitful source of antiques for foreign visitors. Many antique shops were still in private hands and their owners were anxious to obtain hard currency. Inevitably this loophole was closed by the state authorities, who took over most of the shops, and though private antique dealers can still be found, the best things have all gone into the state shops or directly into museums.

A lot of good antiques were in any case 'milked' from the German Democratic Republic just after the Second World War. This particularly affected East Berlin, where Allied soldiers and diplomats contributed to the drain of antiques and where, before the building of the Wall in 1961, there was a brisk westward flow of refugees bringing out their family treasures to sell. East Berlin antique shops therefore tend to have little of interest now; their stocks include a lot of poorly-repaired things, some fakes and a lot of 'combination' furniture (combining part original and part reproduction). Even the bookshops can be disappointing—one so-called 'Antiquariat' in Unter den Linden, opposite the British Embassy, consists of a small room filled with postwar academic tomes in German. East Berlin is certainly worth a visit though, and nowadays it's easy enough for foreign visitors to go across from West Berlin independently of a guided tour: by S-bahn to Friedrichstrasse station, by taxi to Checkpoint Charlie, and thence on foot to pick up a taxi the other side of the Wall, or even by no. 29 bus. However, dealers there generally are reluctant to sell to foreigners, perhaps because they save their best goods for regular Party customers.

The main source for foreign buyers in the German Democratic Republic now is the state-controlled Buchexport in Leipzig, which despite its name deals in a wide range of antiques and works of art as well as books. Buchexport takes hard currency only, and transactions there automatically provide the purchaser with an export licence, necessary for anything of significant value. There is a very low ceiling—100 marks—on purchases allowed to be taken out of the country without an export licence.

If one does find a piece of interest in an East German antique shop, the chances are that it will carry a ticket saying 'not for export'—though it's still worth applying for a licence or checking with a museum to get permission, as the shopkeepers are often overcautious. Almost certainly too it will be highly priced— Persian rugs, for instance, are infinitely more expensive in Leipzig or East Berlin than in London. Oddly enough, some of the best things to look for are, or used to be, Eastern objects such as Chinese bronzes or Tibetan temple ornaments, relics of much-travelled old German families. But, as in several other Eastern European countries, the authorities are refurbishing so many castles as tourist attractions that they are scouring the antique shops themselves in search of authentic objects of the appropriate period.

Leipzig, as an important business centre with its annual trade fair, is well supplied with large antique shops, but the dealers are shrewdly aware of what the market will bear, and prices tend to be high. Near the famous old Auersbachkeller restaurant there is an arcade with several antique shops selling, among other things, Meissen porcelain. Dresden is still a good source for Meissen, but the accent is on the modern product and antique items may well turn out more expensive than in London salerooms. Porcelain is also a speciality of the centre in the Frankfurter Allee for the sale and export of antiques in East Berlin. Most of the great German glass factories used to be situated in what is now the German Democratic Republic, Poland and Czechoslovakia, and Potsdam glass, engraved for the court at Berlin, can sometimes be found at the state run Staatlicher Kunsthandel in East Berlin.

On the whole though, it is probably 20 years too late to make any real finds in East German antique shops.

The trade

Dresden

Dealers

GUENTHER, *Prellerstr 25 (30981)*.
Antiques, furniture.

HOLLAENDER, *Hubnerstr 12 (42791)*.
Antiques, paintings, furniture, Oriental art.

KUHL, *Zittauer Str 12 (55588)*.
Oriental and primitive art.

LOEWE, *Kesselsdorfer Str 25 (86300)*.
Antiques, furniture.

MUELLER, *Regerstr 16 (30622)*.
Antiques, paintings, furniture.

PECH, *Collenbuschstr 25 (36513)*.
Antiques, ceramics, scientific instruments.

ROST, *Buschwitz Str 41 (51547)*.
Antiques.

East Berlin

Dealers

ANTIQUARIAT, *Unter den Linden 37-45 (221939) and 108*.
Rare books, graphic art, paintings, furniture.

ANTIQUARIATSBUCHHANDLUNG 104, *Chausseestr 123 (422979)*.
Rare books.

ANTIQUARIATSBUCHHANDLUNG 112, *Klement-Gottwald-Allee 69 (560576)*.
Rare books.

ANTIQUARIATSBUCHHANDLUNG 102, *Munzstr 1 (429061)*.
Rare books.

BUCHHANDLUNG KUNST UND WISSEN 104, Friedrichstr 127, (426035).
Rare books.

BUCHHANDLUNG FUR KUNST UND WISSENSCHAFT 108, Clara-Zetkin-Str 41 (202220).
Antiques.

KARL-MARX-BUCHHANDLUNG 117, Karl-Marx-Allee 78 and 84 (581455).
Rare and art books.

STAATLICHER KUNSTHANDEL, Frankfurter Allee 84 (583572) and Boxhagener Str 37.

VRH, Schonhauser Allee 9.

ZENTRALES ANTIQUARIAT, Runge Str 20 (272195).

Export centre, Reichstagufer 4.

State shop for sale and export of antiques, Frankfurter Allee 80.

Leipzig

Dealers
BUCHEXPORT, Leninstr 16.
Books, wide range of antiques and works of art. Export licences.
Hard currency only accepted.

FRANK, Nikolaistr 55.
Antiques, ceramics, carpets.

GEBAUER, Madler Passage.
Antiques, carpets, ceramics, jewellery.

KUBE, Gustaf-Adolf-Str 15 (26035).
Antiques, old paintings, ceramics, carpets.

LAGEL, Burgstr 7-13.
Antiques, furniture, china, carpets.

Potsdam

Dealers

STRAUB, Wilhelm-Pieck-Str 7 (8584).

THIEMANN, Friedrich-Ebert-Str 83 (5764).
Antiques.

Museums

Dresden
GRUNES GEWOLBE.
Stoneware pottery.

STAATLICHE KUNSTSAMMLUNG.
19th-century Meissen.

East Berlin
BODE MUSEUM (formerly the Kaiser-Friedrich Museum).
One of the world's largest coin collections with 500 000 coins, medals, banknotes and seals of all periods; Egyptian remains, engravings, sculpture and paintings. Closed Tues. and Sun.

KUNSTGEWERBEMUSEUM.
Furniture, textiles, porcelain, glass, jewellery (especially Berlin iron jewellery) and ceramics made in Germany and the Low Countries from medieval times to the 19th century.

MARKISCHES MUSEUM.
Berlin iron jewellery.

PERGAMON MUSEUM.
Not to be missed for its remarkable—and complete—Greek and Roman temples reconstructed in vast halls. Nebuchadnezzar's Processional Way, from Babylon, is one of the world's great sights.

STAATLICHER KUNSTMUSEUM.
Potsdam glass.

This mid-18th-century mulled wine decanter is an exquisite example of Hungarian goldsmiths' work. It is in the traditional shape of Turkish earthenware vessels

18
Hungary

Introduction

There is hardly a country in Europe which has suffered more from wars, invasions and foreign domination than Hungary. The Turkish and the Habsburg empires in particular left their mark, as they did in most of what is now Communist Eastern Europe. Hungary has been invaded by foreign powers at least 50 times in its history.

The Magyars, who arrived in the 9th century and contributed the most characteristic strand to Hungarian culture, were noted for their strongly-developed decorative instincts. In the 12th century a Persian traveller recorded that their clothing was made of brocade and that their weapons were decorated with silver and pearl. Jewellery, ornaments and arms survive from the early Magyar period. Most medieval Hungarian artists were anonymous. The late gothic period was notable for miniature painting and illuminated manuscripts in which details of weapons, costumes and daily life were faithfully depicted, as well as historical themes. Hungarians see their own Golden Age as the reign of King Matthias Corvinus (1458–90), who introduced the ideas of the Italian Renaissance into Hungary.

Hungarian gold work was famous; a typical Hungarian form consisted of a filigree of twisted gold wire combined with enamel. Enamelling in all its forms was a speciality of Hungarian goldsmiths from Byzantine times to the 18th century. Sculpture and painting flourished in the baroque era; the Esterhazy Castle at Fertod is the finest example of baroque architecture in the country and is known as the Hungarian Versailles.

Ancient peasant arts, some of which survive, were embroidery (sometimes, though rarely, the long embroidered felt coat called the *szur* or *suba* can be found), ceramics (the peasant potter Balazs Badar discovered a brilliant secret new glaze) and wood-carving. ('Herdsmen's art', a typically Hungarian product of the rural past, was noted for its intricately carved tools and domestic utensils.) All these have their modern counterparts. Since 1945 folk art co-operatives have been set up to sell peasant embroideries. There is contemporary wood-carving, and modern ceramics are notable for the work of the husband-and-wife Gorka team, Margit Kovacs and Istvan Gador. Handsome plain black ware is made at Nadudvar.

Graphic artists and cartoonists proliferate; Balint Biro is a master of the woodcut and etching, while Paul Vincze is a notable designer of medals, coins and medallions. Around the turn of this century Hungary produced some fine painters, many of whom studied and worked in Paris and absorbed French influences; the work of Pal Szinyei Merse (1845–1920) reflects Manet.

Books are one of the main attractions for collectors in Hungary, and quite a lot are exported. Hand-painted porcelain from the Herend factory is famous. This was set up originally in 1839, and its present style is chiefly imitation 18th-century Meissen.

There is generally no difficulty in taking antiques out of the country, except for very precious objects. Konsumturist in Budapest sells goods for foreign currency only. Occasionally auctions of important antiques take place, at which a jury decides whether or not an object can leave the country. Budapest has about 25 museums and picture galleries.

The trade

Budapest
Dealers
ARTEX, V. Nador u 31.
State enterprise for the import and export of works of art.

KONSUM TURIST, Hess Andras ter 3 sz and Nepkoztarsaag u 27.
Antiques, Oriental and Far Eastern art, coins, ceramics, sculpture.

KULTURA, Fo u 11 (159450).
Rare books.

Museums

Budapest

CHINESE ART MUSEUM.

EAST ASIATIC ART MUSEUM.

ETHNOGRAPHICAL MUSEUM.
Hungarian folk art, including embroidery, weaving, pottery and wood-carvings.

MUSEUM OF APPLIED AND DECORATIVE ARTS.
Housed in an ornate Secessionist-style building of the 1890s (the outside of which is decorated with majolica tiles from Pécs), the museum has important departments of ceramics and glass, including: 300 pieces of Haban ceramics, Europe's largest collection of the work of this Anabaptist sect, expelled from Switzerland, who were originally cloth merchants and furriers as well as potters (the most popular form of Haban ware is the jug with a flattened body and long neck, only 3000 of which are known to survive); a permanent exhibition of the history of ceramics from Greek vases onwards; 17th-century Italian pottery; Meissen, Nymphenburg, Sèvres and St Petersburg porcelain; and English Wedgwood stoneware pitchers. The textile department keeps oriental carpets, old Hungarian embroidery, brocade, lace, and Italian and French work. The museum is strong in gold and silver, with a permanent exhibition of the goldsmith's art in Europe from the 16th to the 20th century and extensive collections of Augsburg, Nuremberg and Hungarian work of the 16th and 17th centuries. Furniture, bookbindings, fans and old watches are well represented.

MUSEUM OF FINE ARTS.
Comprehensive collection of Hungarian paintings from the 11th to the 18th centuries; romanesque stone-carvings; gothic altar-paintings; a modern foreign department strong in 19th-century French masters such as Courbet, Manet, Monet, Renoir, Gauguin and Cézanne, plus three Rodin sculptures; the Old Picture Gallery, embracing six centuries of Italian painting with many renaissance masterpieces; the most comprehensive

collection outside Spain of Spanish painting, including five Goyas; galleries of Dutch and German masterpieces, including a Holbein and a Dürer; and a small but select collection of 18th- and 19th-century English paintings.

MUSEUM OF NATURAL HISTORY.
Interesting collection of minerals and stones, including semi-precious stones from the Carpathians.

MUSEUM OF MEDICAL HISTORY.
Housed in a beautiful baroque house at the foot of Buda Castle Hill, the museum displays milestones in medical history from the coins, apothecary jars and medical instruments of ancient Greece and Rome, through the cauterizing irons and trepanning instruments of the 16th and 17th centuries, to modern therapeutic equipment. Exhibits include a 17th-century chemist's cabinet with contemporary vessels, 16th- and 17th-century faience medicine jars and an early 19th-century complete pharmacy.

NATIONAL GALLERY, Buda Palace.
The complete development of Hungarian art over 500 years. The gallery's collection of drawings is so extensive that a new display is arranged every three months. It is also particularly rich in engravings—the foreign section alone has 150 000 items including works by Leonardo da Vinci, Raphael and Rembrandt. The speciality, however, is 19th- and 20th-century Hungarian art; the country has many important exponents of 19th-century land-scape and romantic painting, historical genre, impressionism and secessionism.

THE HUNGARIAN NATIONAL MUSEUM.
Rich prehistoric and Roman collections, many interesting items from the 150 years of Turkish rule, an arms collection famous throughout Europe, fine medieval metalwork, ceramics, musical instruments, clocks. The museum also has one of the finest numismatic collections in the world, started by its founder, Ferenc Széchény, in 1802 and subsequently built up with bequests and the discovery of hoards to its present strength of around 250 000 coins and medals. The Hungarian material is especially fine, with many rare gold ducats and medals of the Hungarian kings and Transylvanian princes, but the museum

also has rich collections of Balkan pieces generally, early Austrian and Habsburg coins, papal medals and Greek and Roman coinage.

PHILATELIC MUSEUM.
170 000 valuable Hungarian and foreign stamps.

WAR HISTORY MUSEUM.
Relics, documents and pictures from 1711 to the end of the Second World War, with emphasis on the time of the Hungarian Revolution and War of Independence in 1848/49, such as portraits of the leading generals, copperplate engravings, medals, uniforms and weapons; also a comprehensive collection of hand weapons from the 9th century to the Second World War.

Poland has a long tradition of finely engraved medals and coins. This silver medal bearing the head of King Stanislaus Augustus (1764-1795) was designed and made by J. P. Holzhauser

19
Poland

Introduction

Like Czechoslovakia, Poland remains closely bound into Western culture despite its political orientation. The finest romanesque and gothic architecture is found in Kraków, which was the capital and chief cultural centre until the end of the 16th century. Warsaw did not become an important artistic centre until the late 18th century, when the very name Poland disappeared and the territory was divided between Russia, Prussia and Austria. Poland has been partitioned for much of its history and therefore unable to evolve a truly native art tradition.

The golden age of Polish culture was the renaissance period in Kraków, but gothic art has left a rich legacy—whole towns and villages, dating from the beginning of the 13th century. The earliest Polish paintings go back to the 11th century, and illuminated manuscripts survive. Silver of the 12th and 13th centuries was exceptionally fine, largely Eastern in design. Architecture and sculpture became dominated by Italian influences, painting by German schools. The decorative arts flourished best in the reign of Stanislas Augustus, the last King of Poland (1764–95)—gold, glass, ceramics, furniture, textiles. Typical of Polish artistry were 17th century 'coffin portraits'—a simple, realistic representation of a dead person on an octagonal or hexagonal piece of metal subsequently nailed to the coffin; also carpets using Western motifs such as coats of arms and names in place of Oriental designs (made from the end of the 16th century); and arms and armour. In the latter the Polish speciality was the *karacena*, a kind of chain mail made of iron scales fixed to a leather jerkin and worn by Hussar officers.

Numismatic art has been important in Poland since the 11th

century and the country is a world-renowned centre for antique coins and medals—its contemporary artists in this field also are eminently collectable. Antique silver also is extremely important, and there is some 18th-century porcelain, Silesian stoneware pottery and glass. Some contemporary prints and tapestries may be worth collecting, also wood-carvings and pottery.

Officially the export of antiques or works of art dating from before 1945 is strictly prohibited, but in practice foreigners can obtain permits. The state organization regulating the export of art objects is Desa (Al. Jerozolimskie 2, Warsaw). The Polish antique market is better organized than many others in Eastern Europe. Every piece on sale in the chain of Desa shops is ticketed in white or pink, depending on whether or not it requires an export permit. If it does, one can either buy the piece and leave it in the shop while applying to the Ministry of Culture for a permit, or take it away 'on spec' in which case its price will be refunded if a permit is not granted. A lot of buying and selling of antiques goes on privately. There is no restriction on private citizens selling their possessions, but a foreign visitor might find himself in difficulties trying to leave the country with a piece acquired in this way unless he has acquired an export permit, and it is unlikely that a private citizen is going to sell anything to a foreigner if by doing so he or she attracts the attention of the authorities.

Warsaw, Kraków and Przemyśl are the best centres for antique-hunting. In Kraków, which came unscathed through the last war, there are still old-established families who were wealthy under the old regime and still live in family homes filled with antiques; some of these might be persuaded to sell. Poland is a good place to buy antiquarian books, because old libraries with their early Western books are still being broken up and because it is easier to get permits for books—Antykwariat shops, which are part of the Desa chain, specialize in these.

Specialities

Coins and medals

Poland's tumultuous history has been brilliantly reflected in its coins and medals since the 11th century, and Polish numismatic art was and still is of an exceptionally high order. One of the greatest of all European medallists, Sebastian Dadler, lived in Gdansk and Jan Hoehn the Elder was another distinguished medallist from the same city. The art of coin and medal-making was also highly developed in Warsaw, Kraków (where the Italian 16th-century master medallist Caraglio spent his last years), Torun on the Vistula and Elblag in Pomerania. All produced beautiful examples of the numismatic art. Particularly attractive is the series of coins with views of Polish towns, among them the 'Siege Thaler' of 1629 which shows Torun in flames with the river Vistula in the foreground, and the series of coins and medals from the Middle Ages onwards bearing portraits of Polish kings. Important Greek, Roman and Byzantine coins have also been found in Poland. Medals struck to commemorate great events in Polish history, such as the Peace of Oliwa in 1660, which ended the wars with Sweden, are beautiful and original works of art. Contemporary medallists carry on this tradition. Indeed, some of the best medallic works of the present are produced in Poland—the Copernicus medal of 1971, struck in Torun, is a notable example.

The Wawel Treasury in Kraków's National Museum has a particularly interesting coin collection, formed since the Second World War by the late General Wesierski, which illustrates the whole history of Polish numismatics. There are several numismatic specialists in Warsaw. It is said that one can buy advantageously on the black market in Poland and that there is no problem taking coins out, but this is something not everyone should attempt.

Glass

The finest early 18th-century glass-engraving was done in Silesia, now part of Poland. Techniques, including gilding of cut and engraved glass, were very similar to those of glass makers in neighbouring Bohemia.

Silver

Silver worked by artist-craftsmen was a real passion in times past. Stefan Potocki, Starost of Felin, owned a silver service which filled

22 boxes and in addition possessed 10 cases full of silver spoons, 40 ewers and approximately 200 profusely-decorated wine goblets. King Sigismund in the 16th century had such a rich collection that the Papal Nuncio reported that his treasury held 5000 lb (2268 kg) of silver-gilt objects not in use, as well as fountains and clocks as tall as men. During the mannerist and baroque periods, silver figurines produced by German goldsmiths were very popular—these were often in the shape of birds or animals and made for use as carafes and wine cups. Some old silver is still to be found in Polish antique shops, but it may be difficult for foreigners to take out of the country.

The trade

Gdańsk

Dealers

DESA, ul Dluga 2 (315968).
Antique and contemporary art.

Kraków

Dealers

ANTYKWARIAT, ul Rynek Glowny 43.
Books.

ANTYKWARIAT NAUKOWY, branches at ul Slawskowska 10 and ul Podwale 4.
Books.

ARS CHRISTIANA, ul Maly Rynek.

BWA, pl Szczepanska 4 (20400).

DESA, ul sw. Jana 3 (21722).
Contemporary art.

DESA, ul Rynek Glowny 17 (50823).
Antiques, paintings, furniture, sculpture, carpets, arms. Recommended by knowledgable Polish sources.

Stefan KAMINSKI, ul sw. Jana 3.

KRZYSZTOFORY, ul Szczepanska.

K. PELC, ul Karmelicka 21a.

Poznań

Dealers

ANTYKWARIAT, branches at ul Stary Rynek 48 (54798) and ul Ratajczaka 35 (52131).
Books.

ANTYKWARIAT NAUKOWY, ul Stary Rynek 53-4.
Books.

BWA, ul Stary Rynek 6.

DESA, ul Armil Czerwonej 63 (59422).
Contemporary art.

Przemyśl

Dealers
DESA, pl Wielkiego Proletariatu 15 (5479).
Antique and contemporary art. Recommended.

Warsaw

Dealers
ANTYKWARIAT, ul Nowy Swiat 51 (274760).
Books, numismatics, weapons, silver, porcelain. Recommended.

ANTYKWARIAT, ul Rynek Starego Miasta 4-6 (311681).
Books.

ANTYKWARIAT, ul Marszakowska 34-50 (287705).
Books. Recommended.

ANTYKWARIAT NAUKOWY, ul Swietokrzyska 14.
Books.

ANTYKWARIAT VERITAS, pl Trzech Krzyzy 18.
Books.

BWA, pl Malachowskiego 3.

DESA, ul Nowotki 18 (313648).
Numismatics, medals.

DESA, ul Zapiecek 1 (319918).
Contemporary art.

KSIEGARNIA ANTYKWAYCZNA, ul Nowy Swiat 61.
Books.

Salon PLASTYKI WSPOLCZESNEJ, ul Nowy Swiat 23 (263501) and ul Koszykowa 62.
Contemporary art.

Museums
Kornik

NATIONAL MUSEUM (branch of Poznań National Museum).
Old weapons, miniatures.

Kraków
NATIONAL MUSEUM.
Tapestries, pottery, weapons; valuable collection of paintings including some by Leonardo da Vinci and Rembrandt. The state collections in the Wawel Castle include beautiful Flemish tapestries, gold and silverwork, the Wesierski collection of coins, and Polish embroideries.

Poznań
NATIONAL MUSEUM.
Medieval Polish paintings; paintings from the Flemish, Dutch,

Spanish and Italian schools; furniture, pottery, tapestries and objets d'art of the 16th to 18th centuries.

Warsaw

NATIONAL MUSEUM.
Largest in Poland, containing examples of Polish medieval art and housing the Army Museum with its fine collection of Polish weapons.

This fine antique rug was made in Transylvania, now part of modern Romania

20
Romania

Introduction

The Roman Empire, Byzantium and the Ottoman Empire are the three dominant strands in Romania's history—few places in Europe have such archaeological treasures as this one-time eastern outpost of Rome. The principal regions of modern Romania are Moldavia, Wallachia and Transylvania, finally united after the First World War. From the Middle Ages until the 19th century the Romanian people of Moldavia and Wallachia were dominated by the Turks, achieving independence in 1862. Transylvania, with a large German population, was part of the Habsburg Empire until 1918. Before Romanian art was influenced by Western Europe in the 19th century, it was predominantly religious and Byzantine in character. The unique artistic achievement of Romania was probably its painted churches of the 15th and 16th centuries, and these are a remarkable experience. Their outside walls are entirely covered in biblical scenes painted with pigment which has survived hundreds of years of weathering with an amazing durability and brilliance—the blue is supposedly made from ground lapis lazuli. Bucharest, however, has little of artistic importance in its architecture before the 17th century.

Even before the Second World War Bucharest was the only city in Romania with a strong middle-class community and half of them were foreigners, mainly connected with the oil industry and international business interests. For something like four centuries the richest part of the country was Transylvania with its landed families and heritage of big houses and castles. In recent years German tourists have snapped up most of the remaining antiques. Nevertheless, throughout the whole territory the Romanian peasants developed an impressive folk-art tradition of great beauty.

Romania is a particularly frustrating country for antique
hunters, because while in Bucharest there are for sale valuable
antiques (furniture, icons and paintings) in the Consignatia shops
and rare books (including many old editions of famous French,
English and German books) in the Anticariat booksellers, it is
strictly forbidden to export anything classified as part of the
'national cultural heritage'. Since 1974 this definition has been
tightened to take in even objects and books of foreign origin, if they
are seen as contributing to Romania's cultural wealth. The
national cultural heritage, legally defined, consists of:

a. Goods with a particular artistic value, such as objects or
monuments of architecture, fine arts, which are antique,
medieval or modern and are the craft of acknowledged artists,
Romanian or foreign; also works of unknown artists which are
representative of the national and universal art through their
artistic value, characteristic features and rarity.
b. Goods with a historic and documentary value such as historic
or archaeological monuments; objects or documents of great
importance, outstanding for certain epoques, institutions,
events or personalities; documents of historic character
important for the development of universal history;
manuscripts; valuable national or universal tokens of history,
science and technics; coins; rare stamps.
c. Goods of scientific value such as rare natural pieces which are
preserved only in special collections; monuments of nature;
fossils and rare trophies; preserved or naturalised species.

Even items outside these categories can only be taken out of the
country with official approval, which involves the dealer in
obtaining permission. These are clearly defined by law as
encompassing paintings, sculpture, graphics, ceramics,
glassware, textiles, furniture, books and 'other printings'. Foreign
buyers must be sure to check with the dealer and to obtain written
authority for export—attempts to take goods illegally out of the
country are punishable by two to seven years' imprisonment.

Visitors have to console themselves by looking at the gold work
and embroidery from the 14th to the 18th centuries, icons and
illuminated manuscripts immaculately preserved in Romanian
museums. Bucharest's Museum of Art has a large collection of
feudal art, also 19th-century Romanian paintings.

The trade

Bucharest

Dealers

CARTIMEX, Str Foisorului 41.
Import and export of works of art.

CONSIGNATIA, Str Smirdavi 31.

Antiquarian booksellers

ANTICARIATUL BUCURESTI, Lipscani 6 (144761).

ANTICARIATUL no. 2, Blvd Republicii 5 (1588761).

ANTICARIATUL no. 3, Blvd General Magheru 2 (145296).

ANTICARIATUL no. 4, Bis Enei 16 (154883).

ANTICARIATUL no. 6, Calea Victoriei 45 (130897).

ANTICARIATUL no. 9, Polizu 2 (153593).

Museums

Bucharest

MUSEUM OF ART
Large collection of feudal art, including icons, silken embroideries
and precious metalwork; 19th-century Romanian paintings.

A rare 16th-century icon from Central Russia showing the archangel Michael between St Flor and St Lavr, each standing on a horse, together with three shepherds on horseback

21
USSR

Introduction

Russian art, like most of Russian society except for the Westernized upper classes, remained locked in the Middle Ages until well into the 19th century, with only folk and church art as indigenous flowerings. The society of St Petersburg (now Leningrad) imported its artistic ideas from Western Europe, and during the 18th and 19th centuries much of the glass, porcelain and precious metalwork produced in Russia could have come from any European centre—Paris, Potsdam, Dresden or Vienna. Regional centres of Russian native art such as Novgorod, in which once flourished a famous school of iconography, diminished in importance. Then in the mid 19th century a new wave of Russian artists 'discovered' traditional art forms and at the same time became interested in the representation of Russian life and landscape. In the early 20th century Russian painters were inevitably drawn into the ferment of Western art movements, before the Revolution of 1917 produced revolutionary approaches to the graphic arts also. The major art movement to come out of the Revolution was Constructivism, but this, like the other ideas and experiments in modern art, was stifled by Stalin.

The USSR today has a vast treasury of antiques and works of art in its magnificent state museums, especially in the fabled Hermitage in Leningrad and in the Kremlin in Moscow, where there is a marvellous collection of silver. But the only sources of antiques for sale are the Commission shops—secondhand shops to be found in different districts in Moscow. These are entitled to buy bric-à-brac, pictures or furniture from owners who wish to dispose of them, and they operate rather like pawnshops: the seller receives a guaranteed sum from the shop, the object is put

373

up for sale at a higher price, and the difference between the two is eventually made over to the owner after a deduction for tax. In these shops one can sometimes make finds of 19th-century Russian or foreign objects with the occasional 17th- or 18th-century picture, but in general the items are not of any great interest or value. In any case it is now very difficult for foreigners to get an export licence for anything of pre-Revolution vintage. Western residents, such as diplomats and newspaper staff, may be able to buy the occasional fine piece of Tsarist porcelain in the Commission shops, but they are likely to run into problems with it when returning home.

The state makes sure it buys up any item of real value or historical interest, particularly icons. These are simply unobtainable to casual visitors, as the state purchases whatever is available and, being well aware of market values in London, Paris and New York, lets a trickle of icons out every so often for sale in the West. There is a disused church in Moscow which has been converted to a state icon warehouse; it is literally stacked from floor to ceiling with 18th- and 19th-century icons.

Soviet people themselves are avid collectors and scour the Commission shops, but they operate generally on what is known as the 'granny network'—when someone's relatives are turning out an attic, desirable objects can change hands without involving the Commission shops. Soviet collectors are deeply interested in their own past and have a passion for folk art and particularly for icons.

What then is available for Western collectors? Old Western drawings and engravings, which can sometimes be found in the secondhand bookshops, are one possibility, being of little interest to the Soviets themselves; for instance, there is the Western newspaperman who was able to buy a series of original Hogarth engravings for a song and to take them out without difficulty. The same can be true of pre-Revolutionary prints—attractive views of old St Petersburg and the like. Also, one is quite likely to find volumes of French literature and the broken-up contents of country-house libraries which may have some fine bound volumes dating back to the early 18th century. Victorian and turn-of-the-century books are perhaps the best bet; one former Moscow resident made such fascinating finds as an original Mrs Beeton and a 1900 timetable for the Trans-Siberian Railway. Buyers should look out for the 1914 Baedeker to Russia, a prized collector's piece in Britain; the writer Jan Morris picked up a dog-eared German-language edition in Leningrad's Nevski Prospekt, but it may even be possible to find the English edition which is much more valuable.

Coins are another possibility. The Gold Shop in Moscow, situated on Ulitsa Pushkin just behind the Bolshoi, sells pre-Revolutionary and early post-Revolutionary coins for hard currency only. Some of the gold roubles may have a doubtful provenance; it is thought that immediately after the Revolution the Communists got hold of the dies and made re-strikes of Tsarist roubles. But the silver roubles are genuine and 19th-century Russian copper pieces such as the five-kopeck are extremely handsome. This shop also sells a wide selection of coins from Eastern and Western Europe.

Specialities

This section is likely to be of academic interest only because of the extreme difficulty foreigners face in taking out anything of pre-1917 date, but it may be useful for visits to museums and Commission shops.

Glass

Pre-19th-century Russian glass was chiefly made for the court and nobility and was heavily influenced by Paris and Potsdam styles. Indeed, most 18th-century Russian glass was virtually indistinguishable from the Western forms it imitated except for some distinctive black-stained engraving after 1743 (mainly portraits and monograms). Fine court glass was made at the Imperial factory established in 1777 at St Petersburg (Leningrad). These pieces were sometimes humorously signed S. P. Burg in Cyrillic script and included opaque milk glass very similar to that produced at Bristol. In the 1760s two Moscow glass houses were established. The first was founded by Thomas Maltzov, whose brother Jacob succeeded him and employed Subanov, the greatest of Russian glass engravers. The second, founded by the Bakhmetev family, specialized in fine enamelled and gilded ornamental glass until it was closed down by the Revolution.

Gold and silver

For centuries Russian craftsmen made gold and silver objects for local church and domestic use, such as icon mounts and decorative book covers. Centres of production included Moscow, Kiev and Novgorod. Silver copies of early native wooden drinking-vessels were made for the court, and in the 17th century a silver workshop was established in the Kremlin which produced, as well as native vessels like the *charka, bratina* and *kovsch*, a wide range of dishes, cups, goblets and bookbindings. Typical decorative techniques for 200 years were niello (engraving filled with a black alloy), filigree and polychrome enamel, and chasing. The gold and silver filigree of the 16th century is said to be unmatched in its swirling grace.

The 16th century was the peak of Russian craftsmanship, though a few objects survive; a lot of gold and silver was melted down to provide coinage before the Romanov accession in 1613. The Kremlin workshops were closed in 1700 by Peter the Great, whose enthusiasm for Western art caused an influx of French and English styles into domestic Russian silver.

Moscow was the assay centre and the place of greatest craftsmanship in gold and silver. The earliest hallmarks date from 1651–52, Moscow's mark being a double-headed imperial eagle. However, provincial work done at Novgorod and Solvychegodsk was of excellent quality; examples can be seen in the State Russian Museum in Leningrad, the Kremlin State Armoury in Moscow and the State Art History Museum in Novgorod.

Foreign craftsmen who began to come and work in Russia under the benevolent interest of Peter the Great's patronage of Western art remained outstanding contributors to Russian metal-working, culminating in the great Peter Carl Fabergé. Many beautiful gold boxes were made in the French style in 18th-century St Petersburg, round, oval or oblong in shape and often heavily decorated with diamonds or miniatures. J. Pauzie, a Swiss, and J.-P. Ador, a French goldsmith, were two leading craftsmen making gold snuff boxes. Silver boxes, often ornamented with niello engravings of landscape or architectural views and predominantly circular in shape, were made after 1780.

Gustav Fabergé, the father of Carl, established himself as a jeweller in St Petersburg in 1842, four years before his famous son's birth. The intricately beautiful and ingenious work with which the name of Fabergé is now associated was produced in the years after 1870, such as the celebrated Easter eggs he fashioned for the Tsars and the wonderfully naturalistic flower sprays made of precious metals and carved hardstones. At the peak of his international fame in 1903 Fabergé opened a branch in London, his only branch outside Russia. It closed in 1915 and two years later the Fabergé workshops went out of business when the Bolsheviks seized power.

Icons

The great period of Russian icons ran from the school of Kiev, following the adoption of Christianity in the 10th century, to the school of Dionisii in Moscow 600 years later. The peak of Russian icon art was probably achieved in the 15th century in Novgorod, Suzdal, and Moscow. Novgorod icons were particularly brilliant in colour and composed with beautiful clarity, but from the 17th-century onwards they became more mystical and sombre in colouring as Western influences crept in. Icons, usually in rich gold or silver mounts, were an essential part of the furnishing of every wealthy home. One of the greatest collections now is at the Troitsa Lavra at Zagorsk.

Painting and sculpture

Until well into the 19th century the most important painting and sculpture in Russia was folk and church art. Then a new wave of Russian artists 'discovered' traditional art forms and at the same time became deeply interested in peasant life. The group of painters and sculptors who called themselves The Wanderers and who worked under the patronage of a millionaire industrialist called Mamontov, for the first time began to portray Russian life and landscape, inspired by a sense of social reform. Leading Wanderers were Kuznetsov, Levitan and Mikhail Vrubel, who drew from icon-paintings his feeling for rich colour and abstract formal patterns.

As the fateful 20th century dawned, Russian painters were inevitably drawn into the turmoil engulfing Western art movements. Painters like Larionov, Popova and Goncharova travelled to Italy and France and experimented with futurism and cubism. With the Revolution in 1917 art exploded into the streets; the poet Mayakovsky, who wanted 'bullets to rattle against museum walls', called it 'a living factory of the human spirit'.

The Revolutionary period produced some striking graphic artists, chiefly El Lissitzky, who designed the famous poster showing the red wedge of Communism driving out the white of the old order. The grand old man of Revolutionary art was Kandinsky, who sought in abstract painting to express emotion through colour as directly as the composer does with music. Colour as 'pure sensation' was also the driving force behind Casimir Malevich; both men had been deeply influenced by peasant art and the brilliant colours of icons. Malevich was to carry his theory to the ultimate conception of 'White on White'. The works of Kandinsky (who later left the USSR to live in Germany and France), Malevich and Marc Chagall, who also drew deep inspiration from Russian folk art, are all avidly collected today by Soviet academics, writers and professional people. Many Chagall fakes also circulate in the USSR.

The major art movement to come out of the Revolution was Constructivism, pioneered by the 'artist-engineer' Vladimir Tatlin, the sculptor Naum Gabo and his brother Anton Pevsner. The essence of the theory was that the Soviet artist should 'construct' rather than merely decorate his environment, and modern industrial materials such as plastic, glass and steel were used in constructivist works.

All these ideas and experiments in modern art were, however, condemned by the Soviet Communist Party under Stalin in 1932. Henceforth art was to be cast in the mould of 'socialist realism', both serving the Party and comprehensible to ordinary working people.

Porcelain

The accession of Peter the Great (1689–1725) with his interest in Western styles was the signal for Russian ceramics to develop into more sophisticated forms than the peasant pottery which had been made since primitive times. Peter's daughter, the Empress Elizabeth (1741–62), hired a German named Hunger to experiment with local clays for making porcelain, but it was not until the reign of Catherine the Great (1762–96) that the factory at St Petersburg (Leningrad) produced fine porcelain regularly. It made a wide range of figures showing Russian peasants and tradesmen in national costume, along with tableware distinguished by floral designs and embossed edges to dishes and plates.

When Tsar Alexander I in 1806 imposed a tax on foreign porcelain it gave a boost to many private Russian factories, including one which had been founded in about 1756 by an Englishman named Gardner. Old Gardner porcelain is today ranked with the best anywhere in Europe. The factory supplied personal orders for Catherine and made individual table services for each of the Russian orders of chivalry. Among a wide range of table and ornamental ware, Gardner made biscuit groups of peasant figures, excellently modelled, and tea services for export to Turkey decorated with roses set in white medallions. In the second quarter of the 19th century Gardner ware was characterized by rich gilding on a dark-blue ground and delicate flower designs done in high relief on a white ground. At first the Gardner mark was a G in different shapes, with occasionally a mark similar to Meissen's crossed swords; later it was a St George and Dragon symbol, and later still a double-headed eagle.

The next most important private factory was that of Popov, founded in 1806. It specialized in 'tea house' porcelain in colours such as sky blue, with white medallions encircling bouquets of flowers. Collectors today favour the Popov series showing dancing peasants, but Popov's gilded pieces did not wear particularly well. The factory closed down in the 1870s.

The third-ranking private factory was that of the Kornilov brothers, started in St Petersburg in 1835. Its pieces were distinguished by rich colouring and decoration and were more expensive than those of the other factories. Kornilov ware is known as the aristocrat of Russian porcelain.

From the 18th century onwards most Russian porcelain factories produced elaborately-decorated Easter eggs—perhaps the inspiration for Fabergé's famous series. The peak of Russian porcelain production came in the 1870s when about 70 factories were in operation. However, by the end of the 19th century most had been taken over by the giant Kuznetsov combine, which remained in business until 1917.

The trade

Leningrad

Dealers

ANTIQUITES, Nevsky Prospekt 50.

GALERIE, Nevsky Prospekt 20.

LAVKA KHUDOZHNIKA, Nevsky Prospekt 8 (197645).

Moscow

Dealers

ANTIQUITES, branches at Arbat 19, Gorki 46 and Mira Prospekt.

GALERIE, Gorki 46.

Book dealers, ul Gertsen 13 and Marx Prospekt 1 (by the Metropole Hotel).

Coin dealer (Gold Shop), ul Pushkin (just behind the Bolshoi).
Pre-Revolutionary and early post-Revolutionary coins (hard currency only accepted); wide selection of Eastern and Western European coins.

Museums

Leningrad

HERMITAGE.
Magnificent collection of antiques and works of art.

STATE RUSSIAN MUSEUM.
Gold and silverwork.

Moscow

KREMLIN.
Magnificent collection of antiques and works of art, including gold and silverwork in the Kremlin State Armoury.

PUSHKIN MUSEUM
Fine collection of Impressionists.

TRETYAKOV GALLERY
Masterpieces of Russian painting.

Novgorod

STATE ART HISTORY MUSEUM.
Gold and silverwork.

Zagorsk

TROITSA LAVRA (Trinity Monastery).
A great collection of icons.

Further reading

Bainbridge, H. C., *Peter Carl Fabergé: His Life and Work* (London: Spring Books, 1972)
Gray, Camilla, *The Great Experiment: Russian Art and Artists 1863–1922* (London: Thames and Hudson, 1962)
Hamilton, G. H., *The Arc and Architecture of Russia* (Harmondsworth; Penguin Books, 1954)
Hare, R., *The Art and Artists of Russia* (London: Methuen, 1965)
Oman, Charles, *The English Silver in the Kremlin 1557–1663* (London: Methuen, 1961)
Rice, Tamara Talbot, *A Concise History of Russian Art* (London: Thames and Hudson, 1963)
Ross, Marvin C., *Russian Porcelains* (Norman, Oklahoma: University of Oklahoma Press, 1969)

Although this delightful carving, entitled <u>Newly Weds</u>, by Mato Generalić is quite modern, it forms part of a living tradition of Yugoslav naive art. Without doubt it will become a cherished antique of the future

22
Yugoslavia

Introduction

Yugoslavia, a federation of six autonomous republics, has only existed since 1918 when it was created from Macedonia, Serbia, Montenegro, Croatia, Bosnia and Herzegovina, and Slovenia. Istria, on the north eastern coast of the Adriatic Sea was only ceded to Yugoslavia by Italy in July 1946.

Macedonia, Serbia and Montenegro in the south of the country had been part of the Turkish Empire, Croatia part of the Kingdom of Hungary, Bosnia and Herzegovina part of Austria, and Istria part of the Venetian Republic and then of Italy. Much of the colour and flavour of the resulting mixture remains in modern Yugoslavia.

For twelve centuries the area was a busy crossroads of history. There are classical Greek and Roman remains at Celje and Split, Belgrade, Pula, Heraclea and Lyncestis. Later, Macedonia and Serbia both formed part of the great Byzantine Empire with its capital at Constantinople. From this period survive church decorations painted from the 11th to the 14th centuries. These important frescoes appear to foreshadow the art of the Italian renaissance. In 1453 the Byzantine Empire fell to the Turks and strong traces of oriental culture linger in this part of the country, a legacy of 500 years of Ottoman rule.

There is no mistaking the ancestry of the architecture in Sarajevo, where the Archduke Francis Ferdinand, heir to the Austro-Hungarian empire, was assassinated by the Bosnian revolutionary Gavrilo Princip; a shot that led to the First World War. Today Sarajevo is a notable university town, with a thriving printing and publishing industry. Here there is an oriental-style *souk* marketplace where one may buy, among other things, locally-made Kelim rugs.

Beautiful wall tapestries made of ewes' wool are still to be found in old farmhouses. Other Yugoslav art forms include handmade pottery from Croatia and Macedonia, gold and silver filigree work from the area around Zadar on the Adriatic coast, wood carving and engraving, and embroidery. All these crafts are practised today.

Two famous 20th century Yugoslav sculptors are Ivan Mestrovic, known as the Yugoslav Rodin, and Antun Augustincic.

Especially in the south, the country has been extremely poor, and for this reason the trade in antiques has never really developed. In the northern part of the country in Slovenia, around Zagreb, and in the capital, Belgrade, formerly wealthy families have helped to create a small trade, but a lot of things have been taken by Italian dealers, working across the border. The Yugoslavs do not appear to be greatly interested in antiques—unlike, say, the Russians, Poles or Czechs. There are fewer restrictions on taking items out than in other Communist countries, but not many bargains either. However, the visitor to Belgrade may discover small icons, books, prints, and good folk paintings.

The trade
Belgrade

Dealers
KOMISION, Nusuceva 25.

MILENKOVIC, Branka Cvetkovica 35 and Vitanovachka 7.
Expert in antique icons.

SRPSKA KNJIZEVNA ZADRUGA, Marsala Tito 19.
Books.

Ljubljana

Dealers
ANTIKA, Metsrai trg 19 (22285).

CANKARJEWA ZALOZBA, Miklosiceva c 16.
Rare Books.

KOMISIJA, Invalidsko Podjetje, Satri trg 4.

ZALOZBA MLADINSKA TITOVA, Zalozba Mladinska Knjiga 'Emka', Capova 38.
Books.

Sarajevo

Markets
SOUK.
Craftwork, including Kelim rugs.

Zagreb

Dealers
POSREDIK, Preduzece za Promet Komisionom Robom, Boskoviceva 38 (417828).

POSREDIK, Jurisiceva 5 (37295).

Museums
Belgrade

ETHNOGRAPHY MUSEUM, Studentski tot 13.
Ancient folk art of the region.

NATIONAL MUSEUM, trg Republike 1.
Important collections relating to the history and art of the Yugoslav peoples, including galleries devoted to icons, medieval manuscripts, jewellery and a stunning display of Roman gold coins and Byzantine silver coins.

Dubrovnik

ICON COLLECTION, Puca Street (opposite the Cathedral).

Sarajevo

STATE MUSEUM.
Good collection of Greek, Roman and medieval objects.

Split

GALLERY OF FINE ARTS, Lovretska 11.
Icon collection.

Zagreb

ARCHAEOLOGICAL MUSEUM, Zrinjevac 19.
Large collection of coins—100 000 items.

CROATIAN HISTORICAL MUSEUM, Zrinjevac 19.
Manuscripts, rare books and documents relating to the history of Yugoslavia from the 14th century to the present.

MUSEUM OF ARTS AND CRAFTS, trg Marsala Tita 10.
Yugoslav craftsmanship from the Middle Ages to the present.

STROSMAJER GALLERY.
Specializes in Croatian artists; also a rich collection of Italian and Dutch paintings.

Further reading

Rhodes, Anthony, *Art Treasures of Eastern Europe* (London: Weidenfeld and Nicolson, 1972)

Index